The Stars We Could Reach

The Stars We Could Reach

A Life Story

by

Carolyn S. Hochard

The Stars We Could Reach is a work of creative nonfiction. This story is intended as a composition of personal reflection based on the author's lived experience, and not a factual account. Many of the characters are amalgamations of multiple people with names and identifying information changed to protect privacy. Some event details have been reordered, altered, or compressed, to improve narrative flow.

Author Photo Courtesy of John R. Hochard

Cover Art by Dorota Kudyba Art.
www.Dorota-Kudyba.pixels.com.

For Meg

"And over all the sky—the sky!
far, far out of reach, studded, breaking out,
the eternal stars."

~Walt Whitman 1819–1892

Prologue

My dearest Twyla –

On this, the fifth anniversary of your birth, I sit down once again at my desk to write my yearly birthday letter to you. I will add it to the others, sealed in their cream-colored envelopes and kept safe, unopened, in a wooden box on the top shelf of my bedroom closet. The box is as old as you are and covered with seashells and starfish I've collected and glued onto it. The truth of the beginning of your life is in that box.

It seems like just yesterday we celebrated your very first day with us. You were so wanted. And not a day goes by that I am not reminded in some simple way of the story of you. For you, my love, came into this world as a spark, a bringer of light into the darkest places of my life, and your momma's life, too. You see, your momma and I had each suffered an agonizing loss. We were both filled with a sorrow that knew no bounds. The stars aligned and brought your momma and me together, and you, sweet child, have kept our story bound forever.

You never had the chance to know your older brother and so would not remember that he was called Schuyler. Your momma, too, do you remember her? She loved you so very, very much. When you were just a baby, your momma had to leave you in the care of the woman you now call mother, to go and look after Schuyler. It was the ultimate sacrifice: A woman giving up her heart's desire in the name of love. For fate did not allow your momma to embrace both you and your brother at the same time, in the same place.

Today you are five, and I imagine you are getting so big! I wonder if you will grow up to love horses as much as your momma did. As much as I do. That's how we met one another, you know, through horses—magical creatures who gallop between this earthly-world and the world-of-angels beyond. These noble beasts carried your momma and me into each other's lives.

For your birthday gift today, I will tell you the story of how you came to be. This is a tale of bravery and hardship, of magic and love. There are the bearers of darkness and there are the bringers of light. But before I even get to the part where the miracle that is you enters our lives, I have to go back several years before that time, to the very beginning.

Are you ready...?

Part I

Chapter 1

Susan

A constellation of blood droplets is scattered across the front of her shirt, Susan notices, as she fumbles around inside her purse in a desperate search for her car keys. Her hand has barely touched the driver's side door handle when she hears someone breathlessly coming up behind her. Susan freezes, doesn't turn. Here we go, she thinks.

"Oh, hey, Susan, wait up." She recognizes the voice and turns to see Norma jogging toward her through the medical clinic parking lot. "You were amazing today," her fellow nurse gushes. "I can't believe you had to do CPR on that elderly man who collapsed in the waiting room." Norma finally reaches Susan and stops short, noticing the flecks of dried blood on her coworker's scrub top. "Where'd that blood come from?"

Glancing down again at her clothing, Susan mutters, "It must've been from when the paramedics arrived and started the IV on him; the blood started spurting when they hit the vein."

"Oh, right. Well, you were incredible, jumping in like that. You probably saved that poor man's life, you know."

Susan realizes her friend is going to cast her as the heroine in each retelling of this story. She gazes beyond Norma. A passing spring shower has left the late day air heavy with moisture. Susan watches as the clinical staff trickle out of the medical office building and make their way through the parking lot, calling good night to one another as they weave their way around puddles and on to their cars, then on to their lives outside of work.

Susan is exhausted. The adrenaline that had coursed through her while she was performing CPR earlier that afternoon has faded, leaving her drained. She just wants to go home and stand under the hot shower, wash off the patient's blood, the desperation she had felt while doing chest compressions, the triumph when they got a pulse back.

"All in a day's work, Norma," she says, hoping to bring some finality to the conversation.

Norma misses the tone in Susan's voice. "Listen, I wanted to ask you something," she starts brightly.

Norma's got me cornered, Susan realizes, then adjusts the strap of her pocketbook over her shoulder, smiles with resignation, and turns her attention to her coworker.

"So, my husband has this friend." The tempo of Norma's words gathers speed and enthusiasm as she continues on an entirely different track. "A guy friend...."

Susan groans. "Before you go any further, Norma, I'm not interested in dating anyone right now. After my last relationship, I've sworn off men for a while. I'm happy just living the single life."

"Well, what happened to the 'clock is ticking' rant you went on the other day after we saw all those babies in the health clinic? Listen, I know you were in a bad relationship and that last guy kind of messed with your head, but honestly, I think I might have found the perfect guy for you."

"Norma Jean," Susan sighs, "I'm not interested in meeting someone new. Your John is one in a million, and let's face it, I'm not going to find someone like that for me. I've resigned myself to the fact that I'm going to be an old maid."

"But what about wanting to have a baby, Susan? You're always talking about how much you want to be a mother. If you're hoping for an immaculate conception, don't hold your breath."

Dear Norma, she has always known how to break a serious moment. Susan laughs. "Okay, you're right, I'm not going to hold out for an immaculate conception. But I can be a single mother. I haven't told anyone, but I'm looking into adopting through the foster care system."

"Really? Wow. Good for you. Is that something you want to take on, though? I've heard some of those kids give their adoptive parents a run for their money. Many of them have huge issues bonding with the people who adopt them. Are you sure you want to take that on as a single mother?"

"I'm just looking into it right now, Norma. It might not be the right choice for me, but I've got to pursue it. I've always known I would be a mother, and it doesn't seem like Mister Right will be making an appearance any time soon. My clock is ticking, as you reminded me, and I sort of need to get going if I want to be a mom."

"Well, that's why I want to tell you about this guy, for Pete's sake. Will you just listen for a sec? You can always say no after you meet him."

Susan acknowledges her friend. "All right, Norma, you win. Tell me about this guy." She smiles as Norma takes a deep breath and tells her about her husband's friend.

"I guess he divorced a couple of years ago. He has his own business, a hardware store, and lives in town in a house he built.

I think he might have one or two older kids, but I'm not sure. John went out with some buddies a couple of weeks ago, and this guy was with them. Seems he's interested in getting back into the dating scene."

Susan starts picking at the dried red spots on her shirt, worried the blood is going to set in and permanently ruin her new scrub set.

"I met him once before. Just a genuinely nice person, Susan. No agenda, other than he's looking to meet someone. I think you both might hit it off. What do you say? A double date with me and John and this guy? His name is Paul."

Susan concedes. They make plans to get together at Norma's house the following weekend. The temperatures have continued to get warmer, so Norma and her husband will open their back patio and grill burgers for the gathering.

At last, Susan can open her car door and sink gratefully into the driver's seat.

Susan arrives a little early at Norma's house, a bit nervous but somewhat excited. In spite of her resolve to remain single for the moment, truth be told, she has been a little uneasy about the prospect of adopting through the local foster care system.

Recently, she attended a meet-and-greet as part of the preliminary training to become an adoptive parent. Some of the stories the adoptive parents shared with the newcomers shocked her.

Reactive attachment disorder is just one example of conditions that make it difficult for children to connect with their foster or adoptive parents. Susan wasn't sure she wanted to get involved with something like that. Not that this was the case with every child in the foster care system, but she didn't know how she would handle it as a single parent if she had to deal with it.

"You look so cute in that dress!" Norma shrieks as she opens the door and takes the potato salad out of Susan's hands. "You're adorable. Look, John, isn't Susan adorable?"

John looks up from where he is busy preparing food at the kitchen counter. "Oh, hey, Susan. Make yourself at home. Want something to drink?" He returns to forming hamburgers on a tray, then looks back up. "Do you want a beer? Wine? Or, we have seltzer water. Norma, can you get your friend something?"

"Seltzer water is fine," replies Susan. This seems so awkward, she thinks as Norma hands her a glass filled with ice and seltzer, a little wedge of lime perched on the rim. It's like I'm the last one standing by the bleachers at a high school dance, waiting for some guy to come over and ask me onto the dance floor. The pudgy girl with the pigtails and glasses. God, what a horrible memory, she thinks, wishing she had asked for a drink with alcohol in it.

The doorbell rings, and John's friend, Paul, finally arrives. Susan silently admonishes herself for feeling so giddy at meeting him. He is stocky in build, tan, with a warm smile and kind eyes. He has a shaved head and Susan notices the glint of a small diamond in one of Paul's ears. She finds this sexy. Susan cannot believe she is sizing him up like this after her recent vow to stay single. When Paul reaches for her hand to shake it, Susan feels her knees weaken just a little.

Standing beside Susan, Norma whispers, "I knew you'd like him."

She smiles and then turns to help John carry the burgers out to the back patio, where the grill is smoking. Susan is left with Paul.

"It's nice to meet you," she starts. "Norma tells me you own a hardware store." That's dumb, she thinks. I could have come up with a cleverer opening line.

Paul looks right at her with a silly smile, acknowledging the awkwardness of this setup. "Yes," he replies, "and I hear you're a nurse."

Susan recovers and makes her way over to the fridge. "Want something to drink? Beer? Wine? I think I'm going to have some wine. Can I pour you a glass?"

"Just ice water for me, thanks."

"Sure." Susan pours the water from a pitcher and hands him the glass, ice cubes clinking as her hand trembles slightly. What is wrong with me? Susan thinks. It's not as if this is my first blind date. She smiles.

"What?" Paul asks. "What are you smiling at?"

Relieved that he has recognized her obvious distress, she responds, "This is just so weird, to be set up, you know? Like we're in high school or something."

"I know. I've been so nervous about this. I haven't met anyone since my wife and I divorced a couple of years ago. It's not easy to get back in the game again."

"Right." He has revealed a little about himself, and Susan decides she will, too. With her guard down, she offers, "I recently swore off dating after being in a bad relationship for the past few years. He was an ass, and I finally decided he wasn't worth wasting my life over."

"Oh, I'm sorry to hear that. My wife, my ex-wife, and I," Paul corrects, "split up over my son. Well, that's not exactly true. It was a long time coming, but that was kinda the final straw."

"Your son? Wow, what happened with your son?"

Paul smiles a weak smile and lets out a deep sigh. "It's a long story, but essentially, my son came out to me and my ex-wife when he was sixteen. Parker is gay. And my ex couldn't accept it. He's an only child, smart as a whip, and handsome. I think my ex-wife just couldn't see that for our son. She always expected him to marry someone like her and give her a bunch of grandchildren. We were fighting about it one night, and my son heard us. He thought I was speaking too rough with his mother. He actually took her side. Like she needed protecting, and she latched onto that. Played the victim. She pitted our son against me, driving the final wedge into our marriage. It's been a mess."

"So even though you were defending your son's choices, he ended up siding with his mother, who wasn't defending his choices? That's a confusing one. How are things with your son now?"

Paul pauses before answering. "They're not great. Better. But not great." He lifts his head and smiles again at Susan. "But, hey, enough about that. Let's go hang out with John and Norma. Those hamburgers are calling to me!"

The two of them head out to the patio where Norma has arranged a picnic table covered with salads, chips, and dips, and John is busy flipping burgers. "How do you like your meat, Susan?" he asks, looking up as she and Paul exit the house. "I mean your hamburger? How do you like your hamburger?" He grins.

"Jeez, Honey, way to be subtle," Norma chides playfully. "C'mon over to the table, you guys. Dinner is ready!"

The foursome enjoy the food and drinks well into the evening. John and Paul engage in a long debate about the upcoming baseball season, while Norma and Susan giggle and share first-date stories over their third glass of wine each.

"So, what do you think?" Norma eventually blurts to Susan. "He's cute, isn't he?"

"Shhh," Susan hushes her friend, laughing at Norma. "You

are so loud. I don't want them to hear us. Yes. He is cute."

"You think you'll go out with him again?"

"Oh, I don't know." Susan's head is swimming from the alcohol, the warm spring evening, the lightness of it all. "I'm just getting my legs back under me from leaving my most recent mistake. I feel like I need to spread my wings as a single girl for a while. Plus, he might not even like me."

"Are you kidding me? He likes you! Have you seen the way he's been stealing looks at you all night?"

"You mean it's not because I'm crazy drunk?" Susan throws her head back and laughs again.

"No, Girl. He likes you. I can tell."

Just then, John looks over. "What are you two laughing about? Want to let us in on the joke?"

"Nope. It's a secret," Norma quips as she gets up from the table and puts her arm around John. "A girl's gotta have secrets, you know. That's what keeps you guys coming back for more."

Everybody at the table groans. "Well, on that note," says Paul, untangling his legs from the bench, "I should probably get going home. I've got to open up the store tomorrow morning." He glances over at Susan. "It looks like you've had a bit to drink. Can I give you a ride home?"

"I'm good," she replies, also rising from the picnic table, albeit a little wobbly. "I'm going to help Norma clean up out here, and by then, I should be okay with driving home. I live pretty close by, anyway. Thanks, though."

"Okay. Well, it was really nice to meet you." Paul looks at Susan and smiles before he turns back toward the house. "Thanks for dinner and everything, John and Norma," he calls as he strides out the front door to his truck.

Norma looks at John, "I think that went really well, don't you, Honey? Don't you think that went really well?"

"I do," replies John. He walks over to the cooled grill to put the cover back on. Norma and Susan start collecting dishes and silverware from the table. "Susan, you don't have to do that," John says. "Norma and I've got it."

"You sure? I don't mind helping."

"No, no. You're the guest. We'll clean up here."

"Are you okay to drive home, Sweetie?" asks Norma as she returns from inside for another load of dishes. "John can drive you if you need a ride."

"Actually, to be on the safe side maybe John should drive me home. I'll walk back over tomorrow morning and pick up my car." Susan gives Norma a quick hug. "Thanks, you guys. This was great." She follows John as he reaches for his keys and they make their way out to his car and on to Susan's house a few streets away.

For the remainder of the weekend, Susan busies herself puttering around her little house, airing out the bedrooms, washing windows, and repotting house plants. Her little dog, Ginger, follows her everywhere. "Edith Wharton was right when she said, 'My little old dog, a heartbeat at my feet.'" Susan bends down to pat the Pomeranian's soft head.

Late that Sunday afternoon, Susan returns from her weekly horseback riding lesson. The lessons are a treat to herself after finally getting out of the toxic relationship she'd been in for the past three years. She had moved in with Seth after they'd dated for quite some time. He was sweet and chivalrous until she lived with him. Then he became so manipulative and controlling that Susan had become terribly unsure of herself. She retreated inward, hardly going out with friends, never enjoying any of the things she did before meeting him, like horseback riding.

Susan opens the door to her tiny mudroom and kicks off her riding boots. Happily, she has a moment to put her feet up and enjoy a cup of hot tea. She hasn't checked her phone since this morning and notices a couple of calls from an unknown number. She listens to the messages; it's Paul. He wants to get together for another date, just the two of them. Susan doesn't know how she feels about this; she is flattered but still unsure if she has the energy to start a new relationship.

Susan's mind starts to wander as she sits in her favorite chair, the late day sun warming her face, Ginger contentedly snoring in her lap. Despite being single for most of her adult life, Susan is confident she will be a mother someday. She knows this with every fiber of her being. She knows she will be incredibly caring like her own mother, but she is sure she will not be as temperamental and punishing as her mother could be. She wants to raise a strong-minded, healthy child. Susan wants to leave a part of herself behind in this world through the child she raises. She has thought about IVF, she has thought about adoption, she has even thought about having a one-night stand just to get pregnant. And now here is this guy, Paul. Susan hesitates briefly, then presses the call-back button on her phone.

Paul shows up promptly at six that Wednesday evening for dinner. Ginger barks hysterically when the doorbell rings. As the door opens, Paul hands Susan a beautiful bouquet of flowers as he bends down to greet a bouncing Ginger. "Who is this?" he asks as the dog licks his face, tail wagging. "Those are for you, by the way." Paul looks up at the flowers Susan is now sniffing.

Susan laughs. "Thank you. These are gorgeous. This is Ginger. She's my sidekick. I can't believe how friendly she is with you. She normally doesn't like men. She was a rescue. Came from an abusive home. I got her several months ago, after I was finally out of that bad relationship once and for all. We're kind of two peas in a pod, me and Ginger."

The buzzer on the stove goes off. "Oh, I better get that!" Susan smiles. "I don't want the chicken to burn. C'mon in. Make yourself at home. It's a small house, perfect for Ginger and me."

Paul stands up, Ginger still twirling around and between his legs. He shuts the screen door behind him. "It smells delicious. Anything I can do to help?" He follows Susan into her narrow kitchen.

Susan hands Paul the flowers he brought, "Can you put these in some water? There's a vase under the sink. I need to take the chicken out of the oven. Thanks."

The candles glow on Susan's small kitchen table, and the two sit down to a dinner of chicken piccata, roasted asparagus, potatoes au gratin, and a vegetable salad.

"Oh, my God, you are an amazing cook," Paul says, grinning between mouthfuls. "My ex-wife was a terrible cook; we ate a lot of takeout. Where did you learn to cook like this?"

Susan grins back at Paul, pleased with how well her dish turned out. "My mother and my aunt. Both Polish. Both amazing cooks. And bakers. Wait until we get to dessert."

Paul looks up from his plate, a bite of food balancing on his fork.

"So, tell me about this guy you were living with. The one that you left. I mean, if you want to. You don't have to if you don't want to." He looks sheepish as he glances back down at his fork.

"No, really. It's all right. Well, it wasn't at the time. But it is now. I wasn't someone who dated a lot in high school or college.

I was always heavier than the other girls my age and never got into the dating scene like most of my peers." Susan cannot believe how comfortable she feels opening up to Paul, like she's known him for a lifetime already.

"I think you're beautiful," he interrupts, and his face reddens slightly.

Susan's eyes sparkle as she continues. "In college it was all about my studies. I just never made time for dating. And then a couple of years ago I met this guy, he was like twelve years older than me, a friend of a friend. I had lost a little weight by then, so my self-confidence was boosted. He was charming initially: lots of long phone calls, dinners out, gifts. He even met, and impressed, my parents. After several months of dating, he asked me to move in with him. I was smitten."

Paul looks up, a frown on his face. "Uh oh."

"Uh oh is right! Behind closed doors, in his own home, he was a creep. Manipulative, verbally abusive."

"Did he ever hit you?"

"No, not then. In the end, though, he threw dirt at me one day because he didn't like how I planted some flowers. That's when I knew I had to leave."

"And so you left him? That day?"

Susan takes a deep breath. "No, not exactly. It took me a couple of tries to finally leave him for good. I would go, and then he would make all these promises to change, so I would return and give him another chance. Each time I went back, he was worse. He made me feel like shit about myself, like I wasn't worth anything. All of these mind games."

"God. I'm so sorry you went through all of that. It must've been awful for you."

"Many times, it was. Many times, I felt so worthless after a fight with him that I thought I would be better off dead. My sister said that during the time I lived with him, she was sure I was going to kill myself. She was the one who finally helped me get out of there for good."

"You're such an incredible person, so strong." Paul pauses and continues hesitantly, "I went through a rough patch when my ex and I split up. I was pretty depressed. I felt like I had lost everything: my marriage, my son. I felt like I didn't have anything to live for. I never tried to hurt myself or anything. Instead, I just drowned my sorrows in food, ice cream, to be exact. I've probably gained about thirty pounds in the last couple of years. I need to start exercising to get back in shape. Hey, not to change the subject, but do you like hiking?"

"Perfect segue," Susan replies a little too forcefully, glad to get off the subject of depression and bad relationships. She hasn't yet processed all her emotions since leaving Seth, and she doesn't want to lose her composure in front of Paul, on their first date, no less. "Yes," she says with relief, "I love hiking."

The two spend the next couple of hours conversing over dinner, then enjoying a dessert of chocolate mousse. Paul clears the table while Susan rinses the dinner dishes and stacks them in the dishwasher. "Want me to blow out these candles?" Paul asks.

"Let's leave them going. I love candlelight."

"Yeah, me, too. It's kind of romantic."

"Too romantic? Too soon?" asks Susan, wondering if things are moving too quickly for both of them, although she has a comfortable sense around Paul. She can tell he's a gentle soul. Still, being newly single and out of a rough relationship, she feels somewhat guarded.

"Oh, no, not at all," replies Paul hurriedly. "I didn't mean romantic-romantic. Just, you know, nice, and warm, and comfortable. But not too comfortable. Oh, God, I need to stop talking, I think," he says with an exasperated laugh.

Susan laughs, too. "No worries. Let's sit in the living room. We can talk some more if you want to. I have to warn you, though, Ginger may hop up on the couch and join us. I hope you don't mind pets on the couch."

"Not at all," Paul replies, reaching down to pick Ginger up.

Chapter 2

Hillary

Hillary tidies up the kitchen in her little apartment after a quick breakfast of raisin toast and black coffee. She gives herself a passing look in the mirror, ties back her long dark hair, applies lip gloss, glances at her fluffy cat, Athena, asleep on the bed, and makes her way to her bedroom closet. It's a Monday, but not just any Monday. Last Friday, Hillary's boss, Carl, had pulled her aside at the start of the workday.

"Hillary, hey. Do you have a second this morning?"

Oh, God, what have I done now, she'd thought. So far, things had been going amazingly well at her new job with the large computer programming firm in Albany, New York. Hillary had moved into her cozy apartment six months ago, surprised and delighted that she'd found something close to work that also fit her budget. She had packed her belongings from her stepmother's house, loaded up the back of her old red Subaru wagon, and hadn't looked back, relieved to be out from under that situation.

"Yeah, sure, Carl. What's up?" She had smiled at him, hoping he wouldn't notice the slight trembling in her voice.

"Here, come into my office." Carl shut the door behind them. "Have a seat." He gestured toward the lone chair in front of his large wooden desk, cluttered with a leaning tower of papers threatening to topple over, if not for the balance provided by a nondescript papier-maché paperweight, painted pink and purple—obviously a child's art project.

"I like your paperweight," Hillary had offered, trying to lighten the moment.

Carl looked at the haphazard pile of papers, his train of thought momentarily confused. "Oh, right. My daughter made that for me in elementary school. She's in college now. She never comes to the office, but I haven't had the heart to throw it away." He turned back toward Hillary.

"Listen. I know you've been with the company only a short time, but your work has been exemplary. It hasn't gone unnoticed."

Hillary breathed a huge sigh and finally looked Carl directly in the eyes. She decided not to interrupt him to voice her relief at where the conversation seemed to be headed.

"We have an opening on our consulting team," Carl continued. "It's a fairly new team. Six guys. Our best and brightest. Well, five now. Jefferson just retired. We'd like you to fill the open position, Hillary. It would mean late nights, travel, and putting up with a bunch of immature guys," Carl had chuckled. "But it would also mean a significant pay increase. Management here is really impressed with you and wants to offer you this opportunity. Think about it for a couple of days and let me know."

Hillary hadn't had to think about it. By the end of the day, she had knocked on the door to Carl's office and accepted the position. Carl seemed somewhat relieved that she had agreed to it, making Hillary wonder what exactly she had just signed up for. He stood up and shook her hand. "Welcome to the team," he said with a smile. "I'll introduce you to the guys at our meeting on Monday morning."

That evening, after work, Hillary put on her favorite pair of sweats, poured herself a glass of red wine, and curled up on the couch with her purring cat. As soon as she was settled, she dialed her best friend, Joan, whom she had met years ago at the barn where they rode horses.

"Hey, Girl," Joan said when she picked up.

"Joanie! Oh, my God, you will never believe what happened at work today. Oh, my God!"

"They asked you to design a top-secret program for the Pentagon?" Joan asked. "No, really, what happened at work today? Tell me."

"I got pulled into my boss's office..." Hillary started.

"Oh, shit!" Joan interrupted.

"Well, that's what I thought. But he actually offered me a promotion," Hillary squealed. "Can you believe it? And it comes with a nice raise, too."

"Good for you, Girl!" Joan replied. "I never doubted for a second that you'd go on to break glass ceilings. You are so talented. And smart. Congratulations! Tell me all about it."

The girlfriends carried on late into the evening, Hillary not quite believing she had landed the position so soon after joining the company, and her friend assuring her again and again that she knew all along Hillary would be going places as soon as she got out on her own.

And now it's Monday. THAT Monday. Hillary looks at herself one last time in the bedroom mirror. She is pleased with the face that stares back at her: unblemished ivory skin, full pink lips, perfectly trimmed eyebrows. And then she looks right into her eyes, and she sighs. One is blue, the other hazel. Heterochromia iridium. A condition she was born with. She was made fun of quite a bit as a child because of her eyes, and her stepmother used to point it out to Hillary and whoever of her stepmother's friends happened to be within earshot. "Look at her eyes, will you? I've never seen anything like it, have you? Well, she's not my biological child, you know." And Hillary would look away, blinking back tears.

She has chosen a tight-fitting green dress for her first day with the consulting team, professional, but not leaving much to the imagination. If you've got it, flaunt it, she thinks. Right? Hillary plumps up her lips one more time in the mirror. Smiles at herself. There, she thinks, there is the next CEO of this company. She giggles, grabs her purse by the door, blows a kiss to Athena, and walks out to her car.

The parking garage is a frenzy of cars jockeying for spaces near the elevator entrances. Hillary finds a spot almost at the top level and hurries to the elevator platform to wait with the other building employees for the dingy elevator doors to open. She can feel people looking at her. Men looking at her. She stares straight ahead; she will not return their gazes. Refuses to acknowledge them. Just watch me, she thinks to herself, as she pushes back her shoulders, chin held high.

The glass-fronted conference room grows suddenly silent as Hillary walks in and takes a seat near the middle of the long, polished table. The five other members of the consulting team quickly turn their jocular banter into small talk: weekend events with their families, sports scores, the weather.

"You must be the new girl," one of the team's younger members says as he stares Hillary up and down.

"The new woman, you mean. Right?" Hillary stares right back at him.

A couple of loud whoops from the others around the table. "I guess she told you, huh, Peter?" a middle-aged computer programmer calls from across the room, laughing and jabbing the ribs of the guy sitting beside him with his elbow.

Peter smirks. "My apologies." He stands up and offers his hand to Hillary. "I'm Peter. Welcome to the team."

"Pleasure," replies Hillary, squeezing his hand in a firm handshake. Peter pulls his hand away, shaking it.

"You've got some grip there," he says with a little laugh. "You a softball player or something?"

"No. Horses. I ride horses. And you know what they say about women who ride horses, don't you?"

"No. What?" Peter asks.

"Never underestimate a woman who can control a thousand-pound animal with a mind of its own."

More hoots from the guys around the table. "You better stop while you're ahead, buddy," says one of the other team members. "She's got your number."

"Not that that's too hard to get," another team member chimes in, giving Peter a dramatic wink.

Carl, their boss and team leader, walks in carrying a stack of paper-stuffed manilla folders under one arm, a hot coffee in that same hand, and a box of donuts balanced precariously in the other hand.

Hillary jumps up from her chair at the table. "Need a hand with that, Carl? Here, give me those folders."

"Brown noser," Peter mumbles from the other end of the table, a little put out that the morning banter had been at his expense. Peter is intrigued by Hillary's promotion to the consulting team. He has noticed her at times in the office, heard other men at work talking about her perfect body shape, porcelain skin, and long black hair. They seem a bit afraid of her—her high intelligence, wit, and sharp comebacks when they try to flirt with her. Peter sees Hillary as strong, independent, a challenge to obtain. He squirms in his seat just a little as he becomes aware of the physical arousal Hillary creates in him.

Carl sits down heavily in the chair at the head of the table, clears his throat. "So, you've all met Hillary, our newest team member." He turns to Hillary. "I hope they were polite to you."

"It's great to be here. Thanks for the opportunity, Carl. I look forward to working with the team." Hillary looks each of the team members in the eyes as she speaks. She can't believe the source of strength she feels within herself right now. Ballsy, she thinks. Who is this girl?

Carl launches into a long explanation of a new consulting project the team will be working on with a large medical organization on the West Coast, updating their software. Carl details the project phases, who is assigned to head up each phase, and what they will be responsible for.

Hillary is taking notes on her laptop. She can feel Peter watching her as Carl drones on. She can feel the heat rising on the side of her neck closest to Peter, up the side of her face. She, too, is intrigued. Hillary guesses that Peter is about her age. She finds him a bit mysterious; he's been there, done that, yet he is still young. There's a dangerous edge to Peter that Hillary cannot seem to pull away from. He doesn't remind her of anyone in particular. Perhaps that is why she can see herself with Peter. She shakes her head and tries to refocus on Carl's instructions.

Mary, the woman in the cubicle beside Hillary, loves to gossip. "What I heard," she confides on Hillary's first day with the consulting team, "is that Peter and his ex-wife divorced when their kids were pretty much babies. The ex-wife goes in and out of rehab hospitals, and so most of the raising of those kids falls on Peter, who never really wanted children in the first place, and who has no idea and much less interest in raising them. So Peter gets his poor mother to watch the little boy and girl while he's at work, and then afterward when he goes out to bars. His ex-wife is supposedly in and out of the picture, sometimes moving back in with Peter and the kids, sometimes living elsewhere in a halfway house or somewhere with a new and different boyfriend. It's a shitty life for those kids."

Listening to her coworker, Hillary wonders if Peter resents the fact that he's stuck with his kids. He's still a young man, she thinks, handsome, with dark skin, close-cropped black hair, and a well-trimmed mustache and goatee. She knows Peter has tried to date other women at the company, but Hillary imagines he has no time between work and his two small kids, and then he goes out with the guys after work. Hillary can't stop thinking about him.

When Carl assigns Hillary to participate on the big West Coast medical system project, Peter volunteers to join. It's long days and late nights at the office, designing complicated medical computer programs for delivery on a deadline. Hillary and Peter begin spending more and more time together, getting to know one another on a deeper than work-colleague level.

"My biological mother died when I was young," Hillary tells Peter one late evening as she reaches across the worktable, takes a to-go container from the Chinese restaurant around the corner, and begins digging into the lo mein with her chopsticks. "Cancer, I think. My dad never really talked about her. He got remarried pretty soon after that to my stepmother, and they had a daughter together. My half-sister, Eva."

Peter is madly attracted to Hillary and hasn't been paying attention to what she's saying. "I don't know how you do that," he blurts.

Hillary looks up at him, chopsticks poised for another dive into the lo mein. "Do what?"

"Eat with those things. Those stick-things. Why can't Chinese people eat with a knife and fork like the rest of the world? It's probably because it's cheaper to manufacture those cheesy wooden sticks than to give out a plastic fork and knife with Chinese takeout."

"What are you talking about? Chopsticks are an ancient and elegant way of eating noodles, I'll have you know." Hillary looks up at Peter and smiles. "How do you think those Asian women stay so skinny eating all those carbs? They can only take little bites with their chopsticks, not giant gobs of food on a fork like we do here in America. So really, it's a healthier way to eat, if you ask me. A fashion statement, if you will." Her eyes twinkle.

"Okay, well, it makes more sense when you put it like that. You must eat with chopsticks all the time. Your body is gorgeous." He smiles sheepishly and takes a large bite of a fried chicken finger, then licks the grease off his fingers one by one.

"Well, thank you, Peter." Hillary finds a softness in him, Peter, who comes across at work as a bad boy, with his sarcasm and teasing. She loves that he is the father of two small children. She loves that he rose to the occasion when his wife left and they divorced. She senses a nurturer in this man. She finds herself drawn to this. Drawn to him.

After several months of working in the office, the programming team for the West Coast project is sent to San Francisco, to the medical facility site, to work out a glitch in the system and start training staff members to use the new program. Hillary is the only female on the consulting team, scoring her a single room at a nearby hotel. The rest of the team doubles up and shares rooms.

It is late one night. They've worked hard all day, and their time in San Francisco is drawing to a close. Hillary goes along with the guys to the hotel bar, limiting herself to one drink to keep her wits about her while still taking part in the fun. She notices that Peter is pounding down shots at the bar. He is celebrating, she thinks. He deserves this.

After leaving the bar in the wee hours of the morning, the team heads to their hotel rooms. Hillary is exhausted. They wrap up their work here tomorrow and return to Albany and their regular office lives. She is in the little hotel room bathroom, removing her makeup, when she hears a soft knock at her door. She ignores it. It's late. The knocking grows louder. Hillary walks over and looks out the peephole. Standing there, a bit disheveled but handsome nonetheless, is Peter. She lets him in. He reeks of hard liquor, but she is excited by his dark energy, excited to have this moment together. She is in her T-shirt and pajama bottoms; he is in a button-down shirt and tight jeans. They can't get enough of each other. Hillary drinks in the feel of Peter's tight, muscular arms, inviting lips, and thick, short hair. "Come in," she whispers as Peter places his hands on the small of Hillary's back and pulls her tightly toward him.

In the morning, as sunlight streams through the hotel window, Hillary looks at Peter's peaceful face on the pillow beside her. What a night. She is sore from all of their lovemaking and feels like something has been ignited deep inside her.

Peter's masculine energy burns within her. It is a feeling Hillary has never experienced before.

Chapter 3

Susan

It's their fourth date. Paul surprises Susan with a trip to Newport, Rhode Island, for a day of shopping, touring the mansions, and looking out over the bluffs to the ocean. As they meander along the Cliff Walk, the sweet smell of the rosa rugosa fills the air. Paul's heart is full. He reaches out to take Susan's hand and smiles when her fingers close comfortably around his own. They are both happily exhausted, their skin warm and glowing, as they brush the sand from their feet, slip on their sneakers, and stroll from the beach to a fresh fish restaurant right on the water. They are shown to their table and presented with a multitude of menus for drinks, entrees, and specials. After looking through one menu, Susan laughs as she puts it down and moves on to the next.

"What?" Paul asks.

"Oh, it's so funny, these upscale restaurants, how they have a menu for this and a menu for that, and you spend so much time looking at menus before you even get to what's on their dinner list."

"Do you not like it here?" Paul looks up, somewhat alarmed.

"Yes!" Susan realizes he has misinterpreted her lighthearted comment about the menus. "It's absolutely lovely here." She changes the subject. "What are you thinking of having?"

"Hmmm." Paul continues to gaze intently at the meal selections. "I'm thinking the swordfish. What about you? By the way, I have had the best day with you."

"Me, too," Susan replies. "We get along so well together. Sometimes I feel like I've known you all my life." Then quickly, "Is that weird?"

"Not at all. I feel the exact same way. Hey, there is something I want to ask you about."

"Oh, this sounds serious."

"Well, it is. In a good way."

Dear God, I hope he doesn't ask me to move in with him, thinks Susan. I am so not ready to make that mistake again.

Paul continues, "I know you've told me a little bit about how you've wanted to have a child. And what I want to say is…" He pauses as if at a loss for words. "What I want to say is that we are so compatible, you and me, like you were saying. And I think I'm falling in love with you. And I want to give you a baby." Fearing he has said too much, too soon, Paul looks at his lap and waits for Susan's response.

Susan jumps up from her chair at the table. She squeals and runs over to hug Paul. He is surprised by her exuberance. He holds her to him.

It is October. Susan and Paul are hiking up their favorite trail. The path is steep, but it winds back and forth across the face of the mountain, easing the incline's strain a bit. Even in the crisp fall air, they are sweating with the exertion of climbing. Susan has brought some snacks and cold water in her backpack. She always carries a book of poetry or nature prose when they go hiking, and she likes to read to Paul as they sit and have their small feast once they reach the summit.

Paul is in the lead. He is almost at the top of the trail when he turns around and takes Susan's hand. "C'mon, Suzie," he says, pulling her up the last few feet. And they are suddenly looking out at the world around them. A light mist has settled in some of the pockets of the valley below. In the distance, to the east, Susan can make out the faint skyline of Boston. They are in their own private paradise. Winded after the climb, they inhale the fresh mountain air for a few moments.

"Let's go sit at our favorite spot." Paul leads her across the peak. It is a small grassy patch surrounded by low bushes facing west, so the morning sun is on their backs. They remove their windbreakers and set them on the damp grass to sit upon, both quiet as they take in the vastness of their surroundings. Susan notices a few birds gliding over the wooded valley. She listens to a hawk's long, lonely cry as it soars and dives.

Unzipping her backpack, Susan begins rummaging around inside, pulling out crackers, cheese, and a little chunk of hard salami she grabbed from her fridge before meeting Paul this morning. Paul is hunting around in his backpack. He often brings binoculars so they can focus in on the birds and other wildlife they see on their hikes. Susan is oblivious to what Paul is doing. She pulls out her book of poetry, a collection by Mary Oliver, one of her favorite nature poets.

Paul turns around toward Susan after he finds what he is looking for. Susan is deep in contemplation, with her nose in the book of poetry. He struggles to reposition himself directly in front of where Susan is sitting. She finally looks up from her book and sees Paul fidgeting.

"What?" she says. He is on one knee. *Holy cow! It's happening right now!*

"Suzie," he starts, "my beautiful Suzie. You came to me when I was lost. My world was a dark place, and my heart was broken and tired. You came to me with your smile, and your blue eyes, and your love, and you healed my heart. You healed me. I cannot imagine spending my life without you, Suzie. Will you marry me?"

He pauses. A light breeze blows through the red and orange leaves, stirring them and gently wafting them to the ground around their secluded spot. It is the only sound. Paul holds out his hand toward Susan, and in it is a little blue velvet box with a diamond ring displayed in its crease.

Susan melts. "Of course I will marry you," she says. "You are my heart and soul, and I cannot imagine a life without you." Paul clumsily puts the ring on Susan's finger, then gathers her close. Susan finds herself half crying, half giggling, in this moment of joy, of union.

One evening after work, Susan is busy sorting through her wedding planner, a large binder with papers and sticky notes falling out of it. She is trying to put it in some kind of order while she looks for a piece of paper with the phone number of a musician duo on it. They will have music at their wedding but no dancing; neither can dance, so they easily agreed to cut that out of the wedding day plans. They will have a flute, a violin, and someone to sing hymns. And that will be that.

Paul comes in the door to the house. Their house. Susan has moved in a couple of weeks ago from the little cottage she'd been sharing with her dog, Ginger. Paul is still mildly surprised each time he walks through the door after work to find Susan there, living with him. He smiles to himself. He has never been happier. They have already started to try to get pregnant.

"Hey, Suzie," he calls out, "how's the wedding planner today? I brought us home a pizza."

Ginger flies off the couch, where she has been curled up contentedly next to Susan. She dances on her hind legs, trying to get a better sniff at the pizza box Paul is carrying into the kitchen. Susan also jumps off the couch, following the scent of hot pizza that trails after Paul. She comes up behind him and gives him a huge hug. Paul puts down the pizza box, turns around in Susan's arms, and greets her with a long, deep kiss. His kisses are so passionate, it's like they've been away from each other for many months and have finally come together again.

"I've gotten some of the returns from the wedding invitations," she says, gasping somewhat as she comes up for air. "You really are the best kisser, Paul. Is Parker coming to the wedding?" she asks in the next breath, referring to Paul's son. Susan met Parker and Paul's ex-wife just recently for only a brief moment at his high school graduation. While Parker had been cordial to Susan when they were introduced, she had felt an air of resentment from him as he stood with his arm protectively draped across his mother's shoulders.

She and Paul had arrived together at the high school auditorium. The graduation ceremony was typical: lots of speeches, a long parade of students in their black robes and caps following each other, one at a time, onto the stage to receive their diplomas. Then, there was a huge shout at the end, followed by all those mortarboards excitedly thrown into the air.

Susan had noticed a pregnancy bump under one of the student's gowns, subtly covered by the girl holding her diploma in front of her belly. That's a tough way to start life right after high school, Susan had thought, although deep down, she was somewhat jealous of this young girl's pregnancy. She and Paul had been trying for a while now, and each month, when her period started, she was quietly disappointed all over again.

She and Paul had each scheduled an appointment with a specialist to determine the issue. Susan's gynecologist said everything looked fine with Susan's exam and blood work. She should be able to get pregnant. However, the gynecologist cautioned that she shouldn't wait much longer, as Susan was nearing forty.

Paul scheduled his appointment with a fertility specialist. Susan had a day off from work and came along with him. She sat in the wood-paneled waiting room that hadn't been updated since the 1970s. Susan dug through the stack of magazines on the table beside her. They, too, didn't look like they'd been updated since the 1970s, which she found amusing. She began thumbing through the worn pages of an old *Woman's Day* magazine. Ads for diet pills on every other page, and articles on exercise strategies to lose weight. She laughed at how little had changed from those women's days.

The phone beeped once on the secretary's desk, and she looked over quickly in Susan's direction. The secretary hung up the phone and motioned for Susan to follow her into the doctor's office where Paul had gone. The fertility specialist, a kindly older physician with thinning white hair, wearing a starched white lab coat with his name embroidered on it, sat behind a heavy wooden desk. Paul was sitting in a chair opposite the doctor's desk and looked up without a smile as Susan sat down in a chair next to him.

"I'm afraid," started the doctor, "that Paul's sperm count is very low. And the few sperm that are present have very low motility. That is, they are not strong enough, potent enough, one could say, to swim to the woman's egg, your egg." He glanced at Susan. "There's a very minimal chance that you could get pregnant." He looked apologetically at Susan. She imagined the doctor had delivered this news countless times. He didn't seem impacted by the devastation he had just announced to them. Susan looked over at Paul. He was embarrassed, she could tell. His eyes were cast downward. She reached for his hand. Paul looked over at Susan again, then turned to the doctor.

Quietly, he asked, "Is there anything I can do? Shots or something?"

"I'm afraid," the doctor said once again, "that hormone therapy won't help with this condition. In cases like these, I recommend IVF, in vitro fertilization. If your wife's eggs," the doctor didn't realize they weren't a married couple yet, "are healthy, she should be able to conceive through a donor's sperm. Some couples in this situation have the husband's brother, or other male relative, donate sperm, so the baby is closely related to the father."

Susan and Paul looked at each other. She was slightly hopeful about this news, and he was very obviously horrified.

"I'm sorry to be the bearer of these findings," counseled the doctor as he ushered them out of his office. "Many couples discover IVF to be an excellent alternative for starting a family." He handed them a brochure on fertility options as they exited his office.

Back in the car, Paul had been near tears. "I'm so sorry," he said over and over again. "I really wanted to give you a baby. I'm so sorry."

"Well, let's look into IVF," said Susan comfortingly. "Let's look into it and see what the options are."

Paul shook his head. "I don't want you to have a baby that

isn't mine." He had looked up at her. "I don't want to use another man's sperm. It's not right. Not for me."

Susan felt herself deflating, and her hope began to drift away. No, no. This was not how things were supposed to happen. In large part, she was marrying Paul because he wanted to give her a baby. She knew he would be the very best father to their child. She was marrying this man to start a family. This wasn't how things were supposed to play out. "What about adoption, Paul? There are so many babies and children looking for loving homes. We could adopt one of them."

"I can't think about that right now," Paul quietly replied as he focused straight ahead on the highway taking them home.

Susan pours herself into wedding plans, sure that once Paul sits with the idea for a while, adoption, or even revisiting IVF, will feel like a good option for them. Susan knows that Paul recognizes her strong desire to have a baby. She has told him it isn't just something she wants; it's something her physical body aches for. Her body is designed to bear children, and her body has been telling her loudly that it is time to fulfill this primal drive.

Susan and Paul are keeping the wedding small, with Susan's sister, Lizzie, as her maid of honor and a couple of girlfriends from work as bridesmaids. Paul has asked his friend John, who introduced them that night at the cookout, to be his best man. It has been stressful in some ways to pull even this simple event together. However, Susan is pleased when she thinks of the work that has gone into planning their special day, and she smiles when she thinks of how well she and Paul work and make decisions together.

One thing that still hasn't been determined, and the one

thing causing Susan the most anxiety about their wedding, is Paul's son. Parker is a young man, having just started his first year of college a couple of months ago, and Susan has not yet heard if he will be attending the ceremony. She knows Paul has talked to Parker, told Parker he's met the love of his life in Susan and he's going to marry her. Paul came to Susan after his initial conversation with his son, saying that Parker still held some bitterness that Paul and his mother had divorced. Paul wasn't sure if his son would be attending their wedding.

She asks Paul again as she sits down on the living room floor surrounded by returned wedding invitations, marking off in a notebook who will be coming and who will not, "Is Parker coming, Honey?"

Paul is sitting on the couch, watching a football game on TV, Ginger snuggled next to him, snoring in her deep doggie sleep. A huge play has just happened on the TV screen, and it has caught Paul's attention. "I haven't heard if he's coming yet. If he comes, he'll have to buy an airline ticket to fly back from college."

"Did you offer to buy the ticket for him?"

"I did. He said he didn't know what was happening that weekend at school or if he would need to stay to study for mid-terms or anything."

Susan is a little annoyed that Paul is taking this so casually. She also believes very strongly, as she has not been involved in raising Parker and doesn't know him on any deep level, that it is not her place to get involved in their father-son discussions, even if it is her wedding, too. She turns back to her invitations and doesn't ask again about Parker.

Their wedding day finally arrives. It is a beautiful late autumn morning with a deep blue sky and only a few clouds. This is Susan's favorite time of year, and she is thrilled that the weather has turned out to be perfect. It was forecasted just this morning, that the day would be unusually warm. That's a good thing, Susan says to herself while she packs up her car, as her dress and the dresses of her bride's maids are sleeveless. The beautiful blue sky, with the colorful fall trees in the background, will make for gorgeous wedding photos, she thinks, smiling, her heart full of anticipation.

Susan is the first to arrive at their wedding venue, an old New England inn. The innkeeper, a matronly woman who not only runs the inn but is also the chef for the little tavern there, meets her at the entrance with a warm embrace.

"Welcome to your special day," she says cheerily. She helps Susan with her bags and bundles through the massive wooden front doors. The inn was built about two hundred years ago, Paul and Susan were informed by the innkeeper when they first toured it. Its wide pine plank floorboards were covered in old braided rugs, and the furniture in the sitting room was made of heavy dark wood and padded with soft velvet. The pictures on the walls were faded botanical prints in antique gilt frames. Susan loved it immediately, and they had placed a deposit before they left.

Susan's sister, Lizzie, is the next to arrive, and she finds Susan upstairs in one of the bedrooms, standing in front of the full-length mirror, wriggling to get into her wedding dress. Her sister giggles when she sees Susan, rushes over to help her get into the dress, laces up the back, and gives her a long embrace.

"I am so happy for you," Lizzie says. "I really love Paul, and Mom and Dad do, too. You guys are so perfect for each other."

There. The dress is on; the matching shoes are on. Time for

hair and makeup. The two other bridesmaids, one of whom is Susan's work friend Norma, have joined Susan and her sister. Norma has brought a plate of fresh fruits, cheeses, and fancy chocolates. The second bridesmaid has brought a bottle of champagne.

In spite of the excitement in the air, in spite of the festivity and sisterhood, Susan feels a slight twinge of sadness. She hasn't told anyone, not her sister, not her girlfriends, about Paul and their inability to conceive a child or about his seeming disinterest in IVF or adoption. For an alarming second Susan wonders, am I making a mistake? She shakes her head dismissively as her sister proclaims, "To Susan and Paul's lifelong happiness together! Cheers!" And the four of them clink their champagne glasses together in a giddy toast.

The ceremony proceeds just as she and Paul planned it. The furniture in the sitting area of the inn has been arranged in rows, creating an aisle down the middle, leading to a small altar directly in front of the large glass-paned doors at the back of the room. The musicians start to play Pachelbel's Canon as Susan slowly descends the grand staircase to meet her father at the bottom. She loops her arm through his as he beams at her and proudly leads her down the aisle toward Paul, who is waiting at the front of the room.

Susan's father leaves her at the altar with Paul, who leans over and whispers in her ear, "You look so beautiful."

He is nervous, Susan realizes. There are little beads of sweat above Paul's upper lip. He looks dashing in his tux. His eyes are deep and brown as Susan looks into them and says her vows. When Paul, in turn, confesses his eternal love to Susan, she knows without a doubt that he is the right person for her. There is no mistake, she acknowledges. We are two halves of the same whole.

The couple turns to face their guests after a tender first kiss as husband and wife—so many smiles in the crowd, some tears of happiness, too. Susan gazes at the rows of family and close friends who have come to share in this perfect moment. Her eyes scan the room to the very last row of chairs. None of the guests notice Susan's smile falter slightly as her heart slumps within her chest; Paul's son has not arrived to celebrate their marriage.

Chapter 4

Hillary

Several weeks later, after the consulting team has returned to their Albany headquarters, Hillary is in her apartment one morning, getting ready for work. Her fluffy cat, Athena, has curled up on the exact spot on Hillary's bed where Hillary had been sleeping.

Hillary is picking out some earrings to match her work outfit when she is suddenly seized with nausea and an intense urge to vomit. She runs to her bathroom and chokes up bile. Ugh, what is this? Did she eat something last night that might have given her food poisoning? She thinks back: soup; no, it wouldn't have been that. Could she have a stomach bug? Maybe, but otherwise she feels fine, and once she vomits, the nausea subsides. She finishes getting ready for work and dashes out the door to begin her day.

The nausea and vomiting happen again the next morning. And the next. Hillary talks to her friend Joan. She has confided in Joan about the night with Peter when they were working on the project in San Francisco at the hotel. Joan asks Hillary, "Do you think you could be pregnant?"

"What? No!" Hillary is taken a bit by surprise. She's on the Pill, so she hadn't considered pregnancy. But the thought resonates within her and warms her from deep in her belly. A smile spreads over her face. She had imagined being married first, living in a small house with a small yard in the suburbs. Gardening in the back yard with her husband, Athena sleeping in the sun on a porch swing cushion. Hillary listens to Joan on the phone. She listens without really hearing. She will pick up a pregnancy kit on her way home from work tomorrow and take the test. But she already knows and acknowledges this new life force within her.

The pregnancy test confirms Hillary's feelings. She immediately calls Joan to share this news with her.

Joan, who is very practical, asks, "What will you do, Hill, when you have to work as a single mother? Who is going to take care of the baby? Certainly not your stepmother. Will you be able to afford daycare? What happens when the baby is sick and you have to miss work? What about riding your horse, Calypso?"

Hillary is silent, feeling blasted by all of these questions, accused almost. "I know there are hurdles I will have to figure out, Joanie. But I also know that when I tell Peter I'm pregnant with his baby, he will want to do the right thing." Hillary imagines the joy on Peter's face when she tells him the news. She imagines how he will take her in his arms, hold her tight, and murmur in her ear how much he loves her and this baby. She imagines Peter will ask her to marry him, and she will move in with Peter and his two small children; they will be a family.

As Joan had predicted at the end of that phone call, it doesn't

The Stars We Could Reach

happen that way. Hillary catches Peter alone in the break room at work. It's after the lunch hour, so she knows they won't be interrupted. Peter is fixing himself a cup of coffee, and Hillary sidles up close to him and nuzzles his neck. She looks around quickly. No one is in the room to see them. They have managed to keep their personal relationship out of the work environment, with a quick kiss when no one is looking or Peter patting her ass when she walks by his desk. Keeping their secret has added some intensity to their relationship, giving each of them a sense of power in that they share something no one else knows about. They relish their secret. Or so Hillary thinks.

Peter has told some of the guys from work that he and Hillary have been sleeping together. He is proud of himself for attaining her affections out of everyone else in the office. He is proud of his prowess in finding her, watching her, and having her. He exaggerates their exploits in the bedroom to his work buddies. The more they drink, the greater Peter feels about himself, his manhood, and his physical self. He struts about the office with a new confidence.

Hillary is anxious to share her news. Their news. "I have a secret to tell you," she whispers in his ear.

Peter, leaning against the counter in the break room, continues to stir the coffee in his mug. He seems preoccupied.

"What is it? Is something wrong?" Hillary asks, disappointed.

Gruffly, Peter replies, "My ex-wife has been calling me friggin' nonstop, wanting to come over and see the kids. Doesn't she get that I don't want her to come over?" Emphatically, he adds, "I don't want to deal with her!" Finally, he stops stirring his coffee and looks into Hillary's face. He sees something there that he has never seen before: peacefulness and wholeness. It is so pure. He wants to kiss her glossy, pink lips, to embrace her firm, lithe body. He is aroused. He is in the break room at work. He refrains.

Peter gives Hillary a quick kiss on the cheek and says, "Why don't we go out to dinner later this week after I figure out the situation with the ex-wife? I promise." Seeing the disappointment written on Hillary's face, he adds, "We will go out to dinner, just the two of us, and we can talk. I already know where I want to take you to dinner, Hill." He is feeling chivalrous and continues. "It's a sports bar that I go to a lot. They all know me there. The bartender is great, funny, and always listens. There's a bunch of TVs all around the bar with every game going on at the same time: football, baseball, basketball, hockey." He rattles them off, oblivious to Hillary's blank stare. "It's a slice of America," Peter concludes, "noisy and dark; a perfect place for the two of us to have dinner and drinks."

Hillary is deflated. She lets out a long sigh as she follows Peter out of the break room and back to their cubicles. She wanted to share her news with Peter and see his face soften and smile when she told him she was carrying their baby. Feel the nurturing side of him come out when he embraced her. The nurturing side she knows is in him.

Hillary sits at her desk and tries to work. She is distracted, though. Distracted by this little flicker of life she holds within her. She sheds a silent tear as she gently rubs her belly with both hands. She isn't showing yet. At some point, I will have to tell Carl and the team, she thinks, to let them know that I will need time off for maternity leave. Then the whole place will know. Hillary revels in this quiet moment, just her and her baby sharing a few minutes of peacefulness, hidden in her cubicle. She already loves this baby so much.

That evening after work, Hillary decides to tell her family about her happy news. She imagines that her stepmother will be thrilled with the announcement that she is going to be a grandmother. After all, it will give Anita new status among her group of friends—the group of friends who are always trying to outdo each other with the next best thing. Hillary feels like she will be giving her stepmother something she will appreciate. Finally, Hillary will be special in Anita's eyes.

Hillary excitedly builds up to her announcement later that night when she's on the phone with her stepmother.

"I'm surprised to hear from you, Hillary," Anita barks. "You rarely call me anymore, and mostly out of a sense of duty, I strongly believe," she admonishes. Then continues in an annoyed tone, "Hillary, it's late. I'm watching my shows. What is it that you want?"

"Mom, you're going to be a grandmother!" Hillary explodes with her news. She is practically beaming through the phone as she waits for her stepmother's response.

There is a long pause as Anita processes this information and then says, "How could you, Hillary? How could you go and get pregnant before you are married? How long have you been seeing this guy? How many guys have you been sleeping with? Do you know he's even the father of this baby?"

It's a slap in the face to Hillary. Her hand immediately covers her belly in a protective reflex. I should have known better, she chastises herself. I should have known that no matter what, Mom would find fault with me. I could bring her the moon, Hillary thinks sadly, and Mom would only complain at the darkness left behind in the night sky.

Anita continues with her tirade. "How will I ever hold my head up when my friends get wind of this news? They're going to think I've raised a slut." She pauses dramatically, sharpening her talons. "And you know what, Hillary? I have raised a slut! Just look at you now. Pregnant out of wedlock. You'd better get that guy to marry you."

Hillary can't take it. The wounded child inside her is trying to flee, to get out from under this assault. There was a reason she moved out of that house as soon as she could. There was a reason she worked so hard in college to get her degree and get a good job so she could support herself. "I've got to go, Mom," she says with tears running down her cheeks, and gently hangs up the phone. Not five minutes later, as Hillary wipes the tears away and waits for the Keurig to brew a cup of pregnancy tea to calm her nerves, her cell phone rings. It's her half-sister, Eva. Oh, Lord, Hillary thinks. This is either going to go very well or very poorly. She answers the call.

Eva is breathless. "Hillary! I can't believe you're pregnant! And I can't believe you didn't tell me first." Even though Eva is younger than Hillary by several years, she scolds Hillary for neglecting to share this announcement with her the moment she found out. Eva sounds happy about Hillary's news, happy that she will be an aunt. "Oh, my God! I just got off the phone with Mom, and she is so pissed." Eva laughs at that. She knows she is her mother's favorite and can get away with laughing at their mother.

They talk for a while. Hillary feels close to Eva during this conversation, like Eva will not judge her as her stepmother does, from her lofty Catholic pedestal. Hillary describes how it feels to be pregnant, her morning sickness, how she is still hiding this from everyone at work, and how she knows this baby will be a boy. She shares all of this with Eva, spilling her feelings with her, even though a voice in Hillary's head tells her to rein herself in, not to share too much, and reminds Hillary that Eva is a direct pipeline to Anita. Hillary ignores the little voice and keeps talking.

A couple of evenings later, Peter takes Hillary to the sports bar after work. Hillary is dressed up in her business casual attire as they leave right from work and realizes, as they enter the bar filled with mostly single men dressed in their favorite sports jerseys, that she is overdressed. Peter had brought a change of clothes and looks sexy in his white t-shirt, tight jeans, and black leather jacket. She loves him all over again. Her bad boy. They find a table in a dark corner, and Peter sits with his back to the wall so he can keep his eyes on the various sports broadcasting on the multiple TVs over the bar. This annoys Hillary slightly, but she knows she'll have his undivided attention once she tells him about her pregnancy. Peter orders a beer for Hillary and a whiskey for himself. He is proud to have Hillary here with him. She is so sexy, he thinks, having noticed all the guys turn and look at her when the two of them entered the bar.

Their drinks arrive. Peter is watching a football game on the TV nearest their table, and absent-mindedly talks about work, with intermittent shouts at the TV when one of the referees makes a call that Peter disagrees with. Hillary is not listening to Peter. It's almost the weekend; she doesn't want to hear about work. She wants Peter's attention. She wants to be able to look him in the eyes when she tells him about their baby.

Peter starts digging in when a large plate of cheesy nachos is delivered to their table. He finally notices that Hillary is not eating any of the nachos and hasn't touched her beer. "What's-a-matter, Babe?" he says. "You don't like the beer? You sick or something?"

"No, not sick", she says.

"Well, then what?" he replies, shoveling in another laden nacho chip. "C'mon. This is supposed to be our date night."

Hillary is disgusted by the gooeyness of the nachos. The

spicy smell of the nacho meat and the jalapeños makes her gag. She swallows down some bile. "Peter." No response. "Peter." She waits again for his attention to turn away from the food in front of him. He takes another huge bite. "Peter! I have to tell you something." He finally looks up at Hillary. "Peter, I'm pregnant." He stops chewing, his eyes wide open now and focused directly on Hillary. His mouth is too full for him to respond. He swallows the huge bite of nachos in one large gulp.

"Are you fucking kidding me, Hill?" he cries, a little too loudly. The people at the next table look over.

"Lower your voice, please," she replies. "Yeah, remember when we made love for the first time when we were out in San Francisco working on that big project? Remember that night? I think it happened then. We made a baby."

"Jesus," Peter mutters. "How far along are you?"

"About nine or ten weeks, I think," Hillary says softly. Peter's harsh response takes her breath away. He scowls, and Hillary realizes he is unhappy about this pregnancy. It hits her at that moment that she may end up raising this baby as a single parent after all. What will they say at the office? Will she be ostracized? Will he? She's got to make this work. "I thought you'd be happy, Peter. I'm not asking to get married."

Peter's scowl deepens. "I just can't fucking believe this, Hill. I thought you were on the Pill. What happened?"

"This happened, Peter! Our baby happened. People can still sometimes get pregnant even when they're on the Pill." She is almost in tears. Is he blaming her for getting pregnant? He's been drinking, she thinks; he'll come around.

"Hill, I don't want another kid. I've got two already that are pains in my ass. I never agreed to have a baby. I can't believe you're doing this to me. I'll give you some money toward an abortion."

This comment lays Hillary flat. Anger rises within her. She is so connected to this baby, so deeply in love with this baby. "Fuck you, Peter!" she says, grabs her purse, then quickly gets up, her chair making a loud scraping noise on the wooden floor. Everyone is staring as she storms out.

Thank God we took separate cars, Hillary thinks, tears running down her face. She hears Peter stumbling after her from the bar. He is yelling to her across the parking lot. It's dark, but she has parked under a streetlamp. Hillary quickly finds her car, slides in, and puts the key in the ignition. She backs out of her parking spot with a squeal of tires. She looks in the rearview mirror and sees Peter standing alone under the streetlamp, his hands in the air, mouthing the words, "Come back, Babe, come on. Come back. Come on, Babe." Hillary exits the parking lot and steps hard on the gas. Jerk! she thinks.

It is late when Hillary arrives home. Her heart is still beating fast. She fixes a cup of warm broth and finds Athena asleep on the couch. Hillary lies down next to the cat, covers them both with a soft, fleecy blanket, and falls asleep there, with Athena purring beside her.

The next morning is Saturday, and Hillary plans to meet Joan at the stable to ride their horses. She arrives at the farm early. The sky is pale blue with a blush of pink as the sun rises over the trees. There is a misty fog in the valley below the pastures. The horses haven't been turned out in their paddocks yet. Hillary enters the barn and breathes in the smell of horse hair, molasses, and sweet hay. Ahhh, heaven, she thinks, and walks over to see Calypso.

Calypso lifts her head from her feed bucket when Hillary

calls her name. She gives a little welcoming nicker and pricks her ears forward as Hillary enters the stall. There is a neat pile of hay in one corner, near where Calypso is eating her morning grain, and Hillary sits down on the hay to watch the horse finish her breakfast. She talks to Calypso, telling her about last night. Telling her that there is no way she will ever get rid of this baby, even if it means she raises the baby alone. Calypso lifts her head and nuzzles Hillary's cheek. Her soft, sweet breath on Hillary's face makes the tears reappear. "Oh, Calypso," she whispers to the mare, "what a mess I've gotten myself into."

She hears footsteps in the aisleway and stands up from her spot on the hay pile in Calypso's stall. It is Joan. "What are you doing in there?" Joan asks with surprise when she sees Hillary's head pop up.

Hillary leaves Calypso's stall and meets Joan in the aisle. She tells Joan about Peter's reaction last night after she announced to him she was pregnant with their baby. "I am so angry at him, Joanie! I will raise my baby alone if I have to." It hits Hillary then that she is afraid to raise this baby alone. There are so many what-ifs. What if the baby gets sick and Hillary has to take time out of work to take care of the child? What if something happens to Hillary? Who will take care of the baby? What if, what if, what if. Hillary shakes her head to clear it.

"Hill, I'm just going to come out and say it. I think Peter is an asshole. I'm sorry, but I've always thought this ever since you became attracted to him at work." She couldn't believe sensible Hillary would want to date a guy like Peter. Joan finds him vulgar. Immature, me-centered, irresponsible. "You're like a sister to me, Hill, and I just want the best for you, you know?" She pauses, unable to stop herself now that she's begun, "I figured his response to your news would be something like this." Then she softens and adds, "Oh, Sweetie, I'm so sorry. I'll be there for you any way I can. Let's get our ponies ready and go for a ride, and we'll forget about Peter for a little bit."

The horses are spirited in the cold morning air as Hillary and Joan mount up to ride in the indoor arena. There is no one else at the barn. "We have the place to ourselves," calls Hillary with a smile, and she steers a prancing Calypso through her warm-up exercises.

Joan and her young horse are over at the far end of the arena. Joan's horse is throwing a few temperamental bucks. Nothing serious. Nothing that is going to unseat Joan. She's such an amazing rider, thinks Hillary, as she watches Joan quietly settle her horse down again. Hillary pushes Calypso into a collected trot so she comes up next to Joan and they can talk without yelling across the large riding area.

"God, it's chilly this morning!" Hillary says as she rides up to Joan. "My fingers are freezing, even in my riding gloves. I love it, though, when the horses are a bit spicy like this. They know a winter storm is coming!"

Joan decides to skip the small talk. "I'm worried about you, my friend, concerned for your health and all. Should you even be riding when you're pregnant?" wonders Joan. "What if Calypso bucks you off and you become injured, Hill? What if that were to happen, and God forbid, you lost this baby?"

"Thank you for your concern, Joanie. I feel like I'm okay for now. Calypso will take care of me." She reaches down to stroke the mare's long neck.

"How far along do you think you are?" Joan cannot keep the look of unease out of her eyes.

"I have my first obstetrician appointment next Wednesday," Hillary replies. "I'll ask the doctor when I'm there. I know Calypso knows I'm pregnant somehow. She won't do anything to harm me or the baby." Hillary sets off at a trot again to practice her dressage figures in the center of the arena.

I hope you're right, thinks Joan, as she also urges her horse into a trot.

Calypso feels great, acknowledges Hillary as the two of them connect and start moving as one through more advanced dressage exercises. Once they complete their routine, Hillary and Calypso halt in the center of the arena to wait for Joan and her horse to finish up. "You are the best girl," Hillary says as she reaches down to pat Calypso's warm shoulder. "Thank you for a great ride." Hillary dismounts from the saddle and waits for Joan to do the same so they can untack their horses, brush them down, and turn them out in their paddocks for the day.

After the horses are turned out in their paddocks to nibble the hay piled on the frozen ground, Hillary and Joan return to the barn to put away their saddles, bridles, and brushes. "I love our morning rides together," Hillary calls to Joan, who is heading down to her horse's stall at the other end of the barn aisle.

"I do, too," Joan calls back. "But I want you to be careful, Hill. I don't want to see you or your baby get injured. Promise me that if the doctor tells you not to ride while you're pregnant, you won't. Okay?"

Reluctantly, Hillary replies, "Okay. I know. I'll do whatever the doctor tells me to do." She looks down at her belly and presses her hand over the center, where she imagines her baby to be. "I promise to take care of you always, little angel," she whispers.

The rest of the weekend flies by, and before she knows it, Hillary is back in her closet, selecting her business outfit for the day. Monday, the beginning of another work week. She is apprehensive about running into Peter at the office. He has texted her message after message over the weekend, apologizing for his behavior and begging her to call him back. "I'm sorry, Babe," he typed. "You caught me off guard. I need to talk to you. Call me. Please."

Hillary didn't respond to Peter's messages. She'd thought about the look on his face as she delivered the news of their pregnancy to him: He had scowled. He had actually scowled. She couldn't get that image of his face, his disappointment and anger, out of her mind. She was upset at Peter not only for his obvious displeasure at the thought of being a father again but for the realization that he wasn't the nurturer she had believed he was, that he probably didn't even want to raise the children he had.

Chapter 5

Susan

One early December afternoon, Susan is in the kitchen, chopping vegetables to go into a stew. Cornbread is baking in the oven, and she is humming along to Christmas songs on the radio. Outside, a winter storm blows heavy snowflakes in dizzying patterns around the yard. Inside, the Christmas tree lights are on, and the house smells warm and comforting. Ginger is contentedly snoozing on the rug under the kitchen table. Susan's heart is filled with the happiness of this very moment. So many blessings in my life, she thinks as she peels another carrot.

Paul soon comes in from snow-blowing their driveway for the second time that afternoon. "Boy, it's really coming down out there," he says, standing on the doormat and stomping the snow off his boots. His face is bright red from the cold. "I can't feel my fingers anymore," he says with a chuckle. "It's freezing outside."

"Here," replies Susan. "Hand me your wet hat and gloves. I'll put them in the dryer." Paul passes the frozen items to her. "I made you some hot chocolate. Give me a sec, and I'll sit down and have a mug with you."

Paul bends down to pat an excited Ginger on the top of her head. "C'mon girl, let's sit on the couch and wait for our hot chocolate." Ginger jumps up next to Paul and starts licking his face. "You're tickling me, puppy girl," he laughs.

Susan smiles to herself as she pours the hot chocolate into two mugs. She tops each cup with a swirl of whipped cream and carries them into the living room. As she hands Paul his mug, she asks, "Can we talk about something?"

"Sure," Paul replies, licking a line of whipped cream off his upper lip.

Susan hesitates. She loves what they have together, loves who they are together. She doesn't want to break the spell she believes they are under. She has never been happier in her life. But a strong voice has been rising within her since they returned from their honeymoon, a voice that is all too familiar to her. I will be forty next summer, she realizes. I have to do this now.

The voice within her gives her the strength she needs to blurt out, "I want to revisit having a baby. I want us to talk about starting a family, Paul. We made it through the wedding. We're in a good place now, and my biological clock is still ticking."

Paul stops drinking his hot chocolate. He glances over at Susan, who has joined him and Ginger on the couch. After a long pause, he casts his eyes downward and softly says, "We both work so hard, Suzie. I'm exhausted when I come home at night, and I know you are, too. I already raised a child, and I know how much work it is to have a baby, to be up all night changing and feeding them and then have to leave for work in the morning, to have a toddler that you have to chase after all the time because they're running around and getting into everything. Plus, who would stay home and take care of a baby? You know I can't support us with just my income. I'm getting older, Suzie. I don't have the energy to do it all over again."

Susan notices herself growing very still inside, dark. She pleads with Paul. "But you said we could have a baby together, Paul. You know how much I want to be a mother. You promised me we could have a baby together when we first met. One of the reasons I married you was so we could start a family."

He lifts his eyes and meets hers. "I can't do it, Suzie. I thought I could, but I can't. I'm just too tired."

"But you promised me, Paul! You promised me." Susan senses herself start to unravel, feels her mind slip and tilt. She can't believe Paul is saying this to her. The drive she recognizes within her is so strong, so desperate. Who would she be if she didn't become a mother? Is Paul really rejecting her deepest desire? Is he really telling her she can't be who she knows without a doubt she is supposed to be? She stares at him accusingly, shocked that he is saying this to her.

"Well, Suzie," he says, meeting her stare. "If this is a deal breaker...," and his voice trails off.

Susan feels the breath drain from her lungs. She watches as if outside her own body while a part of the life coursing through her slows to a halt in that one instant. Did Paul just give her an ultimatum: If she pursues being a mother, he doesn't want to be married to her? Something inside her cracks wide open. The silence within her is deafening. Without a word, Susan stands up from the couch and gently places her mug on the coffee table.

She moves in slow motion, silently climbs the stairs, and walks into the bathroom. She closes the bathroom door. She locks it. There are no thoughts left in her head. Her heart is black. She looks at herself in the mirror above the vanity and sees a person without a soul, without meaning. Susan opens the doors to the medicine cabinet, scans each shelf, and selects several pill bottles.

An all-consuming quietness surrounds her. Paul hasn't followed her up the stairs. Methodically, Susan opens an old bottle of painkillers and pours them into her hand. She finds another bottle of Benadryl and another of Tylenol. These she empties into her hand as well. She forces all of the pills into her mouth and starts chewing. She doesn't taste anything. Susan follows each handful of tablets with several gulps of water to ensure that every last pill makes it down into her stomach. Then she turns on the shower to hot and climbs in. Her clothes quickly become soaked and stuck to her body. She hardly notices. She feels nothing. She is nothing. Susan lies down and curls in a fetal position in the tub, the hot water beating on her body, and closes her eyes.

Paul remains on the couch after Susan has gone upstairs, stunned by their argument. He absentmindedly strokes Ginger's soft head. He hadn't realized he had those words in him. He hadn't been sure of the reason he had changed his mind about having a child with Susan, and now he knows. He is tired. Exhausted. He can't father a baby. Paul feels badly about upsetting Susan like this. He knows she has such a strong wish to be a mother. He just can't do it, though. He just can't start over again. He is shocked that he was so stern with her, offering her something of an ultimatum if she continued pushing for them to have a child. Paul has never spoken to Susan like that. He loves her deeply. He wants their lives together to move forward. Paul wonders what Susan is thinking. Is her maternal drive so strong that she will leave him? Will she come around and understand his point of view? Has he just ended their marriage with those words?

Suddenly, the kitchen stove timer buzzes and startles Paul, returning him to the present. He jumps up and walks to the stove to turn off the timer. The kitchen smells delicious. He wonders what Susan has been baking while he was out snow-blowing the driveway earlier. Paul opens the oven door and peers inside. A loaf of cornbread. His favorite. Grabbing oven mitts off the countertop, he takes the bread pan out and places it on the counter to cool.

As he closes the oven door and turns off the baking feature, he glances at the clock on the stove. It has been about forty-five minutes since Susan has gone upstairs. What is she doing up there? She must be really pissed off at me, thinks Paul. He worries that they will end up having a huge fight when Susan comes back downstairs. They haven't had any fights in their relationship yet. They are so compatible. Paul's stomach starts to feel tense. He hates confrontation.

Dirty dishes are in the sink—bowls and mixing spoons and spatulas from Susan's baking. Paul busies himself, rinsing the dishes and loading them into the dishwasher. He tidies up the kitchen counters as best he can. It looks like Susan had been in the middle of chopping up vegetables before she and Paul had sat down to have their conversation. He doesn't want to mess up what she's been working on, so he cleans around it. She'll be surprised when she comes downstairs and sees the sink empty and the counters clean, he thinks, proud of himself, imagining this will make her a little happy at least.

He rechecks the stove clock. It has now been an hour since Susan went upstairs. Paul is growing worried. I should probably go up there and talk to her, he ponders, straighten this out. He dries his hands on a kitchen towel and walks to the staircase. As he passes through the living room, Paul notices that Ginger is no longer on the couch where he had left her. "Where are you, puppy girl?" he calls. Then he hears Ginger whimpering from the top of the stairs. Something is wrong.

Paul runs up the stairs and sees the closed bathroom door. Steam is coming out from under the door in drifting white wisps. He tries the doorknob. Locked. "Suzie," he calls, banging on the door. "What are you doing in there? Are you okay?" No answer. "Suzie," he yells again, louder. Still no answer. Ginger is whining and scratching at the bathroom door.

"Watch out, Ginger!" Paul cries as he runs at the bathroom door and crashes through it with his shoulder. Hot steam and the smell of vomit engulf him. "Suzie!" he yells again as he rushes to the bathtub. He pulls back the shower curtain and finds her lying there in a pool of her own vomit, her eyes closed, her clothes soaked through. Paul turns off the water. "Suzie! Suzie! Wake up!" She doesn't open her eyes. Her lips are blue, and it looks like she's barely breathing. Paul reaches in, grabs her under her arms, and pulls her out of the bathtub and onto the bathroom floor. She moans slightly.

He looks around. There are pills all over the bathroom floor. "Shit!" he yells. "Suzie! What have you done? You have to wake up!" He gently pats the side of her face with his hand to try and elicit a response. "Wake up for me, Suzie!" Still nothing. He is panicking. He watches her chest and sees her take a shallow breath in. Paul quickly pulls his cell phone out of his back pocket.

"Nine-one-one, what's your emergency?" he hears on the other end.

"My wife, Susan, she's barely breathing. I think she took a bunch of pills. I can't get her to wake up," Paul yells into the phone. "You've got to send someone!"

"I'm dispatching an ambulance to your address now," says the voice on the other end of the phone. "I will stay with you on the phone until the paramedics arrive. Can you tell me if she's still breathing?"

Paul is on his knees, Susan's head resting on his lap. He watches her chest. Nothing. Oh, my God, Paul thinks. She's dying. "I don't see her breathing," Paul cries into the phone as he continues to stare at Susan's chest.

"I want you to put your cheek right up close to her mouth. Tell me if you feel any breath," the 911 operator directs Paul calmly.

Paul does as she advises. With his cheek close to Susan's face, he feels a small breath escape from her blue lips.

"I felt it," he says into the phone. "She took a breath."

"Okay," the 911 operator continues. "That's a good thing. I want you to make sure she's lying on her side in case she vomits. We don't want her to choke on it." Then, "Now look around the room. Do you see any empty pill bottles? Can you tell me what she took?"

Paul gently rolls Susan onto her side and places her head softly on the mat on the bathroom floor. He quickly glances around the room. His panic overtakes him.

"When are the paramedics coming?" he shouts at the operator.

"I need you to stay calm for me," the operator says in an even voice. "If we know what she took, it will help the paramedics when they get there. They're about five minutes away from your house."

"There's a pill bottle that says oxycodone on it," he says hurriedly, "and a bottle of Tylenol that's mostly gone. And an empty bottle of Benadryl."

"Thank you, Paul," she replies. "This will really help the paramedics. They should be at your house in just a couple of minutes. The roads are bad because of the storm. They're getting to you as fast as they can. How is Susan? Can you tell me if she's still breathing?"

Paul glances back down at Susan. He can hear the ambulance siren getting louder as it comes toward the house. He puts his cheek up to Susan's lips. He feels a tiny puff. "Yes, she's still breathing." He hears a loud knock on the front door and sees Ginger dash down the stairs, barking. "They're here," he shouts into the phone. "I've got to go."

"Thank you for staying on the phone with me, Paul," he hears on his cell phone as he turns it off, shoving it in his back pocket and racing down the stairs.

Paul opens the front door, and two tall men dressed in blue uniforms stand on the front step. Ginger is barking ferociously at them. "She's upstairs," Paul manages to get out between breaths. "C'mon." His heart is beating fast. He is so afraid Susan is going to die.

The paramedics bound up the stairs carrying their medical boxes and an oxygen tank. They've brought in a stretcher and left it at the bottom of the stairs. Paul closes the front door, and he and Ginger run up the stairs after them.

Both paramedics are kneeling next to Susan. One of them is placing an oxygen mask over her face while the other is taking her blood pressure. "How long has she been like this?" asks one of the paramedics, looking over at Paul standing in the bathroom doorway.

"I don't know," Paul replies in a panicked voice. "A little over an hour, I think."

"Has she ever done anything like this before?" the paramedic continues.

"No, never." Paul is near tears. What has happened? What has she done? Is she going to make it? Thoughts race around in Paul's head. Is this because of what I said to her? Oh, my God, he thinks, I did this to her! He nearly drops to his knees at the idea of it.

"You're looking a little pale yourself," the paramedic tells Paul. "Why don't you sit down while we stabilize her."

There is an old wooden bench against the wall by the bathroom door. Paul pulls it over and sits on it, watching the second paramedic put an IV line into Susan's arm. She winces slightly when the IV needle pierces her skin. She's still alive, Paul thinks with some relief. She's still alive.

"Is she going to make it?" he asks.

"We're getting her ready to transport her to the hospital. She's still breathing on her own, and she has a pulse. So that's a really good sign. We gave her some medicine through the IV to help counteract the effects of some of the medication she took. They'll probably have to pump her stomach in the Emergency Room."

An answer, but not really an answer. Paul chooses to believe there is hope. There has to be. He can't lose her. Not now. Not ever. Tears are streaming down his face.

One paramedic has carried up a backboard. They pick up Susan and strap her onto the board. Paul notices Susan's wet clothes. It is still snowing outside. "Will she get too cold?" he asks.

"When we put her on the stretcher, we'll wrap blankets around her," replies the lead paramedic.

Paul watches as they carefully maneuver their patient down one step at a time. Susan's eyes are still closed. Her head lolls to the side. He can't see the rest of her face because of the oxygen mask over her nose and mouth.

After Susan is placed on the stretcher at the bottom of the stairs and she is wrapped in blankets, one of the paramedics turns to Paul and says, "You can follow us in your car and meet us at the Emergency Room. Be careful driving, though," he cautions. "The side roads aren't plowed too good." The two men steer the stretcher out the front door, down the snowy walk to the driveway, and into the back of the ambulance. They close the back doors, and Paul watches the blinking red and blue lights as the ambulance slowly makes its way down the street toward the hospital.

Ginger has followed the stretcher with Susan on it out to the walk, and she stands in the driveway, watching the ambulance disappear in the heavy snowflakes. "C'mon, Ginger. Do your thing, and let's go inside. I've got to get over to the hospital." Ginger squats obediently in the snow, then turns and runs into the house.

"Okay," mutters Paul to himself once they are inside and the front door is closed against the cold wind of the storm. "She's got food. And she's got water," he says, referring to Ginger. He looks around. The kitchen is just as he had left it before he found Susan upstairs: a partially chopped carrot on the cutting board, a bunch of celery next to it on the counter, the soup pot nearby with potatoes and some carrots already in it. Paul's heart breaks when he takes in these simple things. Things that Susan has brought to their lives. She's my whole life, he thinks. She's got to pull through.

"I'm leaving the lights on for you, puppy girl," Paul calls back to Ginger as he puts on his winter parka and heavy boots. "I'm driving over to the hospital. I don't know when I'll be back." Ginger looks up at him with her deep brown eyes. "She'll be all right," Paul says to her. "Your momma will be all right." He shuts the door and trudges out to sweep several inches of snow off his truck.

Chapter 6

Hillary

On the way to work, Hillary listens to an audiobook about pregnancy she ordered online. She laughs aloud when she hears that her baby is about the size of a prune. She learns that her baby's little arm and leg buds are continuing to develop. Hillary had noticed that morning, when she put on her dress shirt and pencil skirt, that the skirt was a little snugger at the waist than the last time she had worn it. A few more weeks, she thought, and I'll probably be showing. She had smiled to herself.

Hillary parks her car at the office building, wraps her heavy winter coat around her, and enters the large main doors. She squeezes herself into the elevator, just one of a group of silent workers, their coffees in one hand, their cell phones in the other; no one looking at each other, no one speaking to each other. She is glad when the elevator stops on the fifth floor, her floor, and she can emerge from the silent group and join her coworkers at the computer firm.

"Hey, Hill," she hears from the woman in the cubicle next to hers. "How was your weekend? Did you do anything fun? Cold and wintry, right? I stayed in and organized my closets. Did you ride your horse this weekend?" all in one breath.

"Morning, Mary," Hillary replies to her neighbor. "Yeah, I had a good weekend, got to ride my horse." She is not ready to share the news of her pregnancy with her fellow workers. An unsettled feeling washes over her as she imagines the inevitable encounter with Peter today.

At morning staff meeting in the largest of the conference rooms, the CEO begins by addressing the recent national news headlines of a virus rumored to have come from a lab in China, causing masses of people to become seriously sick and even die, that has now made its way to the United States. The room is silent. This recent announcement from every news station, from local to national, has been at the forefront of everyone's mind. Hillary can almost feel a low buzz of anxiety in the room. She listens as the CEO continues.

"I have met with the Board, and we are acknowledging the governor's recommendations to control this COVID-19 virus as best and as quickly as we can." He gazes around the room. "The Board and I feel the best way to do that is to close the office and have everyone work remotely from home. Your team leaders will assist you in deciding which equipment you need to take to set up your home offices. You will have the morning to collect these items from your cubicles, and starting this afternoon, we will all be working virtually. We are taking this outbreak and the safety of all of you very seriously. Let's open the floor for questions."

The buzz in the room becomes louder, the pent-up fear in each of them surfacing. Hillary listens without being able to make out individual conversations, without hearing the questions people are asking the CEO. She frantically looks around the room and finally finds Peter sitting in the back corner with some of the guys from the consulting team. He looks up just then and meets her eyes. She breathes a sigh, somehow comforted by the sight of him.

People are talking in groups now, and a few employees are still listening to the CEO answer questions. The energy in the room feels like a lightning bolt has just zapped through it. Peter stands up and makes his way over to Hillary. She feels her heart rate become faster. How can I be so drawn to him physically, she wonders, and yet so turned off by him mentally?

Peter eventually reaches her and puts his hand on her arm. "Hillary, I texted you a bunch of times. How come you never answered my texts? I was a jerk the other night. I'm deadass sorry." And then, "Can we talk? Later? After this meeting is over?"

His voice is pleading. Hillary has never heard Peter sound so unsure of himself, so vulnerable. She likes it, likes the feeling of control it gives her. Hillary sits up straighter, a little more confident now. "Not here, Peter. Not at work. There's too much going on."

"After work, then?" he asks her.

Pitiful, she thinks. He looks pitiful. The anger and disappointment that had been hardening her heart toward Peter all weekend begin to dissolve. She still loves him and knows she has already forgiven him even before they talk together.

"Yeah, sure. You can come over tonight after we set up our home offices. I'll make us something for dinner."

"I don't want you to have to cook anything, Hill," responds Peter with noticeable relief in his voice. "I'll pick up takeout. What do you want: Thai? Chinese? Pizza?"

Hillary loves that Peter is being so thoughtful. He's coming around, she imagines. He's thought about it over the weekend, and he's coming around.

"You know what I've been craving, Peter?" she replies.

"Salmon. I really, really would like some nice salmon. And white rice."

"Salmon and white rice," he repeats. "You got it."

"Okay, then. I'll see you after work. We've got to get going this morning, pack up our laptops and stuff, and get out of here." She has the strongest urge to follow this with, "I love you, Peter." But she keeps this sentiment to herself, not wanting to rock the boat further. They quickly squeeze each other's hands, and Peter walks back to the group of guys he had been sitting with.

The remainder of the morning is a frenzy of activity and excited conversation in the office. Hillary watches while people walk back and forth by her cubicle, each laden with a bag or a box filled with various articles that are important to them: desk lamps, coffee mugs, and plants poking out from the tops of their piles of items.

"Do you want some help, Hillary?" A voice snaps her out of her daydreaming. It's her team leader, Carl. "Do you know what pieces you need to pack up to be able to set up a home office? I can give you a hand if you'd like."

"I'm all set, Carl." She turns to look at him. A tall, thin man with hair graying at the temples and a rather tired countenance. "Did you know they were going to do this today? Make this announcement and have everybody pack up their stuff?"

"They had a big meeting on Friday afternoon," he replies. "The CEO told us this is what the Board was proposing, given what's been happening across the country, especially in New York City. Have you seen the news? People are getting sick, they go into the hospital, and then they come out in body bags. The death count is unreal. I'm glad the Board is doing this. They probably should have done it sooner. Let me know if you need help packing up, Hillary, all right?" Carl turns and makes his way to a group gathered by the break room.

Hillary takes a box she keeps under her desk for oversized computer manuals, empties it, and starts layering the box with the items she'll need at home: her laptop, programming guides, files, calendar, a picture of her riding Calypso, and her philodendron—whom she calls Phil. "That's about it, Phil," she says to her plant as she looks around her cubicle for anything she might have forgotten to pack up. "We'll have to find you a spot in a sunny window when we get home." She tucks his dangling leaves into the box.

Mary, Hillary's cubicle neighbor, is hurriedly packing up items on her desk. As Hillary puts on her winter coat and picks up her pocketbook, she looks over at Mary, who pulls a tissue from her pocket and sniffs into it. "Mary, are you all right? What's the matter? Do you want me to help you pack up?"

"No, I'm fine," Mary replies, sniffling behind the wadded tissue. "It's just that this has become so real, you know? Having to pack up our stuff like this, not knowing when, or if, we'll be coming back. I know people who have lost family members to the COVID-19 virus. And when I watch the news, I feel like it's happening to other people. Like I'm still safe, you know? But I'm not, Hill. None of us are. Closing up the office like this makes it really real, you know? I'm scared, Hill. I'm scared for me, my husband, and our kids. I'm scared for my friends and all of us in this company. I'm scared for our country. I'm scared for the world." Mary breaks down crying.

Hillary sets down her box and reaches her arm out to rub Mary's back. Hillary has decided that, given the way this virus is spreading and the fact that doctors and scientists are saying how it mutates and grows stronger, she is no longer going to hug anyone at work. "I know, Mary. I'm really scared, too. We have to do what they tell us: stay in our homes and avoid as much public contact as possible. They say we will have to start wearing masks soon when we go out in public."

"Do you think they'll find a cure for this in time?" Mary asks. "Or do you think it's just going to sweep across our country and kill everyone in its path?"

Hillary hears the panic rising in Mary's voice and feels the panic rising in herself as well. She doesn't know what to say to her coworker. Nobody knows what to say to each other about this deadly virus. There are so many unknowns to it. The one certainty is that people are dying from it—too many people. Innocent people who were going about their day-to-day lives, got a cold, ended up on a breathing machine in the hospital, and are now dead. Hillary shudders.

Mary is just about packed up, and Hillary helps throw a few last items into her box. "Let's get out of here, Mary. Let's go home, set up our offices, and stay where it's safer. I'm sure your kids will be super excited to have their mom home with them every day now."

Finally her colleague smiles. "They've got all the schools closing, too, and going remote," she says with a little laugh. "It will be a madhouse with everybody at home all day. I can't even guess how that is going to work!"

They each pick up their boxes and follow the line of their coworkers out of the office and over to the elevators. It is a mass of bodies staring up at the floor numbers above the elevator doors, waiting for floor five to light up and the doors to open. Someone in the crowd is coughing. Hillary looks over at Mary, "I'm going to take the stairs," she says. "You take care of yourself. Good luck with the kids and homeschooling."

Hillary extracts herself from the compressed group of people and heads down the stairs. Five flights, and she is carrying her pocketbook and the heavy box of her office supplies. By the time Hillary reaches the first floor, her arms are aching from holding the box and her legs are burning from the exercise of climbing down that many flights of stairs. She takes in a huge breath as she bursts through the exit door of the office building and into the fresh, cold winter air.

Her apartment is quiet when she enters, fumbling with her keys and the heavy box. "I'm home, kitty," she calls to Athena, nestled in a blanket on the couch. Athena lifts her head and gives Hillary a long look. "Did I wake you, Your Majesty?" Hillary asks in her best British accent as she sets everything down on her kitchen table. "You'd better get used to it. Momma's going to be home with you all day now." Athena tucks her nose back under her fluffy tail and continues her nap.

Winter sunlight fills Hillary's spare room as she rearranges the desk and twin bed location to access the electrical outlets and plug in her laptop. Carl wanted everyone up and running from home by this afternoon. Hillary carefully places Phil onto the windowsill, then sits at her little desk and turns on her computer.

The rest of the workday is spent in virtual meetings, first with the entire staff and the CEO, and then with the other members of the consulting team and Carl. Hillary is amused by the arrangement of the little boxes with everyone's face on her computer screen during the Zoom meetings; like the Brady Bunch, she giggles. Carl doles out assignments to the team, and their work continues, almost uninterrupted by the move. They have some large accounts with foreign medical facilities, who have also gone to the Zoom format during this global pandemic, and it is expected that progress will continue on these projects.

It is dark outside when Hillary wraps up the work she has

been doing for one of the foreign accounts. She gets up from her chair with a groan and stretches. As soon as she stands up, she realizes how full her bladder is and dashes into the bathroom. "Good grief," she says out loud to her baby. "Have you been sleeping on top of my bladder this whole time?" She hears a meowing and looks down to see Athena pushing her way through the bathroom door, her feathery tail curling from side to side, as she sashays her way over to Hillary. "Well, hello, pretty girl." Hillary reaches down to scratch Athena's head. "Let me pull up my pants, and we'll get you some food. You must be starving." Athena purrs loudly.

Hillary flips on the switch to the overhead lights in the kitchen. As she prepares Athena's dinner, she glances at the clock on the stove. "Oh, gosh!" she says to herself. "Peter will be here any minute." Quickly, she places the cat food dish on the floor, clears off the kitchen table, arranges the placemats, and lights a couple of candles. There, she thinks. That looks cozy. Almost immediately, there is a knock at her apartment door. Hillary gulps. Peter.

She hasn't given any thought to what she will say to him. She was so busy with the CEO's COVID-19 announcement this morning and moving and setting up her home office, that she hasn't prepared for their upcoming discussion. A feeling of anxiety floods her stomach. This is either the beginning of something wonderful or the end of something not so wonderful, she thinks as she answers the door.

Peter is standing on her door mat with a bag of delicious-smelling food and a six-pack of beer in one hand, and a single rose in the other. "It's for you," he says as he thrusts the rose toward Hillary. "I'm sorry for being such an ass the other night, Hill."

"C'mon in, Peter," Hillary replies, secretly delighted at the gift of the rose. Peter has never given her flowers before. Her heart melts at the gesture, and she feels the anxiety in her stomach dissipate.

Peter enters the apartment and hands Hillary the bag of warm takeout, which she sets on the kitchen table. He takes off his winter jacket and kicks off his boots. Hillary notices a hole in the toe of one of his socks. "You need new socks, Peter," she says, pointing to the hole with a playful smile.

"I know, I know," he replies equally playfully. "I just need a good woman in my life who can look after me and my holey socks." Peter walks over to where Hillary stands and wraps his arms around her. He pulls her close and whispers, "You are so gorgeous. I've missed you." And he leans in to give her a long, deep kiss.

Hillary is the first to pull away from the kiss. She hadn't wanted to be swayed by his charms so early on, before they could clear the air between them. "Let me grab us some plates and silverware. You want a glass for your beer?"

"Nah, I'm good," Peter replies and cracks the cap off one of the beer bottles.

Although Peter's drinking bothers her, Hillary feels like he almost needs it to have these in-depth conversations, to be able to get in touch with the emotional part of himself. She hopes this time goes better than when they were at the sports bar and she first told him she was pregnant.

Hillary sits down, takes a bite of her salmon, and looks at Peter.

"Before you say anything," he begins, with his mouth full of fried fish, "I want to tell you something." He swallows his food and clears his throat. "I've been thinking. I owe you a huge apology, Hill. I was a jerk the other night. You just caught me off guard when you told me you were pregnant. I didn't expect this to happen. I overreacted. I was a fool, Hill. I love you, and I'm sorry."

"It's all right, Peter." Hillary feels a little sorry for him. She knows it mustn't be easy for him to admit he was wrong. To apologize. "I know, I didn't expect—"

Peter interrupts her. "I'm not done, Hill. Let me get this out." She stops talking and watches Peter as he takes a long swallow of his beer. "I've been thinking a lot since the other night. About a lot of things. About where I am in my life. I'm a single dad with two young kids that I love, even if they are pains in my ass." He gives a slight smirk as he says this. "I'm getting too old for the party life. It's time for me to grow up. I need to take responsibility for my actions." Peter pauses for a breath and continues, "I don't want to lose you, Hill. You're the best thing that's ever happened to me. I want to do the right thing for you and the baby." Peter looks right at Hillary. "I want you to move in with me." He pauses for a moment, and when Hillary doesn't say anything, he quickly adds, "I want us to be a family."

Hillary is speechless. His confession and this proposal absolutely blow her away. She hadn't even considered moving in with Peter, and frankly, given how he had reacted to the news of her pregnancy the other night, she had accepted the idea that she would be raising their baby by herself. This idea that Peter is proposing for her to move in with him, live with him and his two kids, and raise their baby together, rocks Hillary at her core. On the one hand, she is thrilled that Peter has come around, has embraced their baby, and is willing to take his part in the responsibility for the child. And on the other hand, Hillary wonders if he would have asked her to move in with him if she wasn't pregnant. Is Peter asking her to live with him because he wants her to or because he thinks he has to?

"Wow, Peter. I didn't expect that," Hillary responds as she

sets down her fork. "I don't even know what to say. Have you thought about this? Is this what you really want? It would be a huge change of lifestyle for you. And for your kids."

"I've thought about it, Hill. I love you. It's what I want." Peter takes another long swig of beer, finishes the bottle, and opens a second.

"But what about your kids? What will they think about me moving in with you and them, about a new baby brother or sister?"

"Kenzie and Little Pete will love having you move in with us. They already think you're awesome anyways. They can't wait for you to play with them whenever they know you're coming over to visit me."

"What about your ex-wife? What if she wants to come and stay with you and your kids like she sometimes does?"

"She has a new boyfriend who she's all into right now. Me and the kids haven't seen her in a couple of months. She won't be coming around, Hill. Don't worry about her."

Hillary is overwhelmed considering all of this. She hears a quiet voice inside her telling her to pause a minute and think this through, asking, even though this is an amazing proposal, is it the right thing for her and her baby? Hillary acknowledges her inner voice. "It all sounds great, Peter," she says finally. "I have to think about it, though. I have to think through everything and decide if it's the right move." She looks up at Peter. His face has fallen. Hillary realizes he had expected her to say yes right then and there.

"What's there to think about?" Peter asks loudly. And then more softly, "I'm the baby's father. I want to be a part of its life. I want to take care of the baby. And you."

Hillary doesn't know what to say to him. She loves Peter. She really does. And she is impressed by his maturity in wanting to welcome their baby into his life and his kids' lives. She longs to have a family of her own, to raise her child, and to love her child in all the ways her stepmother never loved her, and for her baby to have a father, to know its father. All these thoughts are swirling in her mind, and no one is more surprised than Hillary when she hears herself say, "Okay, Peter. Yes. I will move in with you, Kenzie, and Little Pete. I want our baby to grow up in a family, to know the love of a family."

A huge grin spreads across Peter's face. He quickly pushes back his chair from the table. The chair legs make a loud screech as they scrape across the kitchen floor, and the noise startles Athena, who has been asleep on the couch in the living room. She gives a loud meow, flies off the sofa, and runs down the hall toward the bedrooms. "You just made my day, Hill," he says excitedly as he rushes around to where Hillary is still sitting, pulls her up from her chair, and holds her tightly to him. "I know you're probably already worrying about a million little things right now," he says gently to her, "but it's all going to work out. We love each other, and we're having a baby together. Things'll be just fine. Wait until I tell Kenzie and Little Pete. They will be so psyched when they hear you're moving in." Peter holds Hillary's face in both his hands.

They clear the table, wrap up the leftover food, and put it in the fridge. Hillary then leads Peter over to the couch. He wraps one arm around Hillary's shoulders and pulls her to him. They talk late into the night about the logistics of the move; Hillary has to give thirty days' notice that she will vacate her apartment, she'll need to rent a storage unit for most of her furniture as Peter's house is already furnished, she will need help packing everything up, and Athena will be moving with Hillary. That's not up for debate, she thinks, as she reaches over with her free hand to Athena, who has returned from down the hallway and is pressed against Hillary's thigh, and starts rubbing the cat's soft ears.

Peter ends up spending the night. And even though they are exhausted when they climb into Hillary's bed, they share a moment of gentle lovemaking before drifting off to sleep in one another's arms.

Chapter 7

Susan

Susan hears muffled voices talking to her but can't make out exactly what they're saying. Her brain won't process the words. The voices are loud, and she has a splitting headache. She is aware of someone's face very close to hers. It is as if she is deep underwater and trying to swim up to the voices. She feels like she might suffocate under the deep water before she makes it to the surface to take in a breath of air. Panic rises within her chest; she feels her entire body clench and spasm as she tries to swim out of the depths. Her arms and legs are pumping as hard as they can, fighting to get to the surface to take that breath.

"She's coming around," Susan hears more clearly as she continues to fight her way back from the cold and dark she has found herself in. "Open your eyes, Susan," she hears the voice command. "Can you open your eyes for me?"

Susan tries to focus on the voice and listen to the commands. She feels herself gasping for air as she struggles out of the blackness. She is trying to open her eyes, but they are so heavy. It takes all her strength just to open them a slit. Bright white lights shine all around her. Too bright. It hurts her head more.

She quickly closes her eyes and turns away from the voice.

"Can somebody move this overhead light out of the way," the voice directs again. "Susan, you're in the Emergency Department. My name is Dr. Zimmerman, and I need you to open your eyes for me." Susan turns her face back toward the voice and opens her eyes a bit more this time. A blurry face is gazing down at her. She opens her eyes more fully. They won't focus. She tries to rub her eyes with her hands to clear the blurriness but can't move her arms to her face. Her arms feel tied to something. She pulls hard at whatever is binding them, panic again rising within her.

"We had to restrain you," the blurry face is saying. "You were fighting us, trying to pull out your IV and the tube we had to put in your nose. If you can stop fighting us, we can take off the restraints. Can you do that for me, Susan? Can you stop fighting us?"

Susan relaxes her arms and notices them fall onto the stretcher beside her body. She tries to speak: "Wuhhh?" Her mouth is dry and sticky. She licks her lips and tries again. "What happened?" she is able to get out in a weak voice.

"You took a lot of pills," the doctor tells her. "We had to pump your stomach, and that's why you have that tube in your nose. Your husband found you unconscious in the shower. You're lucky he got to you when he did. He probably saved your life."

At the mention of the word "husband," Susan immediately thinks of Paul. Resentment rises inside her. "Where...is he?" she asks.

Another voice in the room answers; it is one of the nurses. "He's right out in the waiting room. I can go get him for you."

"No!" Susan is surprised at how forcefully that word comes out. And then more softly: "No. I don't want to see him. Tell him to go home."

"You sure?" asks the nurse. "You sure you don't want him to stay with you while we get you ready for transfer up to the Intensive Care Unit?"

"I'm sure," Susan replies. "Tell him I don't want to see him. Tell him to go home."

When Paul first arrived at the Emergency Room entrance, the receptionist at the admitting desk told him to have a seat in the waiting area while she got an update for him. She has been gone for some time, and Paul has become more worried as each minute passes. Did the paramedics get Susan to the hospital in time, he wonders as the receptionist returns.

"So, I was able to find a nurse to give you an update on your wife," the receptionist says as she glances around the waiting room. There is no one else in the area. Probably because of the storm, thinks Paul as he follows her gaze. "He'll be out in a minute to talk with you."

Paul looks back at the magazine he has been thumbing through, an article on turning your backyard into a flowering garden for pollinators. He hasn't absorbed any of what he has read. He can barely make sense of the words as he waits for news on Susan's condition.

Just then, the main Emergency Treatment Area's pneumatic doors open with a whoosh, and a tired-looking nurse walks briskly over to Paul. "Let's sit down for a minute," the nurse says, indicating a bank of chairs opposite the receptionist's desk. Paul looks at the nurse's name tag: "Jared," it reads. "We've been able to stabilize your wife," Jared begins. "We've gotten some IV fluids into her and some medicine to counteract the effects of the pills she took. We also put a tube down into her stomach to pump out anything that was still in there. The paramedics told us that one thing your wife took was Tylenol. Is that correct?"

Paul nods as Jared continues, "She's lucky she didn't take any more than she did. Her liver enzymes are elevated. We're watching to see the extent of injury to her liver."

"Will she be all right, though?"

"We have to wait for more results to come back. Do you know if she was intentionally trying to kill herself? Did she leave any kind of note or anything?"

"No," answers Paul. "There wasn't any note. We had gotten into a fight. She wants a baby, and I told her I just couldn't. And that's why she tried to kill herself." He can barely spit the words out.

The nurse listens as Paul explains, then continues, "We've got several more tests to run. Then we'll probably admit her to the Intensive Care Unit. I'll update you when we know the outcome of those tests. If you follow along the hallway to the left, there's some coffee and vending machines." Jared points down the long corridor off the waiting area and stands up to return through the pneumatic doors and into the Emergency Treatment Area.

"Thank you," Paul says softly. Then, "Take good care of her, okay?"

Paul glances up at the clock on the waiting room wall: 11:30 p.m. Too late to call Susan's sister. Paul doesn't want to worry her until he has more information on Susan's condition, anyway. Her sister will have a lot of questions. What if she blames me, he thinks suddenly, a feeling of guilt seeping into his heart.

Time seems to creep by; the seconds turn to minutes, and then the minutes turn to hours. Paul has gotten two snacks from the vending machines and has looked through all the magazines the waiting area offers. He gets up and starts pacing.

What in God's name have I done he reflects, as he makes eye contact with the receptionist who is typing on the computer behind the protective glass barrier. She meets his gaze and quickly looks away. I would give Suzie anything, Paul thinks, as he continues his pacing, anything. The depth of love he has for this woman who has just become his wife is as deep as his love for his son. Different, but just as deep. This is the one person whose soul he believes he has been looking for his entire life. He hadn't been aware of that longing for his soulmate until he met Susan, until she filled that longing with her smile as bright as sunshine, her eyes as blue as a spring sky, and her laughter like water splashing over rocks. He continues his pacing.

"What's taking them so long?" he asks the receptionist as he circles back by her desk. "When can I see my wife? I want to see my wife." His voice is rising. He is desperate.

"I'll page someone," the receptionist curtly responds.

She presses a button on her phone and speaks to someone on the other end. Within minutes, the pneumatic doors from the Treatment Area open again. An older man wearing scrubs walks through them and toward Paul.

"You must be Paul," he says as he extends his hand. "I'm Dr. Zimmerman. I apologize for the wait. Let's sit down a minute." He motions toward the waiting room chairs. "Susan is going to be okay. Her liver enzymes are starting to come down, and we feel we've gotten all the remaining pills out of her stomach. We're going to admit her to the ICU for observation, and then she'll be transferred to our inpatient psychiatric floor."

"The psychiatric floor? Does she need that?"

"She tried to commit suicide, Paul," the doctor says softly, holding his eye contact with Paul. "This was a cry for help. Your wife is not safe to go home until she can sort through some things."

Paul looks back at the doctor's face. His eyes are deep, tired. I wonder how often he's had to relate news like this to people, Paul thinks to himself. "When can I see her?"

The doctor glances down for a moment and then clears his throat. "She doesn't want to see you right now. She has made that very clear."

Paul feels like the doctor has just struck him. "She doesn't want to see me?" he asks incredulously. "Did she say why?"

"As I said," the doctor responds, "she has a lot she has to work through. It would be best if you headed home, and someone from the ICU will give you a call tomorrow morning. The good news is that Susan is going to pull through," he concludes with a small smile as he stands up to return to the Treatment Area.

Paul stands up also, feeling distraught. He puts on his parka, his hat, and his gloves. He glances back at the receptionist. "Thank you," he says to her, although he isn't quite sure what he is thanking her for. He steps out into the still snowy night air and walks to the parking lot to find his car.

"We're getting ready to bring you up to the ICU," Susan hears the nurse say as he starts moving wires and tubes and tucking them onto the stretcher around her. She lays her head back against the thin pillow. She feels small, vulnerable, like a tiny insect that could be crushed instantly by someone's heavy shoe.

Crush me, she thinks to herself, just crush me and get it over with. Susan closes her eyes as the nurse and an orderly wheel her through the halls and to the elevator. The elevator ride up is quiet and seems to take forever. She keeps her eyes closed. She doesn't want to have to talk to anybody. She has nothing to say. She doesn't want to be here.

The nurses in the ICU are all business. They help Susan slide from the ER stretcher to the hospital bed and busy themselves reorganizing the wires and tubes and reconnecting them to the machines in the room. Susan is cold and starts to shiver. "Here," the ER nurse says as he loads his transfer equipment onto the stretcher. "Here are some extra blankets." Then he gives Susan's hand a slight squeeze. "Take care of yourself," he says, and he walks out of the room.

The compassion from the ER nurse makes Susan want to weep. How can he be so nice to me, she thinks, after the mess I've made of myself. She doesn't cry, though. She won't. She feels an overwhelming sense of exhaustion. They must have given me something in my IV, a sedative, maybe, she wonders as she sinks back into darkness.

Susan wakes several hours later to voices talking all around her, alarms beeping, phones ringing. Her head is pounding. She glances over to the window of her room and sees that the snow has stopped falling and the sun is shining. The air looks cold outside. She pulls the hospital blankets up around her shoulders.

Shortly after, a nurse walks into Susan's room, a different nurse than the one last night. She is young. Too young to be an ICU nurse, judges Susan.

"I'm Stephanie," the nurse says in a bubbly voice. "I'll be your nurse for the next twelve hours."

I don't think I'll be able to stand her for twelve hours, Susan believes, but asks instead, "Can I get something for my head? It's splitting."

Susan feels that if she doesn't say much to the young nurse, the nurse will leave her alone. She can't deal with that bubbliness when she is so miserable. She thinks back to yesterday, her and Paul's conversation, what he had said to her, and the ultimatum he had given her. She begins to notice herself crumple on the inside as she starts to dry heave.

The thick plastic tube is still in her nose, hooked up to a suction canister in the wall behind her. She is going to gag. She feels like she is choking and notices herself panicking. Reflexively, Susan grabs the tube hard with one hand and yanks it out of her nose. "God, that hurt!" she says out loud as she looks at the tube in her hand, covered with blood-tinged mucus. Stephanie comes running into Susan's room.

"What did you do?!" the nurse says accusingly as she rushes over to Susan's bedside. Then she composes herself and in her overly happy voice continues, "Well, the doctor wanted us to remove that tube from your nose later this morning, anyway, so I guess it's okay that you pulled it out a little early. Let's get your face and nose cleaned up."

Susan is left with a plastic basin of lukewarm water, a small soap package, and a washcloth. As she dips the washcloth into the water, she notices her hands shaking. Then, her whole body is shaking. She drops the washcloth back into the basin as sobs overtake her. She thinks of Paul, of how much she loves him, how she loves the way he calls her "Suzie," the way he smiles as soon as he walks through the door after work and sees her, how his whole face lights up. She knows he loves her, but she cannot feel that love within her, cannot find his love within her, cannot find any love for herself.

Who is she for Paul if she is not his wife, his lover? Who is she for herself if she is not a mother? That voice within her that keeps reminding her that she is supposed to bear children had started so quietly and had only grown louder after she met Paul. She knows of women her age who have never had children. But that was by choice, she thinks, as she blows her nose into a scratchy hospital tissue. Her nose starts bleeding. She must have loosened a blood clot. She reaches over to the bedside table to grab a handful of tissues, blood staining her fingers as she tries to stanch the flow. What a disaster I am, she admits as she grabs another handful of tissues.

Later, after Susan has been able to compose herself somewhat and finish washing, the ICU doctor comes in. "Good morning, Susan," she says in a curt voice. Her dark red hair is pulled back severely into a tight bun at the base of her neck. "We have your most recent lab results back," the doctor continues before Susan can return her greeting. "Things are looking better. We should be able to move you from the ICU to our inpatient psychiatric floor within the hour. I'll have the nurse remove the IV from your arm, and we'll have you on your way. You gave us a bit of a scare, Susan," the doctor goes on. "We were very concerned that you might have permanently damaged your liver and your kidneys. Thankfully, you are young and healthy, and your body should fully recover."

The doctor turns and leaves the room. Susan thinks about what she has said, the phrase she had used: "Your body should fully recover." What about my mind, though? Susan wonders. Will that make a full recovery? Or will I be stuck living in this miserable limbo of not fully functioning as a life partner to Paul and not fully existing as the mother I long to become?

Stephanie comes in just then to remove Susan's IV and collect her things so she can be transferred to the psychiatric unit. "It's been a pleasure to meet you, Susan," Stephanie says as she goes about the business of removing the IV catheter from Susan's arm. "I really hope the best for you."

Susan thinks the nurse sounds sincere, even with her bubbliness. "Thanks." She gives a small smile to her, then mutters, "It's been nice meeting you, too."

Chapter 8

Hillary

Hillary loves her little home office in the spare room of her apartment. She loves looking up from her work and seeing outside an actual window rather than looking at the bland walls of her cubicle. She loves that she can get up whenever she has to pee and use her own bathroom. "Baby!" she exclaims at one point, "What are you doing to your momma? Making me run to the bathroom all day?" She plugs through her workday, attending online meetings and talking with her fellow team members, and then returns to solitary work on programming projects that were in progress before the advent of the COVID-19 virus.

At one point, Hillary looks out the window and realizes the sun is setting. It's after five o'clock. Hillary scoots Athena off her lap and stands up from her desk. "Let's get you some food, Miss Athena," she says as she bends down to scratch the top of Athena's head. She laughs as she bends over and realizes it's a little more difficult as there is now a small bump in the way. She walks down the hallway to the kitchen, turning lights on as she goes, Athena following behind her, meowing loudly.

Later that evening, Hillary has had her dinner of leftover salmon. The dishes are washed and put in the sink rack to dry. She hangs her dishtowel over the edge of the countertop, pours herself a glass of seltzer, and makes her way into the living room. She is absentmindedly flipping through TV channels when her phone rings. It's Joan. "Hey, Girl," she says into her phone. "First day working from home is in the books. How was your day?"

"Hey yourself," Joan replies. "Isn't working from home the best?" Joan is a medical coder and has always worked from home. "You can throw in a load of laundry when you're not on a Zoom meeting, go to the kitchen whenever you want to a snack, and you don't have to share a bathroom with a bunch of other women. I'm telling you, you will never want to return to an office. If people ever do get to go back to their offices." Her voice trails off as she considers the current state of affairs in the United States, where the daily death toll from COVID-19 continues to rise in staggering numbers.

"Speaking of bathrooms," Hillary says, startling Joan from her thoughts. "This baby had me running back and forth to pee just about every hour or two. I hope it doesn't stay like this for the rest of my pregnancy!"

"Oh, yeah," Joan replies. "Don't you have your first OB visit this week?"

"It's tomorrow morning. They robo-called me the other night to remind me of the date and time, and the message said I would have to wear a mask to my appointment. Luckily, I found some old face masks in a box I bought when I first moved into this apartment and you and I repainted all the rooms. Remember that? How grungy this place was when I first moved in?"

"Oh, yeah, I do," Joan laughs. "And the smell! Remember that musty smell? It permeated the entire apartment. I don't think those windows had been opened in ages."

"So, I have some news." Hillary's voice becomes more serious. "Peter and I talked last night. And you'll never believe what he asked me."

"Don't even tell me he asked you to marry him," Joan interrupts. "Please tell me you said no?"

Hillary laughs at Joan's comment. "No, he didn't ask me to marry him. But he did ask me to move in with him. He wants us to be a family, with our baby and his two kids."

There is a long pause from Joan, and then she finally responds, "And did you say you would, Hill? Are you going to move in with him? Or did you tell him you would think about it?"

"At first, I was shocked and didn't know what to say. But then I realized it's what I really want, Joanie. I want a family for my baby. I want him to grow up knowing his mother and his father. And his half-siblings, too." Hillary takes a breath, and then, knowing how her friend feels about Peter, she quickly blurts, "I told him yes. I told him I would move in with him."

"Oh, Hill," Joan says with a disappointed sigh. "I know you think you love him, and I know how much you want your own family. But this guy has a lot of issues. For one thing, he's super immature. He's never even around to raise his own kids. Didn't you tell me he leaves them with his mother most of the time? I think you should take a few days, at least, to think about this before you jump into anything permanent with Peter. You can do this on your own, you know, raise a child. Lots of women do."

"Listen, Joan," Hillary replies sternly, "I know you don't like him. And I wish you saw the side of Peter that I see; the soft side, the caring side. But I'm doing this not just for me but for my baby. This is really important to me. And, yes, I do love him. So, yeah, I've made up my mind, and I'm moving in with Peter."

"Sorry, Sweetie." Joan's tone softens. "I didn't mean to come across as all bossy and everything. I love you, you know. I don't want to see you get hurt. But I hear you. And I know you well enough to know that once you've made up your mind, there's no changing it. I'll always support you, Hill, no matter what."

They talk late into the night about all sorts of things: how Joan's husband's construction business has slowed down because of the COVID pandemic, how Hillary's morning sickness isn't quite as bad as it was early on, how another snowstorm is on the way as they head into March. They talk about their horses and share some gossip about women they know from the barn. The girlfriends end their call together in gales of laughter.

Hillary wakes on Wednesday morning to see a few inches of fresh snow on the ground, and the air is still filled with snowflakes. She dresses warmly, prepares a bowl of instant oatmeal and a cup of hot chocolate before she tramps outside to shovel out her car from the parking area on the side of the apartment building. The first few inches of snow are light, fluffy, and easy to shovel. However, the layer below that is hard and packed down. Typically, Hillary keeps her car pretty dug out and accessible to make it to work on winter mornings like this. But now, with the office building having closed a couple of weeks ago, she hasn't had to use her car to commute to work, and it is frozen in its parking space at her apartment building.

In spite of the chilliness in the air, Hillary starts to get very warm, very quickly, while shoveling her way around her car. There is no one else out shoveling their vehicles. There are no cars on the road. It is eerily quiet when, typically, several tenants from the apartment building leave for work around the same time, calling good morning to one another as they each get into their cars with their portable stainless-steel double-size coffee containers in hand. The road would have been busy on a workday morning like this, with cars whizzing by carrying kids to school for drop-off and parents to their various job locations.

Eventually, her old car is dug out. Hillary has left it running while she was shoveling, to heat the inside of it. And when she slides in, the air blows almost too hot on her already perspiring face. She presses a few buttons on the dashboard to turn down the heat, buckles herself into the driver's seat, and backs out of her parking spot. "Off we go!" she says to her baby. "Let's see what the OB doctor has to tell us."

When Hillary arrives at the obstetrics office, her bladder is aching from all of the water she had to drink prior to this visit, combined with the internal pressure of her growing uterus now pressing on her bladder. She puts on the mask that she brought from home and marches into the building. I feel like I'm going to suffocate with this thing on my face, she thinks to herself as she looks up and finds her way to the check-in area. A few other women are in the waiting area, sitting a distance from one another, wearing their masks, and scrolling through their phone messages on their cell phones. The waiting room looks desolate; there are no piles of magazines on the tables, only a couple of boxes of tissues spaced strategically around the room so patients won't have to get too close to each other if they should need to blow their nose. "Maintain a space between patients of at least six feet," reads a sign posted by the check-in window. She notices a large plastic bottle of hand sanitizer on a pedestal and reaches over for an automatic squirt of gel into her hands. Her hands sting as she rubs the sanitizer into them, and even through her mask, Hillary can smell the strong scent of alcohol.

"Next!" a loud voice says. Hillary looks up to see the receptionist looking at her from behind a partition of protective plexiglass.

"Are you Hillary?" the receptionist asks. Hillary nods, and the receptionist hands her a clipboard with a small stack of papers and a pen clipped to it. "Welcome to the practice. Fill these out while you're waiting, and you can bring them back to this desk when you're done. Used pens go in the cup labeled "dirty" when you're done filling out these forms."

Hillary finds an empty seat in the corner of the waiting area, separated from the other pregnant mothers. She fills out the paperwork, checks off boxes for conditions she has or has not had in her lifetime, and signs waivers and the office's HIPAA form. She returns the clipboard and papers to the reception desk and places her pen in the "dirty" cup.

Returning to her seat, she hears a heavy door by the reception desk open, and a young female voice calls out, "Hillary?"

"That's me," she replies as she turns and follows the medical assistant back through the door and down a long corridor of offices and exam rooms. Hillary notices the baby duck and bunny print on the medical assistant's scrub top. So sweet, she thinks to herself and smiles behind her mask.

They stop at a large platform scale in the hall, where the medical assistant asks Hillary to step up so she can get her weight and height. Hillary doesn't have a bathroom scale at home, so she has no idea what her normal weight is and how much she has gained throughout her pregnancy, although she acknowledges that her jeans have been getting a bit snug, and she has started wearing sweatpants since working from home.

Once they arrive at the exam room, the medical assistant tells Hillary her name, and she puts on a pair of exam gloves to take Hillary's temperature, pulse, and blood pressure. "All good," she says as she enters the information into her laptop. The medical assistant looks at Hillary and smiles with her eyes as she gathers her things and exits the exam room. "There's a gown on the exam table. Everything off. It ties in the back. One of our nurse midwives will be in to see you." She pulls the curtain around the exam table and exits the room.

Hillary changes into the flimsy hospital gown. She has been given a sheet to cover her lap, but it is so cold in the exam room that Hillary wraps it around her shoulders instead. Screw modesty, she thinks; it's freezing in here.

She is scrolling through Facebook on her cell phone, catching up on more stories about this new virus, COVID-19. The state of New York has the highest death count in the nation, and the government has officially enacted the mask mandate, she reads. Hillary continues scrolling through the news updates on her phone. She is blown away when she comes across a post about a group of people who believe the virus is a hoax. "You have got to be kidding me!" she says out loud. Are these people watching the body counts rising across the country? Are they not listening to the medical experts?

A quick knock on the door interrupts Hillary's thoughts, and an older woman enters the room. She is well-dressed, with her silvery blonde hair pulled back in a ponytail. "Hi, Hillary," she says, somewhat muffled behind her face mask. "I'm Francine, one of the midwives here at the practice. You can call me Frankie."

Frankie reviews the paperwork that Hillary has filled out in the waiting room. "No current medical conditions, good," she says. "You're not taking any medications. Okay." She pauses and looks up at Hillary. "So then, when was your last period?"

"Honestly, I don't know," Hillary responds. "My periods are

always irregular, so I can't tell you exactly when the last one was." She looks at the midwife's face above her mask. She has kind blue eyes that crinkle at the edges each time she smiles. Hillary likes her immediately. "I'm pretty sure I got pregnant at the beginning of December."

"Not to worry," Frankie replies. "Let's get you up on the table for a quick exam, and then I'd like to get you over to ultrasound so we can take a look at your baby. I do apologize that it's so cold in here today. We're in the older part of the medical building, and the heating system here can be finicky. Would you like a blanket?" Frankie doesn't wait for a reply but reaches into a cupboard in the corner of the room, pulls out a white hospital blanket, and hands it to Hillary, who has climbed onto the exam table and is lying on her back, her hands resting on top of her belly, her feet propped up in the stirrups attached to the end of the table.

Frankie's hands are warm and gentle as she deftly completes her exam of Hillary. "Any history of issues with pregnancy in your family? Any miscarriages?"

"I was adopted by my stepmother when I was younger," Hillary starts. "My biological parents are both dead, so I don't have any idea about that."

"We'll also do some blood work today before you leave. You may want to consider some genetic testing down the road, given that you're in your early thirties and we don't know much about your biological parents." Frankie completes her exam, removes her gloves, and with her back to Hillary, as she washes her hands in the little exam room sink, Frankie says, "Everything looks good here. I'm thinking you're between ten and twelve weeks pregnant, but let's get you over to ultrasound for a more definitive answer. Any questions before I have the medical assistant take you over?"

Hillary is excited by the news that her baby is healthy and that she could be almost halfway through her first trimester. "Will the ultrasound be able to tell the sex of my baby?" she asks hopefully.

"Possibly," replies Frankie. "You'll be able to hear your baby's heartbeat, and there's about a seventy-five to ninety-five percent accuracy with gender identification at this point in your pregnancy. Do you want to know the gender of your baby if they are able to identify it on ultrasound?"

"Yes!" Hillary replies quickly. Peter will be thrilled to know the sex of our baby, she thinks, especially if it's a boy. She can't wait to find out.

Frankie leaves the exam room, and Hillary puts her sweatshirt and sweatpants back on. After a few moments, there's another knock on the door and someone from the ultrasound department arrives to bring Hillary to a small, warm, dimly lit room. Hillary climbs up on yet another exam table and is told to raise her shirt up and pull her pants down below her belly. The ultrasound technologist covers Hillary's legs with a sheet, sits down on a rolling stool by the exam table, and starts entering data into the ultrasound machine located on a portable cart by the head of the bed. The technician then squirts a dab of warm gel on Hillary's stomach. Next, the technician takes the plastic ultrasound transducer and starts pressing it into various areas on Hillary's lower belly and moving it back and forth to capture images of Hillary's baby.

Hillary hears a rapid, rhythmic whoosh-whoosh noise. "That's your baby's heartbeat," says the technician in a businesslike tone as she continues to slide the ultrasound transducer over areas of Hillary's stomach, pressing a little firmer here and there before moving on to another area. "The midwife said you wanted to know the sex of your baby if we could tell. Is that right?" She pauses the back-and-forth movement of the transducer to wait for Hillary's reply.

Hillary is lying with her head turned toward the ultrasound computer screen, and the technician turns it so Hillary can see the fuzzy black-and-white image that is her baby. The technician points out the baby's head and spine to Hillary. She points out the arm and leg buds as well. Then she points to what looks like a small fifth limb bud and says with certainty, "It looks like your baby is a boy."

Tears leak out of Hillary's eyes as she takes in this news and looks at the actual image of the life form growing inside her. Seeing the baby's features makes her pregnancy seem so much more real. Her life has changed forever. She has met the baby inside of her. She is the mother of a little boy.

The technician hands Hillary a tissue to dry her eyes and wipes the ultrasound gel off Hillary's stomach. "Now the fun part begins," she says, smiling behind her face mask, "deciding on a name for your baby."

After an urgent stop at the ladies room to empty her very full bladder, Hillary returns to the previous obstetrics exam area, and Frankie enters to discuss the size of Hillary's baby, his heart rate, and his growth and development at this stage. Hillary hears the words Frankie is saying, but she isn't really listening. I am a mother, she is thinking to herself over and over again. A feeling of peaceful warmth washes over her. Based on the baby's size, Hillary is told she is approximately eleven and a half weeks pregnant. She is told that her baby is due in September. She is given a pile of informational papers and a card for a follow-up appointment. She leaves the OB office and practically floats to her car in the parking lot.

The snow has stopped falling outside and has covered the landscape in a pure white blanket. Hillary arrives back at her apartment, removes her hat, scarf, coat, and boots, and fixes herself a quick sandwich before sitting down at her desk to work the rest of the day on projects for the consulting team. There is one Zoom meeting during the late afternoon, and Hillary literally misses the entire thread of the conversation as she doodles baby names on a piece of paper. At one point, she looks up at the screen and sees Peter staring at her with a questioning look.

He starts texting her cell phone while they are on the Zoom meeting. "So??" he texts. "Did you find out?"

Hillary decides to be coy. "Yes," she texts back. "I will call you after work." And she places her phone face down on her desk while she continues writing and doodling on the piece of paper. She can hear the pings on her phone, alerting her that Peter is sending her text after text. She ignores them intentionally, allowing the suspense to build until they talk when work is over.

At precisely one minute after five o'clock, Hillary's phone rings. "Hey, Peter," she answers. "You're going to be a daddy to a bouncing baby boy! What do you think of that?"

"A boy? Really? That's awesome! And he's all good and everything? Healthy and all that?"

"He's perfect, Peter. Our baby boy is perfect." Hillary is so excited; Peter finally seems to be coming around to the idea of their baby. "What do you think we should name him?"

"Well, we can't name him Peter because that's my little boy's name. What about Edward? That was my father's name. We could call him Eddie."

"I don't know," Hillary responds lightheartedly. "It sounds so old, so common. I want our baby to have a name that's a little different, that makes him stand out. Something like Hunter or Sawyer. What do you think of those names?"

"Sawyer, no, I don't like it," Peter replies firmly. "Hunter, maybe. When is the baby due? What do you want to do about telling people at work? I say we wait as long as possible. I mean, they can only really see you from your boobs up during Zoom meetings anyways, right?" Peter laughs to himself. "I think we should wait until you start to get puffy, you know, later in the pregnancy."

Hillary decides to ignore the "boob" comment. "I think we should tell them now. I'm halfway into my first trimester. They will start noticing that my face is looking fatter at some point. We should at least tell our team leader. Carl will need to plan for when I'm out on maternity leave."

"Oh, yeah, right. I didn't think of that. I guess we have to tell Carl. Maybe we can tell him, and he can keep it quiet for a little bit. We gotta figure out how we'll tell all the guys on the consulting team."

Athena has been padding her paws on Hillary's lap, and now jumps down, meowing madly, and rubbing Hillary's legs. "Listen, I've got to go and feed my kitty. She gets a little pushy when she wants her dinner. We can talk more about this tomorrow. Have a good night, Peter. Daddy-O. I love you."

"Love you, too," Peter replies, softly, quickly. And then ends the call.

Hillary is beaming, she realizes as she sees her face in the mirror that Friday morning. Now that Peter seems agreeable to becoming a supportive father, and they have decided to tell Carl next Monday, this whole pregnancy seems real to her. She constantly talks to her baby and catches herself rubbing her growing belly as she sits in on Zoom meetings for work. She half pays attention to what's happening during these consultation meetings because she's thinking of names for her baby, thinking about decorating the extra room in Peter's house as a nursery for the baby, and humming lullabies in her head.

Her cell phone rings late that Friday afternoon as Hillary is trying to wrap up work projects for the week. She looks down and notices it is a call from Joan. "Hey, hi," she answers. "What's up?"

"Have you looked at the barn Facebook page today?" Joan starts right in. "They're closing the stable to boarders because of COVID. Only the barn owner and staff are allowed at the barn until further notice. She says she'll give everybody regular updates on their horses. This totally sucks!"

"What? Are you kidding? She can't do that." Hillary is becoming heated. "We pay board. We have a right to see our own horses. Can't everyone just wear masks when they're at the barn?"

Joan replies, "I guess with the COVID-19 death toll as high as it is, especially in New York City, lots of barns are doing this. I mean, I can see why. They're just trying to keep everyone safe. I'm going to miss seeing my pony, though. I hope the barn owner sends us pictures often enough so we can see how our two mares are doing."

"Did she say when this boarder ban was going to be lifted? Calypso needs to be ridden regularly, or she will turn into a fire-breathing dragon!"

"I know, and mine does too! No, she didn't give a date when the ban would be lifted. I guess it will be based on what the governor of the state recommends. And, anyway, you shouldn't be riding now that you've got your little bean growing inside you. Did your doctor say anything about that?"

Hillary likes the idea of her "little bean" growing inside her and decides to call him that until she and Peter have a name picked out for him. She laughs. "I love 'Little Bean,'" she tells Joan. "You're going to be the very best Auntie. I'm having a boy." And then she answers Joan's question. "Yeah, my OB says I have to keep moving, but not anything that could harm the baby. So no skydiving for me!"

"And no riding, either!" Joan mocks in a sisterly tone.

Hillary arranges her Saturday morning to start packing up her apartment, determining which things she will take to Peter's when she moves in and which will go into storage. She lets out a long sigh as she stares at the pile of boxes she has gotten from a local supermarket, stacked in the corner of her living room. She looks down at Athena, who is once again pressed against Hillary's thigh, purring as Hillary strokes her head. "No time like the present," Hillary says to Athena as she stands up from the couch and walks into her kitchen.

It's late afternoon when Hillary realizes she hasn't eaten anything since some toast and milk earlier that morning. Her stomach grumbles, and she becomes a little light-headed as she stands up from her bedroom floor, where she has been sorting through clothing and shoes. Hillary steadies herself on the bed as a wave of nausea washes over her. She catches her breath and chuckles; most of the clothing she has packed up doesn't even fit her now. Never mind, she thinks. As her pregnancy continues, her stomach will keep growing. "Sorry, Little Bean," she says, her hand over her belly. "I got slightly carried away with the packing and forgot to feed us."

At her kitchen table, Hillary contentedly sips on chicken noodle soup and nibbles a few crackers. She has been feeling little waves of movement in her belly recently, and it seems now that her baby is happily content with lunch. "Quickening," she says to herself. "When the mother first feels the baby moving inside of her." Hillary smiles. "Right on schedule, Little Bean."

Hillary cleans her soup bowl and spoon, rinses them, and sets them to dry in the dish rack by her sink. She muses over how nice it will be to actually have a dishwasher to do the dirty dishes once she moves in with Peter. Her heart flutters as she thinks about Peter, about setting up house together, about raising a family with him. Peter is due to come over to her apartment later that day to help with the packing, and she plans on asking him to spend the night.

After a quick break on the couch, Hillary reluctantly gets up, shuffles through the maze of boxes on her living room floor, and returns to her bedroom to finish sorting through her clothes and shoes. So many hoodies, she thinks, as she continues to fill box after box with sweatshirts; people must think I'm a mass murderer every time I head out of here. I'm always wearing a hoodie with the hood up over my head!

The late afternoon darkens outside and turns into evening. Hillary is lost in thought, some older clothes from the back of her closet bringing up memories of her childhood at the barn, when she hears the apartment doorbell buzz. She gets up slowly, knowing she will be dizzy from sitting on the floor for so long. The doorbell buzzes again. "Jesus, Peter," she says under her breath. "I can only go so fast here."

"God, it looks like a bomb went off in here, with all these boxes all over the place!" Peter exclaims as he enters the apartment, stepping over piles of clothing, books, and knick-knacks. "You're not bringing all of this to my place, are you? The house is already packed with my stuff and the kids'."

"Relax, Peter," Hillary replies in an annoyed tone, "I'm going to be putting a lot of this stuff into storage. Don't worry, you'll hardly know I'm there. Everybody comes with some baggage," she says cryptically, and turns to walk into the kitchen.

Peter follows. "What are we having for dinner?" he asks. "I could go and get us some takeout."

"Peter." Hillary is a little exasperated. "We're in the middle of a pandemic. No one is serving food to the public right now. There is no takeout!"

"Hey, hey," Peter says more softly now. "Don't get all worked up." He walks up behind Hillary and puts his arms protectively around her and her growing belly. "I'm just trying to help here."

"I know you are." Hillary's tone softens as well. "It's just that there is so much to do. All this packing, and working from home, and everyone dying from this damn disease." Her voice has risen again. "Sometimes it all feels like too much, Peter, you know?"

Peter's embrace tightens around Hillary. "I know, Babe," he half whispers in her ear. "I know." His lips gently brush against the skin on Hillary's neck. He turns her to face him and pushes his lips onto hers.

Chapter 9

Susan

The psychiatric floor is a locked unit, so Susan and the orderly who is pushing her wheelchair have to wait until they are buzzed through the doors. The orderly steers Susan to the nurses' station and checks her in. Susan notices that the psychiatric floor is unlike a regular hospital floor, with patient rooms down each side, equipment lined against the walls, and nurses running back and forth in some intricately organized pattern of daily function and patient care. Here, the hall makes a U shape, with the nursing station at one end. In the center of the U is a large room with windows all around so a person can see any part of the unit. There is a locked room behind the nurses' station, where Susan presumes medications are kept.

The staff wears regular street clothes. Less intimidating, thinks Susan. The patients, too, wear regular street clothes. How do you tell them apart? She muses.

"I'm Sandy, one of the nurses," says a woman approaching from behind the desk. "Let me show you your room so you can get settled." Sandy takes the bag of belongings that had been transferred with Susan when she left the ICU, her still-damp clothing from when they removed it in the ER. Susan stands up to follow the nurse, feeling a little bit wobbly. "This is our Community Meeting Room," says Sandy, indicating the large room with all the windows in the unit's center. "Your room is right over here." She leads Susan into a regular hospital room with no equipment on the walls and two twin beds, low to the floor, next to a couple of wooden sets of drawers.

"This will be your bed." Sandy points to the twin bed farthest from the door and closest to the single, barred window that looks out over the vast hospital parking lot. "Your roommate is Darla. She's in Group Meeting right now."

"You may have noticed everybody here, including the patients, wears regular clothes," Sandy goes on. "We don't allow people to stay in hospital gowns or pajamas all day. We've called your husband, and he'll be stopping by later today to drop off some clothing for you."

"I don't want to see him." Susan turns toward Sandy. "Can he just drop off my clothes and leave?"

"Of course. We'll let you know when he gets here in case you change your mind," replies Sandy as she hands Susan a clean hospital gown and pair of hospital pants, indicating she should change into them. "Morning Meeting just got started. Once you've put these on, they expect you to join them."

"I won't change my mind about seeing him," replies Susan under her breath as Sandy leaves the room. She gets changed into the hospital clothes that the nurse has left for her.

Susan knocks hesitantly on the wooden door to the Community Room. "Come on in," she hears a male voice call out. She opens the door and sees about a dozen people sitting in chairs in a circle. She watches as they turn their heads in unison and stare at her as she enters the room. "I'm Bill," says the therapist sitting among them. The only distinguishing differences between him and the patients are the clipboard of papers he holds on his lap and a hospital name badge clipped to the breast pocket of his shirt. "Have a seat. Group has just started."

When Susan is seated in a chair as close to the door as she can get, Bill announces, "Everybody, this is Susan. Let's welcome her to our community."

"Welcome, Susan," the group replies in discordant harmony.

Susan gives a little wave to the group as she looks around. A dozen faces gaze back at her: sad faces, lonely faces, grieving faces, young and old faces. The room's energy is subdued, as if the people's souls are in a deep slumber while their bodies have shown up for Morning Meeting. God, I don't want to be one of them, thinks Susan; please don't let me become one of them.

Bill, the therapist, turns back to his clipboard and then addresses the dull faces in the room. "Today, I want to talk about coping with depression, about what someone who is depressed can do to help change the way they are feeling in that moment. What are some positive and effective ways we can cope with feelings of depression?" he asks the group at large. "Anybody?"

A young woman, with her face a pale white and her hair dyed jet black, stirs in her chair and says to Bill, "I started going to yoga classes. Not here. Not while I'm in the hospital. But after the last time I was here. After I tried to kill myself, my therapist suggested yoga to help me relax. I found a gym with yoga classes, and I try to go there two or three times a week. I feel like it's helping me to relax more."

"Medication, drugs," a middle-aged man chimes in with some enthusiasm. "My meds really help me not to feel so depressed and anxious all the time. You know, once it takes effect in your system."

Several people in the group nod, acknowledging that

medication has helped with their depression as well.

"I started writing down my feelings in a journal," a third person speaks up, a petite woman with blonde hair, unwashed and hanging over her eyes. "I try to do it every day, you know, to stay on top of what's going on inside of me." Several more heads nod.

"These are all excellent tools to help us cope," Bill addresses the group. "Anybody else? What are some other positive ways people use to help them when they're feeling depressed or anxious?"

Additional voices pop up from the group sitting around the circle: timid voices, pressured voices, tearful voices. I am not like these people, Susan's inner voice keeps saying. How did I get here? And how the hell do I get out of here?

Susan tunes out the voices in the room. She tunes out Bill the therapist's hopeful questioning. They can't possibly understand the loss I'm feeling. The loss of who I am as a female human being. What's the point of having ovaries, of having a uterus, of getting my period every month? I have no purpose here.

The Morning Meeting hour finally comes to an end. People rise from their chairs, some talking with each other as they amble to the kitchen area for coffee; others silent, lost in their own confusion; and still others tearful from the rawness and the depth of their sorrow, guilt, grief. Susan watches them leave, watches out the windows of the large Community Room. She notices the pale young woman with dark hair entering her room down the hall. That must be Darla, she thinks. I wonder what her story is.

"Susan," she hears Bill say, "I'd like to ask you to stay for a few minutes after the group leaves. Can you wait for a second?"

Susan watches as Bill gathers his papers and clips them

neatly on his clipboard. He finds an empty seat and pulls it opposite Susan. She notices his hair is a dull blonde, graying at the temples. His eyes are light, his face pasty white, his lips pale. He wears a beige shirt neatly tucked into his khaki pants. His brown shoes are scuffed and worn. He's so bland, Susan thinks, featureless, like a slug.

"I'm glad you are here with us, Susan," Bill begins. "We have a daily schedule of group meetings and individual one-on-one counseling sessions. We have several therapists who work here. I am assigned to you as your therapist. I see a lot of folks who've been through a suicide attempt, and I look forward to working with you. We'll have our one-on-one session later this afternoon in one of the private conference rooms. You'll also have a psychiatrist, a doctor, assigned to you, who will oversee what medications will work best to help you manage your depression and feelings of wanting to harm yourself. How are you feeling right now? Is there anything I can do for you right now?"

Susan is silent, listening to Bill's therapist voice, soft, with a soothing up and down cadence as he speaks. She isn't drawn to him in any way, but she doesn't dislike him either. "I'm just waiting for my clothes to be delivered. My husband is supposed to be bringing them. I already told them at the desk that I don't want to see him when he comes. I'm not ready to talk to him." Susan notices her heart pounding as anger, longing, and sadness rise and fall within her. She just wants to sleep. To sleep, to die, whatever. She doesn't want to be here in this place, in this world, anymore. She looks at Bill. "Can I go now? I'm exhausted."

"Yes. Sure," Bill replies. "I'll see you later in one of the conference rooms for our session. I look forward to working with you." He gives Susan a small smile as he gets up from his chair and indicates that Susan should do the same. Susan walks out of the Community Room and hears Bill close the door behind them. She makes her way toward her room, toward the little twin bed waiting for her. Her exhaustion is like nothing she has ever felt, and sleep beckons to her like a cooling salve on a festering wound.

As Susan enters her room, she notices Darla sitting cross-legged on her own twin bed. Darla has earbuds in and is busy sketching on a large pad of paper she holds on her lap. Susan can't make out exactly what Darla is sketching from where she stands in the doorway, but it looks like Darla is an accomplished artist. Susan then notices a stack of clothing sitting on her bed, with some sort of stuffed animal on top of the pile.

Paul must have stopped by already and dropped her clothes off. She walks over to her bed and picks up the stuffed toy. It is a Pomeranian puppy—sable, just like her Ginger. Susan gives a half smile as she walks around to the far side of her bed and begins to organize her clothing in the drawers of the little dresser next to it. When she gets to the last item of clothing, she notices a piece of paper sticking out of her pants pocket. She reaches over and pulls out the paper. "I love you more," it says in Paul's handwriting.

Susan feels her heart skip a beat as she folds the little piece of paper and tucks it back into the pocket of the pair of pants. She places the pants in with her other clothing, curls onto her side on the bed, holding the stuffed dog tightly to her, and weeps silent tears until she falls into a blessed, deep sleep.

When she awakens later, the sun is setting and the sky is a dull gray as twilight settles over the snowy world outside her window. She looks at the clock on the wall. Oh, my God! I've got about two minutes to get dressed and go and meet with Bill, she thinks. Susan throws on a shirt and pair of jeans, slips her feet into her sneakers, runs a brush through her short hair, and hurries down the hall to the conference rooms.

Bill is waiting for her in the last room, where there is soft ambient lighting, a slightly worn oriental rug on the floor, and two plush chairs with a small table between them. The space is calming. Susan feels herself relax a little. "Come on in," Bill motions with his hand. He is sitting in one of the plush chairs with a notepad on his lap and a pen in his hand. "It must feel better to be out of that hospital garb and into your own clothes," he says as Susan sits across from him in the other chair.

Susan has seen a therapist here and there in the past for problems like body-image issues, general feelings of depression on and off, mostly related to a particular concern taking place at that time in her life. She had found therapy to be helpful with these things. Someone to talk to. Someone to listen. Susan doesn't believe talk therapy will help her with what she is experiencing now, though. She is doubtful that Bill can pull her out of the pit of nothingness she has fallen into. It is a dark place. A cold place. She has become separated from the rest of the world. Disconnected to the beat and rhythm of human existence. There is no way to climb out of this abyss. She could float there until it sucks her in, body and soul, and she withers and dies there. Susan can't identify with herself anymore. She sits in the chair and watches Bill write notes on his pad of paper as she answers his questions robotically.

"Let's talk a little bit about your husband," Bill says, interrupting Susan's train of thought. "It's Paul, right?"

"I don't really want to talk about him," Susan replies forcefully. "He's the reason I ended up here. He made me a promise, and he broke it. I hate him." And then she finishes softly, "I love him, too."

"Can you tell me a little bit more about that?" questions Bill.

"You know, he's my soulmate. When I first met Paul, I felt I had known him forever. And when he told me he wanted to give me a baby, I knew absolutely that I had found the One. I knew that my life purpose was being fulfilled. I knew, without a doubt, that this was the path I was supposed to be on."

"And now?" Bill prompts.

"Now, my path has ended. There's nowhere left for me to go. How can I be a woman and have all these hormones and things driving me to bear a child? How can I go through this life barren? He promised me we would have a baby together. And then he broke that promise. I feel dead inside, without purpose."

"Before you met Paul," asks Bill, "what was your purpose then? Where were you headed before you had a life partner and potential father for your child?"

Susan is silent for a moment, thinking, remembering. "Before I met Paul, I was committed to my job as a nurse. I had just bought a little house for myself. I would have my little dog with me and adopt a child as a single mother. I was planning for it, planning for being a mother."

"Can you return to that now? Have you and Paul discussed adoption?"

"He won't," Susan says, tears welling in her eyes. "I asked him about that, and he would only want a child that was his own, biologically. Adoption is off the table if I stay with Paul."

"Are you considering leaving Paul?"

"I've been thinking about it," Susan replies, "I've been thinking that maybe I married the wrong person, that maybe I was supposed to stay single, adopt a child, and raise that child, a child of my own, as a single mother."

Tears are streaming down Susan's face now. Bill reaches over to the box of tissues on the table between them and holds it out as Susan plucks a tissue from it.

"That was my original plan before I met Paul." After blowing her nose, she says, "My plan was always to be a mom. There was no question. There was never any doubt."

"And you're reconsidering that option now," Bill confirms. "You're considering leaving Paul because he no longer wants to have a child as part of your marriage?"

"I don't know," Susan says. She reaches for a second tissue as she continues to cry unbidden tears. "I love Paul. I really do. He fills my heart completely. But he broke a huge promise to me. I don't think I can stay in a marriage based on betrayal, based on a lie."

"Was it a lie?" Bill asks pointedly. "Was it a lie? Or was it maybe a promise Paul couldn't keep?"

"Why would he do that to me, though? Why would he promise to give me the thing I want most in this world, the thing that made me marry him in the first place? He went back on his word, and it has destroyed me."

Bill gently steers the counseling session back to Susan's ability to decide what happens next for her. He acknowledges her deep desire to raise a child on her own. They discuss what this would look like logistically, financially. Bill points out Susan's strength and conviction in her strong desire to be a mother. He acknowledges how hurt she must have been when Paul told her he no longer wanted a child with her. He leads her to look into herself, to see that she has options, choices. It is up to her to determine what will happen next on her life journey; she is at a crossroads and ultimately controls what happens from here.

The therapy hour is soon over. Bill asks Susan one last question as she prepares to rise from her chair and depart the conference room. "Would you consider having a couple's session with Paul at some point? I believe it's important for your recovery to face Paul, not only to let him know where you're at with your decision-making process but also to hear what he says about why he changed his mind about having a baby with you. You don't have to decide right now. Think about it."

Susan slowly walks down the hall to her room. "Susan," she hears behind her. "Susan, wait." It's one of the nurses. She has a little paper cup in each hand, one with pills and the other with water. "Hang on a sec," the nurse says, catching up with Susan. "It's time for your meds."

Susan stops and takes the cup of pills from the nurse's outstretched hand. She counts five pills in the little paper cup. Five pills, she thinks to herself; this is what it takes to put Humpty Dumpty back together again—just five little pills. Susan tosses the pills back into her mouth and swallows them all with a gulp of water.

"After dinner, there's a daily wrap-up session in the Community Room," continues the nurse, taking both cups back from Susan and peering into each to ensure that all the pills have been taken. "Then there's some free time before bed. Some people like to watch a movie. Or read. Or talk on the phone to a friend or family member. We have several phones around the unit for people to use. It's usually lights-out by ten o'clock here," she concludes. When Susan doesn't reply, "Well, I'll let you get back to your room." She gives a half smile and then turns and walks briskly back to the nurses' station at the other end of the unit.

Susan continues on her way, lost in thought, mulling over what Bill had said in their therapy session. What are my choices here? I could leave Paul and live in my own place, get pregnant, and raise a child on my own. Could I afford that? Could I afford daycare while I worked? Would I be working just to afford daycare? She enters her room and nods to Darla, who is darting out the door.

"It's almost dinner," mumbles Darla. "We stay on the unit

and eat in the kitchen area. See you in there." And she is gone.

"See you," Susan says to Darla's back. She longs to change into her pajamas, climb into her little twin bed, hug her stuffed dog to her chest, forget that she is here and why, and return to the beginning when she first met Paul. Were there any signs that he wasn't truthful with her when they discussed marriage and a family? Had she missed something that could have saved her from all this agony? Did I fall in love with Paul, she wonders, or did I fall in love with the idea of having a family with Paul? The thought makes her catch her breath. Susan sits on the edge of her little bed, considering all of this until one of the evening staff comes along and encourages her to join the others in the kitchen for dinner.

"You don't want your food to get cold, now," the staff member says in a singsong voice.

"What am I, in kindergarten?" Susan says under her breath as she rises and follows the staff member to the kitchen. She sits beside an older man who smells of poor hygiene and eats with his mouth open. Susan takes a few bites of her meal and then brings her tray to the cafeteria cart parked in the corner of the room. Then, it's over to the Community Wrap-Up Meeting and a movie. Partway through the movie, a comedy, Susan can feel her eyes drooping and makes her way to bed for the night.

The following day is a repeat of the previous day. Susan wonders if all the days are the same here. It already seems like time has stretched out, and one moment blurs into the next. She feels as if her thinking has slowed down, and she wonders if it has to do with the five little pills she obligingly takes morning and evening. I am turning into one of those people. She thinks back to the blank stares she met when she first entered the Community Room. I'm turning into a psych patient. Maybe this is my new identity. Since I'm not a mother, I'll be a psychiatric diagnosis like major depressive disorder, borderline personality disorder, or some other disorder.

That afternoon, Susan meets Bill again in his dimly lit office with the comfortable chairs. "I think I've had a breakthrough," she starts. "Last night, after you and I had our session, I got to thinking about something."

"Oh, yeah? What's that?" Bill looks at her questioningly.

"I think I made a mistake when I married Paul. I think I married him not because I loved him, but because I loved the idea of him, getting married, raising a family, and living in a little house with a little white picket fence and a little golden retriever in the front yard. You know, what's expected of us in our society." Susan recognizes she sounds snippy but can't seem to stop herself. "We get programmed our whole lives as women that our one and only job is to raise a child, to procreate. After all, isn't that the legacy of ourselves we will leave behind? Our children?" She continues her rant, "And where does that leave me? Who will remember me when I'm gone? What impact will I have made on this world if I don't have a child? No one will remember me, that's who! I'll have stood for nothing! My life will have been for nothing. I will have been for nothing." Susan realizes her voice is raised, and tears are splashing down her hot cheeks.

She lowers her voice and whispers, "Sorry." Then, she quickly stands up and walks to the door, preparing to leave.

"Susan. Where are you going?"

"There's no point, Bill!" she says, her voice rising again. "I am nothing. I am not worth anything. Don't bother wasting your time on me. I'm completely and utterly not worth it." She pauses a moment and then, "I'm just going to try and kill myself again when I get out of here, anyway. Don't waste your time." She pulls open the door, then slams it quickly behind her. As she runs down the hall to her room, she hears Bill walking rapidly behind her, trying to catch up. She runs faster. And she doesn't stop until she is sitting on the mattress at the head of her bed, with her knees up to her chest, a sighing, heaving, and sobbing mess.

She hears Bill stop at the doorway to her room. "Susan." He is out of breath from walking so briskly. "Susan, come on out. Let's go back to my office and finish our session even if you don't want to say anything else, even if you don't want me to say anything else. Let's finish our time together. You are worth it, Susan. You may not see it right now, but you are so worth it."

Several other patients gather around Susan's doorway when they hear the commotion and peer in at Susan to see what will happen next. "I hate this fucking fishbowl!" she yells. "Go away!" She buries her head in her arms.

One of the female nurses has worked her way into Susan's room. "Susan, it's Sandy. Remember, we met when you first came in yesterday? Listen, we can't have you yelling like this in your room because it triggers some of the other people here. Can I give you something to help you to relax a little bit? Would that help you right now, Susan?"

Susan looks up at Sandy's kind face with her own red, puffy, tear-stained one. Once again, she watches from seemingly outside herself as her life is draining out of her. She has no more energy, no more light, no more soul. I am nothing, she thinks silently. I am nothing. She does not react as the needle pierces her skin or hear a word that Sandy or Bill or anyone is saying to her. She lets go, lets the darkness consume her, and she remains that way for an indeterminate amount of time. Breathing. But not living.

When Susan finally returns once again from the darkness within her, she realizes she is lying on a hard mattress, on her back, with lights above her. She feels groggy and worn and empty. Her tongue is as dry as sandpaper, and when she opens her mouth to ask for water, hardly any sound comes out. She hears people talking in the room. And when she looks around, she realizes she is in a curtained-off cubicle. She can hear the whoosh of oxygen and heart monitors from various beds around the large room of curtained cubicles. Susan tries to push up off the hard mattress to get a better look around her, but her arms are weak, and she falls back on the stretcher.

"Oh, hey there," says a cheery voice as someone in scrubs peers around the curtain at her. "I'm one of the nurses here. You're in the post-anesthesia area. Glad to see you're coming around."

"I'm where?" Susan manages to whisper incredulously. What the hell had happened to land her in the hospital recovery room?

"You've just had your first ECT treatment. Electroconvulsive therapy. You did really well. We'll have you out of here and back up to your unit in a little bit."

"Shock therapy!" Susan manages to spit out. "What?"

"Yeah, you had been in a state of catatonia for a couple of days and weren't eating or drinking or responding to anyone. They tried to give you stronger medications, but you were not swallowing them. It sounds like nothing was working to bring you around, so your doctor ordered ECT in hopes that this treatment would help you."

Susan is in disbelief. Back in nursing school, she had learned about ECT treatments for patients with severe depression. Reading about the procedure in school, it had seemed rather barbaric. She didn't even know it was still done. She's never even heard of someone who had had shock therapy. She acknowledges the flood of sadness that overtakes her. She closes her eyes as tears slip down her cheeks.

In a matter of minutes, Susan hears a familiar voice; Bill. "Hey there, Susan," he says kindly, looking into her eyes. "How are you feeling? Tired, I bet. You'll start to feel better once the sedative they've given you for the ECT procedure wears off. Let's get you back upstairs." Susan notices that Bill has brought another person with him, a nurse she recognizes from the psychiatric unit. The nurse unhooks Susan from the heart monitor and readies her for transport back to her room.

Susan keeps her eyes closed for the entire trip down hallways and up in the elevator, and through the locked doors of the unit, and back to her bed by the window in the corner room at the end of the hall. Bill and the nurse chit-chat over her as they steer the stretcher along. So casual, thinks Susan, like they do this every day. Maybe they do? she ponders.

The nurse helps Susan sit up and step off the stretcher. Susan immediately becomes dizzy, and the room starts spinning a bit. "Just go slowly," says the nurse. "Once you're back in your bed, I'll get you something for the dizziness."

"Thank you," Susan sighs as she climbs into her bed and pulls the blanket over herself. The exhaustion she feels is overtaking her, and her eyes close heavily. She drifts off to sleep, awakening only when the nurse returns with more medication. Almost immediately, her mind succumbs and releases as she falls again into a deep sleep.

Chapter 10

Hillary

"Kenzie, Little Pete, c'mon down and get your breakfast before home school starts!" Hillary calls Peter's kids from down in the kitchen of Peter's house. Our house, Hillary has to keep reminding herself. The two children clomp down the stairs and race into the kitchen.

"I want waffles," shouts Little Pete.

"It's a school day. We only get waffles on Sundays, Stupid," Kenzie admonishes her brother. Little Pete starts to cry.

"Hey, that's not nice, Kenzie. Say you're sorry to your brother. We're running late this morning, so it's cereal and milk with a banana for breakfast."

"I don't have to do what you say." Kenzie pouts and crosses her arms defiantly across her chest. "You're not my mother, you know."

Hillary sighs. This has been going on with Kenzie since she moved in with Peter a few months ago. Peter assured her it was only temporary, that Kenzie just had to get used to the idea of another female living in the house. But it hadn't gotten better.

Hillary still feels resented by the little girl.

She pastes a smile on her face and turns to Kenzie. "You're right. I'm not your mother. But I am the adult in the house right now, and it's the right thing to do, to apologize for calling your brother a bad name."

"How come Daddy can sometimes call Little Pete stupid, then? If it's a bad word?"

Hillary concedes to herself that Kenzie does have a point. "Nobody should call anybody stupid, especially if they love them. Now tell your brother you're sorry so we can get ready for school."

"Sorry," Kenzie mumbles, barely audible, to her brother.

Little Pete doesn't even look up from his cereal bowl to acknowledge his sister's apology. Probably so used to it, Hillary guesses. She's heard Peter call his kids that, and worse.

Kenzie and Little Pete push back their chairs and dash from the kitchen, leaving empty cereal bowls and glasses of orange juice, half full, on the table. Hillary is about to call them back to clear their plates but then picks up the bowls and glasses herself.

Moving in with Peter and his kids has been a much harder transition than Hillary had anticipated. At first, it had been fun: waking up each morning and making breakfast for the family, getting the kids ready at their home computers for school during the COVID-19 pandemic. Peter had seemed to enjoy it, too; helping Hillary prepare meals, offering to go out and do the grocery shopping so she wouldn't risk exposing herself and their unborn baby to the virus. It had been a sweet first few months.

And then everyone's true colors started to show. Little Pete threw temper tantrums whenever he didn't get what he wanted. Kenzie was just plain mean to her brother and Hillary. Some of the language the little girl used, Hillary assumed she'd learned from her father. And Peter started leaving more and more of the running of the household to Hillary: the meal prep, the laundry, the cleaning, even the disciplining of the kids, such as it was.

Hillary is exhausted. Her belly is getting bigger by the day, her lower back aches and her feet are swollen. One evening, after she has tucked the kids into bed, reading one extra story and then another to Little Pete to keep him from having a tantrum, she all but falls onto the couch cushions next to Peter.

"Hey, watch it!" he cries, not looking away from the baseball game on television. "You'll make me spill my beer."

"Peter," Hillary starts. "Peter. I can't keep going like this."

Peter doesn't respond, continues watching the game.

"Peter," a little louder this time.

Still no response.

"PETER!"

"What? Jesus! You don't have to yell, you know. I'm sitting right here." He gives Hillary a stern look while taking a swig of his beer. "What the hell is the matter with you? You look friggin' possessed or something."

"What's that supposed to mean, Peter? I'm six months pregnant. I work full-time. I'm making all the meals, cleaning the house, pretty much raising your kids."

"Hey," Peter turns to fully face Hillary now, "leave them out of it. They're good kids."

"I didn't say they weren't, Peter. I feel like I'm doing everything around here. I can't keep up with it all. Peter, look at me. I'm exhausted!"

"I do stuff around here, too. Who takes out the garbage? Who cleans the litter box for a cat that isn't his? Who gets the groceries? Don't tell me I don't do enough. Aren't I entitled to a little downtime with a beer at the end of the day? I work hard, you know."

"Yes, you do. We both do. I'm just... This baby is taking a lot out of me. I feel like I'm tired all the time."

"Well, why don't you ask your baby doctor about it? Maybe she can give you something. You know, to pep you up."

"They can't give me anything, Peter. I don't feel like I'm getting enough rest with the kids' schedules, school at home, and then work. And I can't get comfortable to sleep at night because of my belly."

"Don't I know it." Peter takes another swallow of his beer, returns his focus to the television. "You keep me up all night, tossing and turning like you do. And that damn cat of yours scratching on the bedroom door at night."

"Athena's used to sleeping in my bed with me. It's going to take her a little while to adjust to sleeping in her cat bed in the living room. She's not trying to keep you awake on purpose. She's a good girl."

"She's a pain in my ass, is what she is," Peter concludes, reaching for the remote to turn up the volume.

"Aaand I guess we're done with that conversation," Hillary says under her breath.

"What?" Peter says, staring at the television.

"Nothing. Nothing at all," Hillary mutters to herself as she slowly pushes herself up off the couch. "I guess I'll just go pick up the kids' toys, get their lunches made for tomorrow, and read in the bedroom."

Peter turns once again toward Hillary. "Listen, if you're not happy here, you don't have to stay, you know." He is practically yelling over the volume of the television.

Hillary's voice catches in her throat for a second. She looks over at Peter on the couch. "And where would I go, Peter? I'm pregnant with our child. Remember?"

"Well, stop moping around all the time, complaining about this thing or that thing. You have a house; you have a family. Isn't that what you told me you always wanted? If this isn't enough, I don't know what else I can give you, Hillary."

"It's enough, Peter. I don't mean to complain. It's just a lot, you know? A lot to go from being a single woman in my own apartment to living in a house with you and the kids and a baby on the way. I'm grateful for everything you do for me; I really am."

"Well, then shut it, will you? I'm trying to relax and watch the game. Unwind from the day."

"Yup. Right. You got it." Hillary shuffles into the kitchen and begins to tackle the dinner dishes.

Asshole! She thinks as her hands dive into the soapy dishwater and reach for a glass, then rinse, then arrange the glass among all the others on the top rack of the dishwasher. He's the one who likes the dishes to be practically already sparkling clean before I even put them in the dishwasher. Why isn't he here doing the dishes, Hillary asks herself. I'm not the maid for Peter and his kids. What the hell? Is that what he thought the arrangement would be when he asked me to move in with him? Hillary pauses her mental tirade, looks around at the stack of dirty dishes yet to be washed. She steps back from the sink, removes her rubber dish gloves, leaves them on the kitchen counter. She closes the dishwasher door, silently walks into the bedroom she shares with Peter.

The cell phone rings once, twice. Then, "Hey, Chickie! How's the momma to be?"

"Oh, Joanie," Hillary practically wails into her phone. "You were right. I made a huge mistake."

"What mistake, Hill? What are you talking about? Are you all right?"

"I never should have moved in with Peter and the kids. I should have listened to you! And now here I am, stuck with this jerk, taking care of his house and kids, and big as a whale to boot. I didn't sign up for this, Joanie."

"Okay. Take a deep breath. Let's be logical about this. Tell me what's going on. Did Peter do something to you? Did he hit you or anything?"

"No, nothing like that. I'm just sick of taking care of the house and the kids and Peter! I never have any time to myself, but he gets to put his feet up at the end of the day and watch his sports. The kids rely on me for all their meals, help with their homework, refereeing when they fight. I'm beat, Joanie. I work all day, too. I need some downtime, too."

Joan pauses on the other end of the phone, then replies, "What you need is to carve out a space for yourself. Is there a spot in that house that nobody else uses? Somewhere you could stick a comfy chair or something and be able to put your feet up for a few minutes?"

"Yeah, in the basement. It's called the laundry room." Hillary gives a rueful chuckle. "I can promise no one will look for me there."

"No, seriously. You need to set some boundaries with these guys. Didn't you tell me there was a spare bedroom in Peter's house?"

"There is. It's down the hall from the kids' rooms. Except it's filled with all this crap—boxes of old clothes, toys, a couple of twin beds. I think there's even an old TV in there. It would take quite a clean-out to make that space livable. And I don't know what Peter would say."

"Hill. This is your house, too, now. Who cares what Peter will say? He probably doesn't even know about half the junk in that room. Why don't you talk to him about it? I can come over some weekend day when he and the kids are out, and we can clean up that room, and it can become your room. Your private space."

"That sounds like heaven. I could have Athena sleep with me again. I miss her little fluffy self, shoved under my armpit at night. And Peter was just saying I'm keeping him up all night with my tossing and turning. He should try being pregnant!"

Chapter 11

Susan

When she awakens, Susan pushes back the covers and sits on the edge of her bed, facing the window that overlooks the parking lot. It's another gray winter day, late afternoon, by the looks of the light through the heavy clouds. It's going to snow, she thinks, as she stands up slowly and gingerly takes a few steps over to the windowsill. She peers down at the parking lot, at the people walking in and out of the doors on the ground level, bundled up against the winter cold, going about their daily lives. Standing there, she suddenly realizes her bladder is full. Susan quickly turns to walk to the bathroom and almost falls. She catches herself on the end of her bed and makes her way across the room, holding onto furniture for balance as she goes.

Susan notices that Darla's bed is perfectly made with clean sheets and a clean pillowcase. The few effects patients are allowed to have in their room are gone from the table by Darla's twin bed. Her drawing pad and pencils aren't there, either. She must have gone home, Susan concludes. How long was I out of it? Fragments of voices and glimpses of medical personnel flicker on the edges of Susan's memory. People talking to her, coaxing her to take more medication, coaxing her to eat, to wash. She can't put the pieces together in any order that makes sense. Huge gaps are missing from the story. She desperately tries to follow a thread of thoughts to pull together the jumbled voices in her head. A familiar voice softly pulses through the distorted sequence of events Susan tries to recall. Paul. Paul had been here! When? She couldn't remember.

She flushes the toilet, washes her hands, walks out of the room, and down the long hallway, holding on to the railing along the wall. I feel like I'm a hundred years old, she says to herself as she shuffles along. She had looked at herself in the bathroom mirror when she was washing her hands and didn't recognize the pale, drawn face looking back at her, her empty eyes with brown circles underneath them. She had run her brush through her greasy hair to try and neaten her appearance. It didn't help much. When Susan finally reaches the nurses' station at the other end of the hall, she can't find anyone. I really need to shower, she thinks. I look gross. I probably smell grosser.

A few chairs are lined up along the wall, across from the nurses' station, where people wait for their medications. A middle-aged man wearing a sweatshirt and sweatpants sits in one chair, watching Susan. She walks over to a chair a couple away from the man and sits down to wait for someone to appear who can give her some items for showering. Susan has been told that the unit staff kept soaps, toothbrushes, toothpaste, shampoos, and hair dryers locked up behind the nurses' station. If a patient needs a razor to shave their legs, they have to request one and then return it immediately after showering. She was told that a staff member stands outside the shower room and waits for the patient to hand them the razor when they finish using it.

The middle-aged man is a noisy breather. Sinusy. Susan

hates nose whistlers. She looks over at him, catches him watching her. The man immediately turns away when Susan looks over at him. He looks so sad. So deeply, deeply sad. "I'm Susan," she says to him. "Do you know when someone will be back at the desk? Have you been waiting a long time?"

The sad man turns and makes brief eye contact with Susan. "I'm Russ," he says. "I've only been sitting here for a few minutes. I think someone will be back soon."

"Nice to meet you, Russ. How long have you been here? On the psych unit?"

"Only a couple of days," he replies solemnly. "My wife left me. She took our kids. She found another man, and she moved in with him. I'm so depressed. I don't know how I'll live without her and my children. I didn't even see it coming. I'm such an idiot."

"I'm so sorry, Russ. That's got to be really hard." Susan tries to sound comforting. "I tried to kill myself. I honestly don't know how long I've been here. I got my head zapped, and I can't remember anything."

"Zapped?" Russ asks.

"Yeah, electric shock therapy."

"Did it hurt?"

"No, not really. I don't remember it, actually. I woke up in the recovery room, and they informed me that they had just given me electric shock therapy. I don't even know how I got there."

"Why'd you try to kill yourself?" Russ looks back in Susan's eyes. "You seem like such a nice person. Why would you want to kill yourself?"

Susan pauses for a moment. You wouldn't have a conversation like this with just anyone you meet on the street, she thinks, psych ward shoptalk. "My husband," she starts, looking back at Russ's open face. "He promised me we'd have a baby together, and after we got married, he changed his mind and told me no. I kinda freaked out. Lost it. Tried to kill myself and ended up here, getting zapped in the head."

"Is it helping? Getting the electroshock therapy? Is it helping you?" asks Russ.

"I don't know," she replies. This was my first one, I guess. I don't know if I have to get more, but I hope not. It screws up the way you think. I feel like someone scrambled my brain."

Just then, the door to the medication room behind the nurses' station opens, and Sandy, the day nurse, and another nurse Susan has not seen before walk out. "Sorry to keep you waiting," Sandy says, "I was just giving end-of-shift report. Laura is the evening nurse tonight. She'll help you both in a second." Sandy gathers up her coat and pocketbook. "Have a good night, Laura," she calls as she uses her name badge to buzz herself out the locked door. "See you tomorrow, Russ, Susan." And the heavy metal door slams shut behind her.

Laura turns to where Susan and Russ are sitting. "Who's first?" she asks.

Russ immediately responds, "She is," indicating Susan.

"Oh, thanks, Russ." She smiles at him. "I just need some things to shower," she explains to Laura. "I feel gross."

"Okay, let me find one of the aides to take you," Laura replies to Susan. "And how about you, Russ? What can I do for you?"

"I think... I need some bandages," replies Russ softly, looking down at his hands in his lap. They are covered with blood.

"Oh, my God, Russ!" Laura grabs a pair of rubber gloves and runs around from behind the desk. "What happened? Did you cut yourself? Russ, what on earth did you use to cut yourself?"

Susan stares incredulously at Russ's folded hands. How had she not noticed the blood? How had she not seen the stains on Russ's shirt and pants? Oh, my God, she thinks to herself, I've lost it. I have absolutely lost my mind. "Oh, Russ," Susan says, looking at him, "I'm so sorry. I am so sorry."

Laura ushers Russ into a treatment room and leaves Susan sitting alone in the chairs along the wall. There is a small puddle of blood on the vinyl chair Russ had been sitting in and some drops along the floor leading to the treatment room. One of the aides walks quickly by, notices the blood, and looks at Susan questioningly. "Not mine," she says, pointing to the treatment room. "They're in there."

"Okay, hang tight," the aide responds, "I'm going to see if Laura needs any help, and then I'm going to call housekeeping. Are you all right with waiting for a minute?"

Susan nods. Poor Russ, she thinks, suffering in silence like that. I guess we all do, in a way. Put on our game face and show up for life, all the while living with our pain hidden inside us. The world is a sad place. A sad and lonely place.

She watches as housekeeping shows up with her cart and cleans up the blood from the chair and the floor. The smell of disinfectant lingers in the air. The aide returns soon after, gets Susan her showering items, and accompanies her to the shower room. He stands outside the door with no lock and waits for Susan to finish her shower, dry off, get dressed, and come back out. Susan hands the aide her items. He checks off that she has returned them all and carries them back to one of the cupboards behind the nurses' station to be locked up until Susan needs them again. Such is the life of a psych patient, Susan thinks. Nothing is my own—nothing except my crazy thoughts and my depression.

After breakfast the following morning, Susan is scheduled to meet with Bill and her psychiatrist, Dr. Phillips. Susan met Dr. Phillips once before, on her second day on the unit, when he was making rounds with the staff. She'd studied the psychiatrist's short stature, trim physique and trim mustache and beard. His neatly coiffed hair had a slight wave to it, and the whole picture in profile, Susan concluded, was one of a Roman bust.

When Susan arrives, Bill is already in the room a few doors down from his office and welcomes her to sit at a large table. They make small talk for a few minutes, explaining how yet another snowstorm is predicted for that night and into the following day, until the door to the room opens again, and Sandy, the nurse, walks in. Susan looks at her questioningly, and Bill says, "This is a meeting for you and your care team, this morning. We're just waiting for Dr. Phillips to come along."

Sandy sits down next to Susan and gives her a comforting smile. "We're going to talk about your treatment plan going forward and start making plans for your discharge."

Susan panics inside. My friggin' discharge, she thinks. They've zapped my head, for God's sake! How can they possibly think I'm safe to go home? And what about Paul? Susan hadn't seen him in she wasn't sure how long. Had he known about the ECT therapy? Had he called into the unit to check on her? She has no idea. The thought of Paul makes her heart warm for a quick minute, and tears well in her eyes. She misses him, she realizes. She misses his smiling brown eyes and big bear hugs, and she misses hearing him calling her Suzie.

"Don't worry," comforts Sandy, placing a hand on Susan's shoulder. "We're not sending you home tomorrow. This is just a meeting with your team to start planning for your discharge. Putting some goals together for you while you're here on the unit and continue to work to get better. Everyone is here to support you and make you feel safe. We're not going to push you out of the nest before you're ready to fly again," Sandy concludes with another comforting smile. She reaches to the middle of the large table, grabs a box of tissues, and hands it to Susan so she can dry her eyes. The consoling gesture, the thought of leaving this place, and the thought of Paul, make yet more tears slide down Susan's cheeks.

The door creaks once again as it opens, and Dr. Phillips walks in and sits next to Bill, directly across from Susan. "Good morning, Susan," he starts. "We're glad you're here. You had your first ECT treatment yesterday. How are you feeling?"

Susan observes Dr. Phillips's hands as he spreads them on the conference room table. She can't help but notice his perfectly clean and rounded fingernails. I bet he gets his nails done, she muses. He has a thick gold wedding band on his left ring finger. I bet he and his wife get manicures together. This idea strikes Susan as amusing, and she smirks briefly before answering Dr. Phillips.

"I feel tired," she says regaining her composure, "and my thoughts are jumbled. It's like I've missed a few days of my life, and I can't seem to get them back no matter how hard I try to remember them." And then, with a little bit of anger in her voice, she says, "No one told me they were going to do this to me. No one asked my permission. I'm not some lab rat you can just do experiments on, you know! Who gave you permission to do this to me?"

"Well, that's one of the things we wanted to talk to you about today, now that you're feeling better. Forgetfulness, fatigue, brain fog; these are all normal side effects of ECT. For most patients, these memory lapses eventually clear up in a few weeks; for a few, they can remain longer. But to answer your question, let's back up a little bit. You had what we call a psychotic break. This can happen to patients for a variety of reasons, some of them organic in nature, some related to a great trauma in their lives, or an episode of major depression. Four days ago, you had entered into a state of depressive catatonia. You were awake but mostly unresponsive. You weren't answering our questions, you weren't eating, you were drinking very little."

"We could only give you medications by injections," adds Sandy. "It wasn't safe to give you any pills because we weren't sure you would swallow them and there was a concern you might choke. At that point, we had to consider sending you back to the Emergency Department for IV fluids."

"The team met to discuss the best and safest treatment for you," Dr. Phillips continues. "And because we were only able to give you a limited amount of medication, mostly sedatives, by injection, we had to come up with a plan to bring you out of the state of catatonia you were in. Electroconvulsive therapy has been shown to have excellent results in circumstances like this."

Bill looks at Susan from the other side of the table. Is that concern she sees in his eyes? Pity? "Susan, we had to invoke your healthcare proxy because you were not in any condition to make decisions on your own behalf while you were in that catatonic state. Paul is your healthcare proxy, and we invited him in to discuss your treatment options."

Susan has been holding her breath throughout the conversation. She takes a huge gulp of air and then interjects in one long breath, "You did what? Paul was here? Did he see me? I don't remember any of that."

"Yes," Bill replies gently, "Paul was here. And he did come to see you. We thought it might help you to hear a familiar voice, but you didn't respond to him."

"So, we discussed the pros and cons of various treatment options with your husband," Dr. Phillips picks up the conversation, "from trials of medications to ECT to doing nothing at all. There is no guarantee how long a patient will stay in a state of depressive catatonia. Your team and your husband agreed that the best course of action would be to try the next step to return you to a functional mental state. Medications weren't helpful. The only thing left to try was ECT. And your husband agreed with the team."

"Paul agreed to this?" Susan is dumbfounded. Paul had been here? He had seen her in that state. She looks at the team sitting around the table. "Paul was here?" her voice sounds desperate.

"He loves you very much," Sandy turns to Susan and says softly. "He did this out of love for you. He told the team that even if you never wanted to see him again, he wanted you to have your life back, to be able to go on and live your life how you wanted to live it."

"He said that?" Susan is filled with emotion: grateful that Paul gave permission for the ECT treatment that brought her out of the depressive catatonia, angry that he made the decision without her, frustrated that her mind had gone to a place where she wasn't in control of her own choices and decisions. She slumps in her chair; she feels weak and vulnerable.

"He did," says Sandy.

Dr. Phillips clears his throat. "Let's talk about your treatment plan going forward. You have had a remarkably positive response to your first ECT treatment. And we've got you stabilized with a standard combination of antidepressant and mood-stabilizing medications that seem to be working for you. As you know, being a nurse, it can take several weeks for some of these medications to have a noticeable effect on your mood. We'd like to continue with the ECT treatments, if you are agreeable to that. Two or three more treatments while you're an inpatient and then a continued series on an outpatient basis, supportive counseling with Bill here and then continuing again, on an outpatient basis, and the medication regimen that you're on. Would you be open to giving that a try, Susan?"

Susan is silent, taking in all of this information. The idea that she will have to continue on psych medications, the idea that she will have to have more ECT treatments here, and then even more ECT treatments on an outpatient basis. What had happened to her? To her life? To her old self? I really have become one of them, she thinks sadly, recalling her first day on the unit and seeing the blank faces of the other patients in the Community Room, looking up at her as she walked in. The new patient. The patient that still had some fight left in her. The patient who had yet to have her mind twisted and turned with medications and talk therapy and shock treatments. They knew, Susan acknowledges to herself, they knew I was the next guinea pig to walk through the door. They knew I would end up just like them. And now here I am.

Dr. Phillips concludes the team meeting with Susan after she has acknowledged his proposed treatment plan. She feels sick inside, tired, and empty. I'm now a psych patient, Susan says to herself. Forever after, going forward, I will always have the identity of a psych patient, a person with a medical diagnosis of major depression, a person who went into a catatonic state, a person who had to have her head zapped. A freak.

Susan tucks in her chair at the big table and turns to leave the room. Bill approaches her. "You did a great job in the meeting, Susan. Really, you are on the road to recovery here. Let's meet in my office later today to discuss all of this, the ECT, and how you feel. Two o'clock. Okay?"

"Sure. All right," Susan replies. She looks up at the clock on the wall as she leaves the conference room. Morning Meeting has already started in the Community Room. She shuffles down the shiny linoleum hall and cracks open the door. Ten faces turn to look at her. Some of the faces have become familiar. Susan thinks she notices a look of recognition, of camaraderie almost, in those familiar faces. These are my people now, Susan thinks, as she looks for an empty seat around the circle. Her eyes meet one familiar face: Russ. She gives him a smile and sits down next to him. Russ looks over as she settles into her chair and gives her a half-smile in return. Susan notices his wrists are wrapped with white gauze. Clean, startlingly white, like a flag of surrender Russ wears for all the world to see.

Another therapist leads the meeting, a young woman Susan recognizes from the psych unit. This morning's topic is commitment: commitment to each individual's treatment plan, commitment to recovery, commitment to moving forward from whatever brought each person to the psychiatric unit in the first place. Susan isn't listening to the young therapist, isn't paying attention to the discussion from the other patients who raise their hands to answer the therapist's questions. She is thinking of Paul, of what it must have been like for him to see her like this, to see his wife in a state of deep depression, of having to make the decision for her to have shock treatments. Was he remorseful? Did he acknowledge what had happened to Susan after what he had said to her, after he broke his promise to her about having a baby, a family? Did he still love her after all of this? Did she still love him?

Again, tears pool in Susan's eyes as she thinks of Paul and their relationship. Russ notices and quietly places a warm hand on Susan's shoulder. It makes her cry harder. People can be so kind, she thinks. Even in the darkness of their own despair, they can reach out and offer compassion to another struggling person. There is still goodness in this world. She gives Russ a slight nod of acknowledgment and smiles to herself. I will go on, Susan realizes at that moment. In some way, shape, or form, I will go on from here.

Morning Meeting concludes, and people slowly rise from their chairs around the circle, some gathering in small groups to talk and offer support to one another. Susan and Russ are still seated. "How are you doing, Russ?" Susan asks him softly.

"I'm doing pretty good." He looks away. "Better than the last time you saw me. They've got me on some heavy-duty medications now. The meds kind of knock me out, but they're making a difference with my depression. And I've got a nice therapist. She's helping me to recognize that I can go on from this. That there is still life out there for me." Russ looks at Susan again. "It's like I have to define my new reality; I have to find my place in it, you know?"

"I do know, Russ. I absolutely do know." Susan and Russ rise to leave the Community Room. "I'm glad you're feeling better. I was worried about you," she says as she turns down the hall toward her room.

"I'll see you around," Russ says to her as he walks in the opposite direction.

"Yeah. See you."

The rest of the morning passes quietly; Susan spends some time in her room reading a book she found in the unit's library—a set of shelves in the back of the kitchen that holds a variety of novels, their covers tattered, their pages worn. Susan was delighted when she found *A Wrinkle in Time*, by Madeleine L'Engle, among the other titles. It's one of her favorites from when she was younger. She loved the idea of L'Engle's tesseract: the theory that time could be bent, wrinkled, shifted, to allow you to pass from one moment, one reality, into another, and almost instantly you'd find yourself in another place, a new reality, a different fate.

The day nurse has given Susan her pills, and lunch in the unit kitchen has come and gone. Before Susan realizes it, it's time to go and meet with Bill. As she leaves her room and walks toward Bill's office, Susan suddenly notices that she is looking forward to talking with Bill, rearranging some of the thoughts in her head, and putting some away on a shelf, no longer needed, to define her new reality. Damn, she thinks and shakes her head, this ECT stuff really does work.

Bill gets up from his chair when Susan enters and greets her with a big smile. She smiles back, acknowledging a spark of happiness within her. "You look like you're feeling better, Susan," he says. "Here, have a seat. Let's talk about how you're doing," Bill gestures toward the chair Susan always sits in for these sessions in Bill's quiet, dimly lit office. She notices a new Himalayan salt rock lamp on the corner of Bill's desk. It gives off a soft, warm, orangey glow. Nice, she thinks to herself, comforting.

Susan allows herself to relax. She lets out a slow, deep breath, "I'm actually doing better," she responds. "I feel positive, ready to move forward. And a little scared, too, about moving forward."

"That makes me happy to hear, Susan," Bill replies, "happy that you're in a positive, more open place. How do you feel about the treatment plan that Dr. Phillips proposed? Are you okay with receiving more ECT treatments? It's a big step to commit to this type of treatment. How are you feeling about that?"

"You know, if you had asked me two weeks ago if I would ever consider having my brain zapped, I would have laughed at you and said, 'Absolutely not!' I used to think this type of treatment was so archaic. But, you know, it's making a difference for me. Even after one treatment, I'm noticing a huge difference. It's like I was dark inside, all black, and now there's a spark of yellow in me, a spark of hope."

"Excellent. That's great, Susan. You had us worried for a while there. I thought they were going to have to send you off the unit for medical treatment. I'm so glad the ECT is working for you. Let me ask you this: You mentioned that you are ready to move forward; let's talk about what that will look like and what your life will look like when you leave the unit."

Susan gulps. Her stomach flip-flops. "I don't know where I see myself after I'm discharged. I feel like I have to redefine myself, incorporate all that just happened, and redefine who I am. It makes me nervous to think about that."

"Well, let's just theorize for the moment. Nothing is cast in stone. Where would you like to see yourself when you leave the unit? If you could imagine anything you wanted for your life going forward, what would it be? Will you return to your job? Will you still be with Paul? What would you like to happen for yourself, Susan?"

She closes her eyes for a moment. She can hear her heart beating rhythmically in her ears, notices a gentle sensation of warmth rise and surround her heart. She recognizes this feeling of gentleness and warmth. It is love. It is love for Paul. And it is love for life.

"I don't know about my job," she says as she opens her eyes and looks at Bill. "I don't know what they know about all of this, what happened, and where I am. I have to think about that. But I do know that I miss Paul. I do know that I love him. I would like to imagine Paul and me still together. I don't know what that will look like. I have trouble imagining going through the rest of my life as a childless woman. I have trouble accepting that as a definition of myself. I don't know if I'm ready to commit to that. I don't even know how to commit to that."

"That's completely reasonable," Bill responds, "completely

understandable. You've focused a lot of time and energy of your adulthood preparing to bear a child and be a mother. And, if I hear you correctly, to stay with Paul, with the man you love, will require you to close a door on that dream, that focus, and open a door to an unknown. It will require you to take a step into the unknown. And that can be very scary."

Susan nods, and Bill continues, "So that's one reality. The reality if you choose to stay with Paul. What if you don't stay with him? What would that reality look like? Would you have a child on your own? Find someone else to father your child? I imagine you've thought of this possibility as well. Tell me what that looks like."

She closes her eyes again, sighs. She has indeed thought of this other reality: the reality of leaving Paul, of getting pregnant through in vitro fertilization, and raising a child on her own. And she has thought of how she could afford to do that, if she could afford to do that. Where would she live? Who would take care of her baby when she was working? Could she move back in with her parents? No, probably not.

They have their own lives since Susan and her sister moved out and went away to college, got married, and started their own lives. She didn't want to imagine what they would think of their daughter getting pregnant through IVF, moving in with them, and then having a newborn living with them. No, that wouldn't work. And what if her child got sick? She would miss work to stay home and care for her child. Who would pay the bills?

She thinks that having a child and raising a child is quite a difficult financial proposition and says to Bill, "Honestly, I don't think I could afford to raise a child by myself. I know a lot of women do. They make it work somehow. I just don't see how I could. And I'd miss Paul. If I went and left him, I would always miss him. The moment I met Paul, I knew he was my soulmate.

I know that sounds corny, but it's true. We are meant to be together, two halves of one whole. I love him with everything I am." She pauses, thinking of Paul. "When he was here, when I was out of it, what did he say? Was he disgusted with what had become of me?"

"Oh, no, not at all," Bill says quickly. "Your husband, Paul, was desperate to try and reach you. He sat on your bed next to you. He held your hand. He pleaded with you to come out of the state you were in. That man loves you dearly. He had tears in his eyes when the final decision was made and he agreed to have you undergo ECT treatments. He was terrified that this was the last resort treatment for you. He had the doctor repeatedly explain what would happen in an ECT session. He wanted to know if you would feel anything. If you would remember anything. Paul had the doctor review all the potential side effects of ECT treatment, both short-term and long-term. Paul was very deliberate in his questioning of your care team. He wants the best for you. Like I said, he had tears in his eyes when he signed the consent form for the ECT treatments to begin."

"Did he apologize or anything? Say he was sorry for causing all of this? Did he own any of this?" she asks a bit forcefully.

"We didn't get to that in that particular meeting; it was more about what we needed to do sooner rather than later to help you medically. But it brings me to a question I've wanted to ask you: Would you consider having Paul come in for a session with you and me? You have many unanswered questions, and I imagine he does, too. It would be extremely beneficial for both of you if you could see each other and talk about what happened in person. And I would be here to moderate the conversation. I would be your advocate if you need me to be."

"Yes," Susan responds without any thought. She doesn't need to think about her answer to Bill's question. "Yes, I would like

Paul to come. I would like us to have a session together, with you."

"Great. I'll give him a call after our current session is over. I'll see if he can come in tomorrow. I'll let you know as soon as I do. How does that sound to you?"

"It sounds good," Susan replies, and then, tentatively, "do you think it would be all right for me to call him? Like today? From one of the phones on the unit? Or should I wait until he comes in for our session with you?"

"I think," Bill says, "that if you're ready to talk to Paul, you could call him anytime. I think he would be so glad to hear from you. He calls the unit every day to check on you, you know. To get an update on how you're doing."

"Really?" Susan is surprised, "He does?"

"He does. And he's asked to come and see you several times since your ECT treatment. But we wanted you to make that decision. As soon as we wrap up our session, I will call him about a meeting tomorrow. Okay?" Bill looks at Susan and asks, "How does that make you feel? The idea about seeing Paul? Speaking to him?"

"I'm happy. I'm frightened. I'm a little angry."

"Angry at what? At Paul? What happened? Both?"

"At both, I guess," Susan replies after a brief pause. "I'm angry that he broke his promise to me. I'm angry when I think about if I will stay with him; it's like he got what he wanted: a wife and no baby, and I got nothing, no baby and no getting to be a mother. Yeah, I'm angry about that."

"Did he say why he changed his mind about having a baby with you? Why, in the end, he had to break his promise to you?"

"He said he was just too tired, that he had already raised a child, and was just too tired to start over again and raise another one. He's in his late forties and thinks he's too old to have another baby, which I get. But why did he make that promise to me in the first place? Why did he put those words out there when he was going to take them back in the end?" Susan's voice is rising now, her anger flooding her thoughts.

"Do you think, maybe in the beginning, he thought he could do this? That he loved you so much and wanted to give you your greatest wish? And in the end, he realized he didn't have the energy to do it all over again?"

"Why did he have us go to the fertility doctor, then? The one who told us that Paul didn't have enough sperm, or enough strong sperm, to get me pregnant? I feel like he led me on. Like it was a trap to get me and keep me, and then once he knew he had me, he went back on his word."

"What I'm hearing," Bill says calmly, matter-of-factly, "is that you believe Paul went back on his word to you intentionally? Am I hearing that correctly?"

"Yes," Susan replies, her voice lowering slightly, "Yes, that's what I'm trying to say. That the person who is supposed to love me the most in this world intentionally went back on his promise. How can he truly love me if he did something like that? How can I ever trust his love for me again? Maybe I was just a fool for falling for it." Susan spits out the last sentence with a tone of disappointment in her voice.

Bill looks over at the clock on his desk. "It's past time for our session to end, Susan," he says softly. "My next patient is scheduled for right now. Think about this: Do you think Paul perhaps didn't do any of this with intention? Do you think perhaps it was a miscommunication in some way? That you heard one thing, and maybe he meant it differently? Would you be willing to think about this after you leave my office today, and we can discuss it tomorrow? With Paul?"

Susan takes a breath and lets it out slowly. She feels like Bill is rushing her out a little, but she doesn't want to hold up the next person's session. "Yes. All right. I'll think about it and maybe ask Paul when he comes in tomorrow."

"Good. I'm here until five o'clock today if you need to reach out to me. Or the staff on the unit. If strong feelings start to come up about our conversation today, I want you to reach out to the staff. They're here to help support you."

"I know," Susan replies quickly, her hand on the door handle to pull it open. "I will." As she leaves Bill's office, she practically bumps into the next patient, a nervous young man, waiting outside the door for his session with Bill.

Susan returns to her room, sits on her bed, tucks her legs under her, and opens *A Wrinkle in Time* to where she had left off. She knows the story well. A young girl named Meg, her younger brother Charles Wallace, and her school friend Calvin, were looking for her father—who had gone missing on a science mission—to save him. But it wasn't without risk; it wasn't without danger. The story tells of being willing to step into the darkness, following your heart into that unknown because it is the only way to find what you seek. The story is about being open to the unexpected and risking everything to alter fate for the greater good. The story is about self-discovery. And, ultimately, the story is about love, giving and finding love.

Susan can't concentrate on the characters today or get involved with their struggles; too many thoughts are swirling through her mind. Paul. What had he thought when he had to sign that consent form for her ECT treatments? She imagines it must have terrified him in some way; he didn't have a medical background, and Susan wonders what he had imagined about the idea of electrical impulses being sent through his wife's brain. They must have told him the side effects: confusion, short-term memory loss. Would she have made the same decision if the roles were reversed? Would she do anything, in the end, to save him, even if it meant that saving him would free him to move on without her? Would she, like the character Meg in *A Wrinkle in Time*, take that leap into the dark void, into whatever dangers awaited, to save the person she loved most?

Another thought hits her: Is she willing to travel through the time and space of her own unknown? Is she worth the risk of saving herself? Does she have enough love within her to alter her own fate? Or is the darkness too deep? Is the passage too risky? Is the unknown too painful and heavy to push through?

Am I worthy of this destiny? Susan thinks to herself as she stares out the window of her room at the darkness of another winter evening. What's out there for me in that vast universe? Susan is starting to feel her stomach turn at the thought of moving on from all of this, of leaving behind the familiar path she had been walking, of turning off that path and surviving in a life she has never imagined, a life without a child. A life in which she will never become a mother.

"Time for your evening meds, Susan." A voice brings her back to the present. The evening nurse enters the room and brings over the two small paper cups that have become so familiar to Susan; one with the five pills, the other with just enough water to gulp them down. "You've got about an hour of free time before dinner," offers the nurse as she collects the paper cups, examines the one that had been filled with pills to make sure nothing is left at the bottom, and makes her way out the door and down the hall to the next waiting patient.

Susan stands up from her bed. She knows with complete faith what she has to do next. She walks down the hall to an area of three small cubicles in the wall, each with a phone hanging from one side of the cubbie and a small chair against the opposite wall. Susan enters one of the cubicles and sits in the plastic chair. She stares at the phone momentarily before picking up the receiver and dialing the familiar number of Paul's cell phone. She holds her breath as she counts the rings: one, no answer; two, no answer; three, what was Paul doing? He always had his phone with him.

And suddenly, there is his voice. "Hello?" he asks. "Hi, this is Paul. Can I help you?" Susan realizes Paul must not recognize the number she is calling from. He thinks this is a business call.

She takes a breath, "Hi Paul, it's me. It's Susan."

Silence on the other end of the phone. Is he mad at her? That she hadn't wanted to talk with him for this long? Is he turned off by what had become of her? Her weakness. Her vulnerability. "Paul, are you there?"

She hears a sniffle and then, in a whisper, "Yes. Yes, I'm here. Suzie?" Paul's voice gasps, "Suzie. It's you." He sniffs again, trying to quietly conceal that he is crying.

A flood of emotions rushes through Susan the moment she hears Paul's voice. She becomes almost dizzy at the strength of her feelings. Her breath catches in her throat for a second, and then in a rush, "Paul. I miss you. I miss you so much. I... I'm sorry I didn't want to see you. I'm sorry it took me so long to call you. I needed to process things, you know? I'm trying to get my head on straight. I'm not sure I'm there yet. But I miss you, Paul. I really, really miss you."

"Oh, my God, Suzie," Paul replies through his sobs. He can't hold back the tears any longer. "My heart aches for you. Are you okay? How are you feeling? I'm sorry I made that decision about the electric shock treatments. I didn't know what else to do. I was losing you, and nothing they were trying was working. They told me it was the best option to bring you back. I hope you're not mad at me. I honestly didn't know what to do. I had to save you. Are you all right?"

"Yes. I'm okay. Well, as okay as I can be. I still have so many feelings, Paul, so many questions. Did Bill call you? Are you coming in tomorrow?"

"Yes. If that's what you'd like. I will be there. I want to be there. God, it's so good to hear your voice, Suzie. Bill said ten o'clock tomorrow. You don't know how happy I am to hear your voice. I didn't know if you'd ever talk to me again. My life has been so empty without you. The house has been so empty without you. Ginger looks out the window every day, waiting for you to come home."

"Oh, my little Ginger!" Susan cries, thinking of her sweet dog, the dog that has been with her, by her side through so much. Her little dog loves Susan without question, without judgment. "Is she doing all right? Are you spending lots of time with her?"

"We have our little routine," Paul replies. "She's doing fine. She just misses you. We both do."

"Give her kisses for me, will you?" The call is almost too much. Susan senses her mind beginning to freeze at the many thoughts and emotions she is experiencing: missing Paul, anger at Paul, loving Paul, being hurt by Paul. Suddenly, Susan has nothing left to say. "I've got to go," she tells Paul quickly. "It's time for dinner here, and I've got to go."

"Sure. Okay," Paul responds, not picking up on Susan's sudden shutting down of the conversation. "I'm really glad to hear your voice, Suzie. I thought maybe I never would again. I'll see you tomorrow at ten."

"Yes. Bye, Paul."

"Love you. Bye, Suzie."

Susan gently hangs up the phone without responding with her usual "love you more." She is exhausted. Defeated. *Am I giving in to a life demanded by someone else? Am I about to lose* my true self in the process of forgiving Paul? Do I love him that much, she thinks? Do I love him more than I love myself? What about my wishes? My desires? Susan thinks again that perhaps she isn't ready to give up on her own dreams, isn't ready to recreate her own reality in order to fit into the life of someone else. Do Paul's desires outweigh hers? Is it a cop-out if she stays with him?

Susan is immobilized by this reaction to speaking with Paul. Uncertain. Stuck.

One of the unit aides walks by on the way to the kitchen and notices Susan sitting on the chair in the cubicle, blankly staring out at nothing, an empty expression on her face. "Hey, Susan," she says, approaching the cubbie. "It's time for dinner. Everyone is already in the kitchen eating. C'mon with me. We'll walk there together."

Susan stands and allows herself to be guided by the arm to the community kitchen. The large room is a blur of colors of clothing worn by the other patients, of the smells of the meal, of the din of several conversations taking place at the tables set up in the kitchen. She can't focus. Can't take it all in and process it. Nothing is making sense.

She sits in front of a tray of food, the plate covered by a metal lid to keep the food warm; a carton of milk is in the upper left corner. A small bowl of fruit in the upper right corner of the tray. Just like every dinner here. Always the same. Always consistent—and reliable. Susan removes the metal lid and stares at the gray, unidentifiable meat on the plate; the instant mashed potatoes, sticky, no lumps; the stack of dull green beans, their typical vibrant color cooked out of them by too much boiling. She replaces the lid and reaches for the carton of milk.

Chapter 12

Hillary

It had worked! Hillary now has her own room in the house, her own bed, her own space. Athena is seldom found outside the spare room these days, snuggled up on one of the pillows on the twin bed in the spare room. Hillary had approached Peter with the logic that he would get a much better night's sleep if she wasn't keeping him up all night with her tossing and turning. She had made it about Peter. And it had worked. There was even a lock on the door to the spare room. Hillary couldn't be happier. With the room decorated in light blues and greens, starched white curtains hanging in the dormer window, a small bureau, and a desk in one corner, Hillary finally feels at peace. Kenzie and Little Pete have even started leaving her alone when they know she's in her room with the door locked. It really feels like heaven.

By mid-summer, businesses have started to relax their COVID isolation rules and open their doors again. Plexiglass has become a mainstay dividing people from face-to-face encounters everywhere, from banks to restaurants to grocery store cash registers. It is a strange way to live, Hillary has to admit, but at least commerce is back on the upswing and people can get out of their houses after being cooped up for so long indoors. Happily, the barn owner at the farm where Calypso is boarded has opened the barn back up to riders as well; as long as the huge doors at either end of the long aisleway remain open, people can come and go to visit their horses. Masks are even optional at this point at the stable. And while most prefer to ditch their masks, sick of the stuffy feeling of breathing through cloth or paper, Hillary continues wearing hers whenever she goes outside the house. She has heard of some pregnant women who have contracted COVID-19 and ended up having miscarriages. She is not about to risk her or her baby's future against the many still unknown effects of this disease. He is all she can think about these days.

Hillary has decided to drive to the barn to feed carrots to Calypso. Several of her barn friends, including the barn owner, are sitting under the shade of a large oak tree. "C'mon over, Hill," one of them calls. "We've got a spot saved for you over here."

"My word," Joan blurts with a chuckle, sitting among the ladies under the oak tree. "You look like you've swallowed a watermelon, whole." Everyone laughs, including Hillary, happy to be back among her friends at the barn.

"Trust me," she says. "I feel like I've swallowed one!"

School is out for summer break. The morning air is already thick as pea soup and hotter than Hades. "Gotta love global warming," Hillary says under her breath as she rummages through the refrigerator, looking for something cool to drink for herself and the kids.

"You believe that stuff?" Peter walks into the kitchen just

then. "Global warming and all that hogwash. Icebergs melting. Gimme a break."

"Well, we don't have to agree on global warming, Peter, to agree that it's a hot one out there today. Are you going to take the kids to the lake this afternoon? They've been asking."

"Oh shit! I totally forgot." Peter walks around to stand beside Hillary in the cool air from the refrigerator. "I told Jimmy that I'd stop by his place this afternoon. Couple of the guys are getting together for beers and a cookout. Can you take them?"

Hillary stiffens, straightens up, and firmly closes the refrigerator door. She turns around and finds herself face to face with Peter. "You're kidding me, right?"

"What? No. Why can't you take them, Hill? You're not doing anything anyways except sitting around with your feet up in the air conditioning. I haven't seen the guys in a while. And it's an outside party, so you know, no COVID."

Hillary silently asks herself where to begin with this one as she draws a large breath. "First off, you can get COVID-19 just by standing next to someone with it. It doesn't matter if you're inside or outside. We talked about this already, Peter. I don't want to risk contracting this virus and making me or the baby sick. There are more women having miscarriages now with COVID. I don't want to be one of them. So far, our baby boy is strong and healthy. I don't want to chance it. Anyway, Frankie is coming by later this afternoon for a checkup on me and the baby. I already told you that, too. I can't take the kids to the lake."

"Oh, so what am I supposed to do? Tell the guys I can't come? Or tell the kids they don't get to go to the lake? You're putting me in a hard spot here, Hill, you know that?"

"You'll have to figure it out, Peter. Now, move out of my way. I'm going to make some lemonade for the kids. You want some?"

Peter sulks. "No." He reopens the refrigerator and grabs a

beer. He hasn't even had breakfast yet.

Hillary spends the rest of the morning simultaneously playing Legos with Little Pete and dressing and re-dressing Barbie dolls with Kenzie. Kenzie is slowly starting to warm up to Hillary, realizing she is a constant in the otherwise chaotic lives of herself and her little brother.

Later, Peter announces that he will take the kids out to the lake early, stop and get them each an ice cream, and then leave them back at the house while he visits the guys for the cookout. He is starting to resent the fact that Hillary is changing up the lifestyle he and the kids had going for themselves before she moved in. Frankly, he wonders how he is going to stand it when there is a crying baby in the house. If Hillary thinks I'm gonna wake up in the middle of the night to change its diaper or feed it, she's got another thing coming, he tells himself. I never wanted another kid in the first place. Jesus, he thinks, running his hand through his hair and shoving a bite of cold pizza into his mouth as he looks for the keys to his truck, how did I end up the father of three brats? I'm too young to be trapped like this. I'm too smart. I've got a career to think about.

"Let's go, Kenzie, Little Pete! Grab your swimsuits, and let's get going! I'll be waiting in the truck for you. We gotta get a move on to the lake."

The kids scramble through the house after their father, grabbing swimsuits, towels, swim goggles, plastic buckets, and shovels.

"Hey—" Hillary runs out the door after them, a bottle of lotion in her hand, "don't forget to put on sunscreen, you guys."

She stands in the driveway and waves as Peter puts his truck in reverse and peels out onto the road, a puff of smelly black smoke escaping from the exhaust pipe. As soon as the truck is out of sight, Hillary's shoulders relax and she breathes a huge sigh of relief. "It's just you and me, Little Bean," she says, rubbing her swollen belly, "at least for a little while."

Inside, the house is cool, shaded by some large old maple trees. Hillary loves afternoons like this, though rare now, when it's just her and her baby, with Athena asleep on the rug in a patch of sunlight. She plunks down on the sagging sofa in the living room, puts her feet up, and opens the book she has been reading. A book about past lives. Hillary finds this fascinating: that a soul might have inhabited another, or several other, bodies, and lived several different lives before occupying its present host. She lets her head fall back on the soft cushions and imagines who she might have been in another life—a fair maiden, perhaps, riding her trusty white steed through the castle grounds. Of course there would be a horse, she thinks, and quietly giggles. Waiting for her knight in shining armor to come riding out of the forest...

An insistent banging suddenly rouses Hillary from her reverie, and she realizes she has dozed off. She looks at her phone. It's two o'clock. Oh, my God, it's Frankie at the door! She hasn't gotten anything ready for her home appointment. "Coming," she shouts as she manages to hoist her bulk off the sofa and waddle to the front door.

"Hey there, Momma," Frankie says with a smile, then envelopes Hillary in a hug. Frankie always wears a mask when she comes to visit Hillary for her checkups, knowing the risk of spreading COVID-19 between any of her pregnant mothers. "Look at you!" she exclaims. "You're huge! How are you feeling?"

The two women make their way slowly upstairs to the spare room, now Hillary's room, Frankie lugging a large duffle bag with her, containing all of the supplies needed to do a home examination on Hillary. "I've been feeling good, I guess," Hillary replies to Frankie. "Tired. Fat." Both women laugh.

"Well, that's all normal, to be expected. Let's set things up on your bed and get you examined." Frankie helps Hillary climb onto the bed after she has spread clean disposable pads over Hillary's blankets. Athena wanders in and meows.

"I hope you don't mind an audience."

"Not at all," replies Frankie, gloving up. She lifts Hillary's baggy t-shirt and spreads gel on her belly, listening for the whoosh-whoosh of the baby's heartbeat with her ultrasound doppler. She finds it, smiles. "Hear that, Momma? Your baby is happy and healthy in there."

As Frankie continues her exam, she asks, "So, how are things with Peter? Has he watched any of the home birth videos I left for you guys last time? You're right on schedule for September, so I want you both to be as prepared as possible."

"I'm working on him," Hillary replies, still smiling to herself, knowing her baby is healthy.

"How about a name? Have you two decided on anything yet? When I asked you before, Peter had wanted Edward and you had wanted something a little different. Schuyler, right?"

"Yeah, we're still locking horns about that one. Everyone knows someone named Ed or Eddie. I want our baby to stand out. To be remembered. I've always loved the name Schuyler. I call him that sometimes, anyway. When Peter's not around."

Frankie snaps off her rubber gloves. "All right, Momma. Things are looking good. It's imperative that Peter knows what to expect and what to do until one of the midwives gets to your house when you go into labor. Promise me you'll get him to watch those videos. Even if you have to make a bowl of popcorn and sit down and watch them with him." Frankie chuckles. "Seriously, though. This is really important."

"I know. Don't worry. I'll make sure Peter is ready when the moment arrives."

Summer vacation has come and gone, and the kids are back at school even before Labor Day. This year, due to the COVID-19 virus, their school desks are separated by plexiglass partitions. And they rotate: half the class in the classroom in the morning, while the other half of the class tunes in on their computers from home, and then in the afternoon, the reverse. Buses aren't running yet, so the queue to drop off and pick up children from school has parents waiting in their cars, lined up around the block, for far longer than anyone has time for.

So frustrating, Hillary thinks, as she waits in her car to drop off Kenzie and Little Pete. Thankfully, both are in the afternoon session at school. Hillary agreed to do the drop-offs, while Peter reluctantly agreed to pick them up when school got out for the day. This schedule is impacting their work lives, not to mention their home life. Hillary is backed up on a project she has been spearheading for the consulting team with an overseas medical company in Japan, and she often finds herself working late into the night, after the kids are tucked in and Peter has fallen asleep watching "Survivor" episodes and drinking bottle after bottle of beer—a whole case in one evening sometimes.

Hillary has turned one corner of her bedroom into a nursery for the baby; there is nowhere else in the house to set anything up, so she quickly and happily decided that the corner of her bedroom by the dormer window, would be the perfect spot to set up the baby's crib. Schuyler's crib.

Friends from work and the barn have held virtual baby showers for Hillary, sending gifts to her house and offering their congratulations from the screens of their laptops or cell phones. Her stepmother and half-sister even pitched in and sent a pack-

and-play to Hillary for when the baby is a little bit older. Hillary is grateful for this, their offering. Anita still hasn't seemed to embrace the idea of being a grandmother and keeps herself at arm's length during the infrequent phone calls from Hillary, who is excited to share news of the baby's health and movement and imminent birth.

Her half-sister is somewhat more excited about Hillary's pregnancy, calling herself 'Auntie Eva' and asking question after question about how big Hillary's belly is getting (watermelon), whether she and Peter are still having sex (no), and how much does Hillary think it's going to hurt to deliver a baby (ummm, I'm not sure). At least Eva's interested in Schuyler, and Hillary is pleased about this. Perhaps the birth of this baby will allow the sisters to become closer.

This past weekend, Peter has finally set up the crib, with a small bureau and changing table next to it. Joan has sent Hillary a rocking chair to match the set, which is also tucked into the corner of the room. Hillary's theme for the baby is stars and moons. She finds herself spending more and more time arranging things in the baby's nursery: stuffed animals lined up at the bottom of the crib, soft blankets washed and folded in one drawer of the bureau, while adorable baby outfits ranging from newborn size to one year are neatly arranged in another drawer. A mobile of soft felted yellow stars circling a soft felted blue moon, plays "Twinkle, Twinkle, Little Star" when she winds it up. I'm nesting, she thinks. This feels so right.

It is late one Friday night, nearing the end of September. Hillary has kept herself awake since coming up to her bedroom hours ago. She can't get comfortable; she's tried a pillow between her knees, a pillow under her belly, blankets on, blankets off. She is restless, although she can't understand why. The day had been so perfect; she had finished her work for the consulting team in the early afternoon and had gone out for a walk to enjoy the brightness of the blue autumn sky, the changing colors of the leaves against it: the bright reds of the maples, the dusky oranges of the oaks, and the deep yellows of the beeches. The air smelled of apples and fallen leaves, a sharpness from the cold filling her chest with each deep breath she took. The feeling of change was all around her, was within her.

Hillary had come home from her walk exhilarated, cheeks flushed, gently carrying several perfect fallen leaves she had collected on her walk. "Peter," she had gushed, "you have got to get outside before the sun sets. It's so gorgeous out there!"

"Can't, Babe," he mumbled, not looking away from his laptop screen. "Too much goddamn work to do. Someone's gotta pay the bills when you're out on maternity leave."

"God, Peter, we talked about this. I will still get a paycheck when I'm out with the baby. It might do you some good to pull yourself away from that computer screen and look up at the blue sky." She had walked up behind him and was rubbing his shoulders.

Peter shrugged off Hillary's hands. "Not right now, Hill. Can't you see I'm in the middle of something?"

"Suit yourself, then. I'm going in the kitchen to bake us an apple pie. With the kids away at your mother's for the weekend, maybe we can spend a little time together. Light some candles, have pie and ice cream in front of the fireplace. Doesn't that sound nice?"

"Yeah, whatever." Peter dismissed Hillary with his voice.

Hillary had spent the remainder of the afternoon making

the pie dough from scratch, rolling it out, and peeling apples for the filling. She even took a paring knife and cut little heart-shaped holes in the top crust to vent the cooking apples within. Afterward, leaving Peter sitting in front of the TV with his beer and watching a sports show, Hillary went upstairs and took a hot shower, rubbing lavender body wash all over her large belly.

When Hillary came downstairs after her shower, she found Peter asleep in his recliner, his head drooping on his chest, an empty beer bottle rolled under the coffee table. She smiled to herself, tenderness overcoming her, and placed a quilt over Peter before going back upstairs to her own room to read before falling asleep. The baked apple pie was untouched, and the candles never lit.

Only, Hillary finds she cannot sleep. There is a deep, dull pressure in her lower body, she is hot all over, and she can feel the muscles in her lower back cramping with some regularity. Braxton Hicks contractions, she assures herself, having experienced them on and off for the past few weeks of her pregnancy. Frankie had said these were normal and nothing to be alarmed about. Hillary finally finds a somewhat comfortable position lying on her side, propped here and there with various-sized pillows, and drifts off into a fitful sleep.

She awakens around three in the morning. Her lower back is screaming with pain, and as she slowly sits up on the edge of her bed, she realizes the bottom sheet is soaked. Quickly, Hillary turns on the bedroom light and takes note of a large area where she had been lying, which is wet and almost pink-tinged in color. Before she can react, she is hit with another intense burning pain in her back. She braces her hands on her lower back and tries to breathe through the contraction. Her face is dripping with sweat, and she is suddenly nauseous.

Hillary glances at the clock on the bedside table again:

three-fifteen. Her contractions are about ten minutes apart. She wraps her arms around her belly. "Looks like today is your day, Schuyler." Then she pushes herself off her soaked sheets and, once standing, immediately vomits onto the braided rug beside her bed. As she gingerly walks across the bedroom to find a towel to wipe up the rug, she is seized by yet another contraction. "Breathe, Hillary," she talks herself through the intensity of the pain. "You got this now. Just breathe." The contraction passes. Hillary is panting.

She is on the floor, on her hands and knees, wiping up the vomit with a towel, when Peter throws open her bedroom door. He rushes over to her. "You all right, Hill?" His voice is anxious. "I saw the light was on in your room. Jesus! What is that smell?"

"I'm all right. I just threw up. I'm in labor. Peter, our baby is coming!"

"Now? Like right now? Shouldn't we call someone? What do I need to do?"

"First, you need to take a deep breath. Then help me up off the floor. It's going to be fine. Frankie said not to call her until the contractions are five to six minutes apart."

Peter grasps Hillary under her arms and pulls her to a standing position. "God, you're sweaty," he announces. "Your face is dripping."

"Can you help me into the bathroom, Peter? I want to wash my face and put on a clean nightgown."

"Do you think that's a good idea? Walking to the bathroom? Why don't you lie down, and I'll get you a face cloth."

"Walking is good for me during labor. It helps the baby move through the birth canal. Plus, my bed is soaked. I think my water must have broken when I was asleep. While I'm in the bathroom, maybe you could change the bottom sheet on my bed?"

"Umm, yeah. Okay. Where do we keep the sheets?"

Hillary laughs. "In the closet outside of the bathroom. Ohhhhhhh." Another contraction envelopes her lower back and belly. Hillary practically doubles over. "Peter, can you rub my back," she says between rapid breaths.

"What? Yeah, like this?" He digs his thumbs into her shoulder blades with some force.

"Owww. No! My lower back. Rub in circles with the palms of your hands."

"Like this?" He is rubbing his hand back and forth across Hillary's lower back.

"Kind of. Thanks." The contraction has passed, and Hillary makes her way down the hall to the bathroom.

Hillary looks at herself in the bathroom mirror. Her face is flushed and beaded with sweat, her long dark hair matted to her cheeks and neck. "Whoever said birth was a beautiful thing?" she says and laughs at her image. She wishes she could call her mother right now, someone who had gone through the birthing process. Someone who could give her encouragement, tell her not to be afraid of the pain, someone who would say over and over again to her, "I love you, and I am so proud of you." But her own mother has long passed, and her stepmother would only be angry at Hillary for waking her in the middle of the night. She returns to her bedroom, where Peter is sitting in the rocking chair, rapidly rocking it back and forth and strumming his fingers on its armrests.

He looks up as Hillary enters the room. "I think you should call Franklyn, or whatever her name is. I don't know if I can deal with this, Hill. What if something goes wrong?"

"It's Frankie, not Franklyn. Nothing is going to go wrong. Everything is right on schedule. We just have to time my contractions. And if you could gently rub my shoulders when I sit down, that would feel great."

Her contractions continue, deep and intense, her belly and back tightening into a forceful knot each time, and then a pause, a release. Hillary catches her breath, looks over at the clock. It is about six o'clock in the morning. She has been laboring for almost three hours now, and while the contractions are still only about nine to ten minutes apart, they are lasting longer. The pain is sharper. She is not sure she can endure the progressive pain of this labor, not sure she has the fortitude or mental capacity to do this. Hillary reaches for her cell phone.

"Hey, Girl," she hears from the other end of the call, "it's early. Everything all right?"

"Hey yourself, Joanie. I'm glad you're a morning person. Guess what?"

She can hear Joan brushing her teeth with her phone on speaker. "What?" The word comes out garbled around the toothbrush in Joan's mouth.

"It's time. It's happening." Hillary winces as another sharp contraction grips her lower belly. She can feel the sweat dripping from her forehead down the sides of her face.

"What's happening?" Joan is still absentmindedly getting ready for the day.

"The baby, Joanie. The baby is happening!" It comes out a little louder than necessary, Hillary trying to suppress her physical agony behind what she hopes comes across as happiness in her voice.

"Oh! Oh, my God! Like right now? Are you doing okay? Is Peter there? Is he helping? Do you want me to come over?"

The contraction has subsided. Hillary moves onto her side on her bed and chuckles at her friend. "Yes. I'm all right. It hurts like I can't even tell you. Peter is outside, smoking."

"What? Smoking? I thought he gave that up a while ago,

before you moved in with him?"

"Well, he did. He said watching me in labor is too stressful for him, so he went out for a smoke. It's just as well. He's been fairly useless since I went into labor."

"Is your midwife there?"

"Oh, gosh, no. It's not even close to time to call her yet. My contractions are still about ten minutes apart."

"I'm coming over. If you're not going to call your midwife, and Peter is being a ding-dong about the whole thing, you should have somebody with you. I'm coming over."

"Joanie, you don't have to do that. Really. It's going to be a while. They say the first baby always takes a long time to come. I'm fine. Really."

"Too bad, Girlfriend. I'm coming over. Do you want me to bring you anything? Something from Dunkin's?"

"Well, I already threw up once earlier this morning. But a glazed donut sounds really good right about now, and a chocolate milk. Do they even sell chocolate milk there?"

"If they don't, I'll stop at a convenience store on my way. I'm out the door. Be there in twenty. Hang tight, little Schuyler, Auntie is coming!"

As soon as Hillary hangs up the call, she lets out a loud moan. Her back is aching and burning at the same time. "Deep breath in, hold, blow it out slowly," she coaches herself. The pain is making her eyes water.

She can hear Peter, who has remained downstairs after coming in from smoking, pacing from the living room to the kitchen and back again. It's starting to get on her nerves. "Peter!" she calls. "Can you come up here for a sec?"

He bounds up the stairs, pokes his head around her bedroom door. "Yeah? You need something?"

"Yes, Peter. I do need something. I need the father of this

baby to help me through this. Can you grab me another cool face cloth? And maybe rub my back some more?"

"Umm, yeah. Okay. I guess. I really don't like this kind of stuff, Hill. You know, I wasn't even in the room when Kenzie or Little Pete was born. I had to step out. I'm just not good in situations like this. Have you called the midwife yet?"

"No, not yet." Hillary's belly seizes once more in another long contraction. Peter continues to stand in the doorway to the bedroom, watching.

"Jesus Christ, Peter! Don't just stand there like an ass while I'm in agony. Go wet a face cloth with cool water. I'm sweating like a racehorse here. I'll need you to help me put on a dry nightgown while you're at it. In my dresser, second drawer."

"Okay! Okay. You don't have to boss me around. I'm trying to help, you know. I just got done telling you I'm not good at this sort of thing. I really think you should call the midwife."

"STOP telling me to call the damn midwife! I will call her when it's damn time to call her." Hillary lowers her voice, tries to calm her nerves with another deep breath. "Anyway, Joan is on her way over."

"Christ, that witch! You invited her over while you're delivering a baby? I'm not staying up in this room if she's here. That woman hates me. And to tell you the truth, the feeling is mutual."

"Would you shut up for a second! This is not about you. For once in your goddamn life, can you make this about someone else? I asked her to come, Peter, to give you a break. Okay? So you better be nice when she gets here."

"You're so tense. I'm just doing what you asked me. Here," he hands Hillary the wet washcloth.

"I know you're trying, Peter. But this is hard. It hurts, and to be honest, I'm scared. I need someone to be with me. All right?"

She reaches her hand out to Peter. "Can you help me get this wet nightgown off and change into the clean one?"

Peter grasps her hand in his and helps pull Hillary up to a sitting position on the side of her bed. Immediately, she is wracked with more pain. "Rub my back, Peter, please?" she says through a grimace. The contraction lasts several long seconds, and when it passes, Hillary is even more soaked with sweat than before.

Gingerly, Peter reaches behind Hillary's back and starts tugging on her wet nightgown, pulling it over Hillary's head. The cool air in her bedroom feels like a salve on Hillary's hot bare skin. She looks up to see Peter staring at her, grinning.

"What?"

"Your boobs. They're huge." He reaches out to grasp one of her breasts in his hand. Hillary slaps his hand away.

"Stop it, Peter! Now is not the time. Help me put on my clean nightie. Joanie will be here any minute."

Chapter 13

Susan

The following morning dawns bright and clear, not a cloud in the sky. "I want to be out there," Susan says to herself as she dresses for the day. She gazes out over the parking lot as she does every morning. In the center of a little rotary by the main entrance to the hospital, several floors below where Susan is looking out her window, she notices a small pine tree, staked on two sides so it won't blow over in a storm, decorated with holiday lights. "Christmas!" she says out loud. It must almost be Christmas. How long have I been here? she thinks with alarm. Did I miss Christmas altogether? She doesn't think so. The other patients would have been talking about having Christmas while on the unit, wouldn't they?

Susan can't stomach breakfast and has only a Styrofoam cup of weak black tea before entering the Community Room for Morning Meeting with the rest of the patients and whichever staff member must have drawn the short straw. Susan finds Russ sitting alone in one of the chairs around the circle. She sits down next to him. He turns to smile at her, their familiar greeting at these meetings.

"Morning, Russ," she says quietly. "How are you this morning?"

"I'm doing okay," he whispers back, glancing over at the staff member leading the meeting to ensure their side conversation isn't being detected. It isn't. "You?" he asks.

"My husband is coming in for a meeting later this morning. I'm freaking out a little."

Russ instinctively reaches over to give Susan's shoulder a comforting pat. "Good morning, Russ and Susan," the group leader interrupts them. "Please, no side talk during the meeting, all right?"

The meeting drags on. The group leader is soft-spoken and timid, and nobody around the circle pays attention as she drones on about patterns of life: good patterns, bad patterns, changing patterns. Whatever patterns, Susan thinks, as she continues worrying about her meeting with Paul, which will take place in less than a couple of hours. What will I say to him? Do I need to apologize? Will he apologize? She is lost in thought when she hears chair legs scraping on the linoleum floor as patients get up and head to the door to exit the Community Room. Thank God, the meeting is over.

Russ stands up to leave as well. "Good luck meeting with your husband today," he says. "Come and find me if you need to talk later."

"I will. Thanks, Russ." What a kind soul, Susan thinks, following Russ out of the room. So gentle and so sincere. I hope he makes it out there after he's discharged. She worries that there is a pretty good chance he will not. The world will destroy him. Susan doesn't think Russ is strong enough to survive, to navigate the dangerous waters that rage outside of the safe walls of the psych unit. Am I strong enough? she wonders.

The next hour flies by, and Susan finds herself walking once again down the long corridor to Bill's office. She can hear two male voices talking as she approaches. She recognizes Paul's voice. It stops her dead in her tracks. Her mind reels. She misses him so deeply. She loves him so deeply. And she is angry at him so deeply. Susan takes a slow breath in, exhales, and enters the room.

Paul is sitting in a third chair Bill must have brought in for the meeting. Susan glances at Bill, who gives her a reassuring smile as she walks over and sits in her familiar chair. She can't make eye contact with Paul. She feels his presence, though, strong, questioning. All she can think about is rushing over and hugging Paul, burying her face in his chest, and never letting go. Susan takes another deep breath. Bill is speaking, and she turns her attention to him.

"Thank you both for coming in to meet together today. I want to set a few ground rules before we begin; this is a safe space for both of you, and what you say here and what happens here in this room is confidential. Let's make sure that we hold that safe space for one another. When one person is speaking, let's wait for them to complete their thought before talking over them. Let's embrace this meeting together with openness and with kindness. The fact that both of you are willing to be here now, together, speaks so much about your commitment to one another, your commitment to come to some sort of resolution, whatever that might look like in the end. Let's begin. Paul," Bill asks, turning toward him, "You've taken the morning off from work to come in today. What are you hoping to get out of today's meeting?"

Paul is silent. Susan glances at him out of the corner of her eye: He is wearing a nice sweater and a new pair of jeans. He has a new pair of sneakers on. He's trying to look his best, she realizes; this is important to him. She feels her eyes well up realizing he is doing this for her, for them, for their marriage. Susan quickly looks at Paul's face. His head is bent, he gazes at his hands in his lap.

After a long minute, he speaks softly. "My hope is that we can talk about what happened and figure this out and move forward from here." Paul lifts his head and meets Susan's eyes. "I miss you, Suzie," he says. "I miss you and want you to come home. I want us to be able to work through this so we can go on with our lives together. But I also don't want you to come back if that's not what you want to do. I want you to be able to find happiness. I hope it's with me, and Ginger, but I understand if it isn't." Paul's eyes are watery as he speaks, and a single tear leaks out of the corner of one eye as he finishes what he's saying.

"Thank you, Paul," interjects Bill. "And Susan, what do you hope to get out of this meeting?"

She turns her face away from Paul's gaze and looks at Bill. A slight pause, and then, "I don't know what I want to do as far as Paul's and my relationship going forward. I feel like so much has happened—so much big stuff. Our relationship will never be the same again. *I* will never be the same again. I guess I need Paul to acknowledge that. I need to hear Paul apologize for changing our relationship like this, for changing me like this. I need to know he's sorry."

"So, what I'm hearing," Bill summarizes, "is that in order to move on, there needs to be some acknowledgment about the events that led up to this, to Susan's suicide attempt and hospitalization. Is that right?"

"This whole thing has really fucked me up," Susan jumps in. "I can't go forward with anything until I hear Paul apologize for doing this to me." She looks again at Paul, this time with anger in her eyes. "Why did you do this to me? I'm supposed to be the person you love most in the world. Why did you make that promise to me that you would give me a baby? Why did you go back on your word? It wasn't fair! I feel like you used that to get me to marry you, and then once we were married, you took it back. You broke your promise to me, and it really fucked me up!" Susan's voice is raised. She takes a breath, tries to steady her roiling emotions.

"All right. Let's give Paul a chance to say something here." Bill's voice is calm. The calmness of it annoys Susan. Isn't he supposed to be on her side? Doesn't he see that Paul is at fault here?

"I didn't mean to hurt you, Suzie." Paul looks at her, sadness in his eyes. "When we first talked about having a baby together, in my mind, it was a baby that would be our genetic child. When we found out that I couldn't give you a baby, I thought that was the end of it. I didn't think about there being any other options, like in vitro, or adoption, or anything. I wanted a baby with you, that was ours. I thought you understood that."

Susan is seething. "You thought I understood that?!" she asks. "Well, clearly, I didn't! You already have a child. You already got what you wanted. You didn't stop to consider what I wanted. Paul, you know how important it is for me to be a mother. We've only talked about it a million times together. How did you think I would feel when you went back on your word? What did you think would happen? That I'd just agree? Give up my hopes and dreams so you could have your life, the way you want it?"

"Let's pause for a minute here," Bill says quickly. "I hear a lot of 'you' statements in what you're saying, Susan. Let's give Paul a chance to tell his side of things."

"I thought our life together was what you wanted. I thought when we found out we couldn't have a baby together, that we would go on with our life together. I thought we were enough for each other. I guess I didn't think it through." Paul looks at Susan imploringly. "I'm sorry for that, Suzie. I'm sorry I couldn't give you what you wanted. I'm sorry I wasn't enough."

"Oh, don't go playing the martyr here, Paul!" Susan continues. "That was one of the main reasons I married you: because you wanted a baby so we could have our own family." As she says this, she realizes how it will sound to Paul, that she married him not for love but for a baby. She feels like a jerk for saying it.

"So, you didn't marry me because you loved me?" he replies. "You just wanted a baby?"

"No! That's not what I'm saying! I'm saying that one of the reasons I fell in love with you was because you said we could have a baby. I thought you'd make a great father to our child and a great husband to me. I had this idea in my head of starting a family. And I loved the idea of starting a family with you. And now," her voice softens, tears spill down her cheeks, "and now, I don't know if I fell in love with you or with the idea of you."

Susan realizes, as the words come out of her mouth, how true they are and how much she has just hurt Paul by saying them. But she feels vindicated by that, vindicated by knowing she has pierced his heart. Because truthfully, she acknowledges, he had splayed her heart wide open when he broke his promise to her.

"Let's pause here for a sec," Bill says to both of them. "Those are some strong accusations I'm hearing. Do you mean that the idea of a husband and a family is what you fell in love with? If it hadn't been Paul, could it have been someone else? Someone who was able to give you a child?"

Susan has a sense that she might vomit. She can't believe those words have come out of her, that she has spat this venom at Paul. But she also feels she needed to let him know how much he hurt her. Bill is right to question her; did she just want to hook up with someone to have a baby? Was that it for her? Was she that shallow?

"No," she replies, trying to calm her voice. "I mean, yes. In a way, I did want to meet someone who could give me a baby. My biological clock is screaming at me to bear a child. I can't control this directive from God, from the universe, from whomever! I can't control what my body is directing me to do. It's almost not a choice but an anthropologic duty for a woman to have a child, at least for me. At least that's how I feel. When I first met Paul, I thought he was a nice guy. He had already raised his son. He was a devoted father to him, giving him everything he could. Parker is his pride and joy. And I thought to myself, what better person to be a father than someone who had already shown what an amazing father he could be, someone who had already launched a child into young adulthood?"

Susan pauses, takes another breath as she continues. "But Parker isn't my child. I didn't raise him. He never knew me as part of his childhood. I'm meeting him as an adult. As an adult with his own experiences and boundaries. Parker has a mother already. I will never be his mother."

"But," Paul speaks up, "he does love you. You're still getting to know each other. But he does love you."

"That may be the case," Susan replies somewhat dubiously, "but he is still not my child. He was never my baby. That's what I don't think you understand." She looks again at Paul, her voice calmer. "You already have this experience of having your own child. And if I stay with you, if I make that choice, I will be denying myself that experience. I'm not saying that's not the choice I will make in the end. I'm just saying that I will make that choice with tremendous regret. If I stay in our marriage, I will always carry this regret. I will carry it to my grave, Paul."

"Well, I don't want you to regret marrying me." Paul reaches for a tissue to dry his eyes. "I just want you to be happy, Suzie. I love you so much. I love you with everything that I am. And if you don't feel the same way, it's okay. I understand. I want you to find happiness in your life, and if it's not with me, of course I'll be devastated, but I'll understand. If I can't be who you need me to be as a partner, I understand. And if that means that our marriage is over, I understand."

"But that's just it, Honey." Susan feels such empathy toward Paul when she hears him say those words, wanting her happiness above their marriage, above what he wishes for with her. "Somewhere along the way in this relationship, I fell in love with you. Just you. Not the idea of you. But you. Somewhere along the way, I realized with my whole heart, my whole being, that you are the person I am supposed to spend my life with, that you are my soulmate. Not everyone finds that in life. And I know, in spite of all of this shit that I'm going through, that I am blessed because I have found my soulmate. I love you, Paul. I will always love you." She reaches for his hand and squeezes it. Paul squeezes her hand back. "So, no matter what happens," Susan continues, "I feel like we must find a way to forgive each other. I believe that no matter what, we are meant to be together. It's going to be hard for me to move on from here. It's going to hurt—a lot. But I almost have no choice. My fate is to love you. You are my heart."

Paul stands, still holding onto Susan's hand. He gets down on one knee directly in front of where Susan is sitting, reaches for her other hand, looks up into her eyes, and, between sobs, gushes, "I'm so sorry, Suzie. I'm so sorry for all of this. I'm so sorry I can't give you a baby. I'm so sorry you tried to hurt yourself. I'm so sorry you're here. I want to do whatever you need me to do to help you heal, get better, and come home to me and Ginger. I may not be able to give you your greatest wish, Suzie, but you have all of me. You carry my soul in your heart."

Susan takes Paul's face in her hands, gazes down into his deep, sad eyes, the familiar kind, brown eyes she had first fallen in love with. "I don't know how I'm going to do it; get through the pain of not raising a child. I physically have no idea how to even deal with the sorrow I have around that; my heart is in such a dark place when I think of that. I'm scared, Paul. I'm scared of what will happen when I get out of here and return to the real world. I don't even know how to exist as a childless woman, a woman whose heart is that of a mother."

She looks up to Bill, who has quietly been watching the two of them, the beginning of the rest of their lives together unfolding before him. "How will I do that, Bill? How will I go on outside of here? I still don't feel like I'm going to be safe, you know, outside of here, outside of a locked unit. My sadness still consumes me. It's like I'm split down the middle; I love Paul, and I know I want to spend the rest of my life with him, and I'm grieving the rest of my life as well, a life where I don't know who I am anymore. It's like I have no identity anymore. I am still so lost."

Paul stands up, still holding one of Susan's hands, and returns to his seat beside her. Bill speaks: "First of all, I want you to recognize, Susan, how strong you are. How strong you are to be able to survive what happened when your idea of the future you and Paul would have together took a turn you didn't expect, didn't even see coming; how strong you are to be able to feel this pain, this raw pain, and still acknowledge the love you have for Paul, for your soulmate; to be able to identify your love for this man." Bill glances at Paul, who is quietly nodding in agreement with what Bill is saying. "We are here, all of us, me, Dr. Phillips, all of the nurses and aides and counselors; we want to help you find your way, Susan, help you to put the pieces together to start to rebuild a healthy life for yourself. The hardest thing you have ever done, harder even than pulling yourself back from a suicide attempt, is the work that starts now."

Susan lets go of Paul's hand and sinks back into her chair. She is exhausted—exhausted at what has taken place just now between her and Paul, exhausted at surviving her world slipping away before her, exhausted at holding on tight in the darkness, exhausted at swimming her way to the surface for that first deep breath of air, to sustain herself through all of it. She is exhausted at recognizing there is still a life force within her that wants desperately to carry on and live. She is exhausted from recognizing her continued love for Paul, from beginning to forgive him and forgive herself. Susan feels she can no longer go on with the conversation. There is too much to process, and she needs to be alone to do that.

Bill must notice this in her and steers the conversation to the current moment.

"Susan, this has been a lot. And you look tired. I know you have a lot of thinking to do about all of this. And, Paul, you do as well. Let's wrap up this morning's meeting together. Incredible work. From both of you." Bill continues, getting back to business, bringing both Susan and Paul back to the present, "Susan you have another ECT treatment tomorrow morning, Thursday. And then, if it's okay with both of you, I'd like to schedule another meeting with the three of us for Friday. How does that sound? Will that work for you, Paul?"

"I'll make it work," Paul replies with conviction. "Would it be all right if I visit Suzie tomorrow after her treatment?" He looks at Susan. "Would you like me to see you tomorrow, Suzie?"

Before Susan can reply, Bill interjects, "If you do come tomorrow, Paul, I recommend you come later in the afternoon. I believe Susan's treatment is around nine in the morning, and these treatments often leave people tired and foggy for a few hours."

"Right. Of course. I could come anytime," Paul replies. "Would you be okay if I stopped by later in the day tomorrow, Suzie?"

Susan looks over at Paul and says, tiredly, "Yes. Yes, I would like you to come tomorrow afternoon."

And then to Bill, "I didn't know I had another treatment tomorrow. How many more do I have to have?"

"Dr. Phillips wanted you to have at least three ECT treatments while you're an inpatient so we can monitor for positive results and any side effects like memory loss. He wants you to continue receiving ECT as an outpatient. We can talk more about this plan this afternoon, Susan. I'll check in with you later today to see how you're processing things. Sound good?"

"Yes. It sounds good. I feel like I could sleep for a hundred years after this session," she jokes meekly. "Are we all set? Would it be all right if I returned to my room for a bit? It must be close to lunchtime."

"Yes, we're all set here. You can go to your room and have some quiet time before lunch, Susan. Paul, will you stay here for a moment longer so we can schedule a time for our next meeting?"

Paul looks over to Susan, who has gotten up from her chair. He stands and wraps her in his arms. "I love you more than anything, Suzie," he murmurs into her ear. "It's going to be okay. It's all going to be okay."

Susan melts into Paul. She feels at peace in his embrace, at home. And then, quickly, she pushes back a bit. "Hey, I've been meaning to ask someone when Christmas is. It must be soon, right? Or did it already go by? Did I miss Christmas?"

"Nope," Paul replies, happiness in his voice. "You didn't miss Christmas. I know it's your favorite holiday. I'd never let that happen!" he says playfully. "December twenty fifth is a week from tomorrow. Ginger and I have the tree up and everything. And there are some presents for you already under it. I hope you can be home for Christmas, but we can celebrate it when you do come home."

"Oh, phew!" she responds with a little laugh. "I definitely want to be home for Christmas. "Do you think that can happen, Bill?"

"I think it's a definite possibility, Susan. Let's see how the rest of this week goes, and then your team will meet again about the next steps in your treatment. We can talk more about this when I check in with you later today. Okay?"

"Yes, sounds good." Susan gives Paul a quick kiss on the lips, gently untangles herself from his embrace, and leaves him and Bill to decide on the next meeting time.

Early the next morning, Susan wakes up groggy. Head Zapping Day, she thinks. I wonder what I should wear? She laughs out loud, softly, so as not to wake her new roommate; an older woman, overweight, disheveled, with matted hair and sorrowful, droopy eyes. The woman had arrived yesterday without a word, taken to her twin bed, and fallen promptly asleep, snoring loudly. Susan couldn't stand the loud snoring, and it took a strong effort not to rush over to the woman and shake her out of her deep sleep. She must need it, though, Susan had thought to herself. Either that, or she's sleeping to escape her current reality. It makes Susan curious about what the woman's current reality might be.

One of the aides interrupts her thoughts, standing in the doorway of the bedroom with a wheelchair and announcing to Susan, "Your chariot has arrived. Let's get you down to your treatment, Susan."

Susan is embarrassed. "Why do I have to ride in a wheelchair like an invalid when I'm perfectly capable of walking to the pre-op area on my own two feet?"

"Hospital policy," the aide replies. "In case you fall or something. You know, liability. The hospital doesn't want a big lawsuit."

"It's all about liability. And money," Susan grumbles as she climbs into the wheelchair.

By now, the procedure is somewhat familiar to Susan. She hops up from the wheelchair and onto a stretcher behind the curtain of her cubicle in the pre-op area. The unit is clean, very bright, and smells of disinfectant. She can hear murmurs of other pre-op patients talking with their loved ones before they receive their anesthesia and drift into a blissful sleep while whatever life-saving procedure modern medicine has deemed necessary is done to them. She wonders what the nursing staff thinks of her. An imposter. Not needing surgery per se, just getting her head zapped. Life-saving nonetheless, she thinks.

Someone arrives to start an IV in Susan's arm. They make small talk: the weather, Christmas, that sort of thing. Within moments, Susan notices herself relax deeply. She is still aware of the sounds of the pre-op unit, but that awareness is secondary to the sense of utter calm and quiet within her. She closes her eyes. Two people enter the cubicle, and Susan feels the stretcher jerk as the brakes are released, and they are on their way to the treatment area.

"Good morning, Susan," the doctor performing the procedure says to her. Susan opens her eyes sleepily and smiles at the face looking down at her. "We're going to give you another small dose of anesthesia, and then we'll perform the ECT. It shouldn't take long. We'll have you back upstairs before lunch. Any questions before we begin?"

Susan feels the warmth of the newly injected anesthesia move from the IV into her arm. She shakes her head no. Blissfully, she allows herself to let go into nothingness.

First, she hears the beep of a heart monitor. Then she hears voices around her, speaking softly. "She's coming around," one of the voices says. "Hi, Susan. You did great. You're all set. We're just going to take out that IV, and we'll get you back up to your unit. How are you feeling?"

"Fine," Susan manages to mutter.

Her thoughts are coming at her with jagged edges. Bright colors are flashing behind her closed eyes. She takes a deep breath and tries to still her jumbled mind. She turns her attention toward the fingers of her right hand and spreads them out on the sheets of the stretcher. They feel crinkly, rough. Ahh, she is grounded again in reality. Susan lets out a sigh.

The staff on the psych unit lets Susan sleep off the effects of the anesthesia, and it isn't until lunchtime that she awakens, the noonday winter sun streaming through the bars on the window of her room, willing her to wake up and take notice of the day. Susan stretches. Her head is pounding. She sits up too quickly, and the room begins to spin. She notices that she might throw up. This is like being hung over. Times a hundred, she thinks to herself, and slowly makes her way to the bathroom to wash up before going to the kitchen for lunch.

Her eyes are having difficulty adjusting, and Susan's vision is blurry. She finds her lunch tray and sits at a table for four. It is the table she has been sitting at since she arrived on the unit. The location of the table and the location of her chair at the table have not changed. However, the table's occupants revolve almost daily as patients are discharged from the unit and new ones arrive to take their places. A never-ending wheel of depression, thinks Susan, as she lifts the metal cover off her plate of food: a bland-looking turkey sandwich with wilted lettuce on dry white bread.

"How unappetizing," she says to herself and takes a tasteless bite.

Susan's new roommate comes over and sits across from her at the table. The roommate shoves her sandwich into her mouth in large bites, followed by loud gulps of milk. Susan looks up at her. The woman is wearing the same clothes she wore yesterday, and her long gray hair remains matted to the back of her head, clearly unwashed, unbrushed. "I'm Susan," Susan starts, after swallowing the dry bite of turkey sandwich. "What's your name?"

The woman's eyes dart from her plate toward Susan. The woman then takes the remainder of her sandwich, a good quarter of it, and shoves the entire thing into her mouth. She is trying to chew, but there is so much food in her mouth that her cheeks are puffed out like those of a chipmunk, and small pieces of sandwich fall onto the woman's stained pink T-shirt. On the front of the T-shirt is a picture of Tweety Bird. Susan notes how distorted Tweety looks all stretched out over the woman's ample bosom. The woman quickly pushes her chair back, gets up, and walks out of the kitchen.

Well, that went well, Susan thinks, shaking her head and returning to her sandwich. Typically, Russ sits at her table for meals, and Susan wonders where he is. He is usually right on time for meals, but he is nowhere to be seen today. Susan wonders if Russ has been added to the Head Zapping Program and is sleeping off his anesthesia.

In her room, Susan has just settled onto her bed and picked up where she left off in *A Wrinkle in Time*. She feels her mind let go as her imagination takes over and the book comes to life.

"Hey, Beautiful," she hears from the doorway.

Susan smiles as her heart leaps into her throat. Quickly, she places a bookmark to hold the place in her book where she left off. "Paul!" she cries happily. "Hang on. I'll be right there."

He is wearing a winter parka and his snow boots.

"Is it cold out?" she asks, walking to where he is standing just outside the door to her room.

"Yeah. It's pretty nippy out there. More snow is predicted for tonight. I just got the snow blower gassed up before coming to see you. I couldn't wait to get here."

"Oh, sure, I bet you couldn't wait to meet your wife for a date in the psych ward," Susan says a little sarcastically.

"I just couldn't wait to see you and tell you I love you, that's all," Paul replies with a smile as he wraps his arms around Susan.

She quickly pushes him away, saying, "I think they frown upon public displays of affection here." And laughing, "Let's find a quiet, empty room to sit and talk. I've missed you since yesterday. I'm glad you're here. I miss being at home with you and Ginger."

"Nothing would make me happier," smiles Paul, clomping down the hall beside Susan, his boots leaving wet puddles behind him. "Hey," he says, quickly changing the subject, "what's with your new roommate? I watched her pick her nose and eat it while standing in the doorway waiting for you."

"Ewww, that's so gross!" squeals Susan. "I don't know. She doesn't talk to anyone. I don't know anything about her. She freaked out and left lunch when I asked her name. You gotta get me outta here. I don't think I can stand too many days in the same room with her!"

They arrive at a small, empty conference room. Paul sits at the table across from Susan. "Well, that's something I wanted to talk to you about," he starts. "Bill said I could take you home for a few hours this weekend, on a day pass, if you're up for it. See how it goes." He looks at Susan expectantly.

Susan is a little taken aback. Bill hadn't mentioned this when they had spoken again yesterday after her meeting with Paul. "Are you sure?" she asks, "Bill didn't say anything to me."

"He wanted us to talk about it together first. See how you feel about it. And then he said we could tell him when we meet with him again."

"And when is that?"

Paul looks down at his watch. "In about a half an hour." He glances up at Susan, who is fidgeting in her chair, clearly flustered. "Are you okay with that? We can change the meeting if you want. What's wrong, Suzie?"

"As much as I want to get out of here, it feels like too much, too soon, Paul. I'm scared. I still don't know if I'm fully comfortable with myself. I still don't even know who I really am. And my mind is all jumbled from the ECT treatments. It's like the world is spinning so fast around me, and as soon as I can finally focus on one thing, the whole thing shifts and starts spinning again. What if I can't keep up?"

Paul reaches across the table for Susan's hand. "It won't always be like this, you know. They said that after you stop the electroconvulsive treatments, it takes a little while, but then things settle down, your memory starts to return. I really think it's helping you, Suzie. You seem so much better than before you started the ECT. I'm here for you, and we can take things as slowly as you need to. I love you so much, Suzie. I want you to know that—how much I love you."

Paul and Susan spend the next twenty minutes softly talking with one another. Susan asks about Ginger. "She's good. I've had to snow blow a path through the yard for her," reports Paul. "Her little Pomeranian legs are too short to make it through the snowbanks. She can't wait for you to come home and give her a belly rub," Paul concludes, looking into Susan's eyes. "Come on, Suzie. Let's go to Bill's office."

They settle themselves into the plush chairs in Bill's office. Bill smiles at each of them before opening up the therapy session with, "It's so nice to see you two arrive together today. I want to start our meeting with your thoughts on how things are going for you as a couple and as individuals since our last meeting. Susan," Bill turns and looks directly at her. "How are you feeling today? You had another ECT treatment this morning, correct?"

In spite of the anxiety about returning home that she expressed to Paul earlier, Susan replies, "I feel like I'm doing better. These treatments make me tired, but in a good way."

"In a good way?" Bill prompts.

"Like a deep tired, not like the agitated tired I felt before I started doing ECT. That kind of tired was physically painful, like the only way to find some respite was to crawl out of my own skin."

"And how about now? Do you still feel in physical pain now?" asks Bill.

"No, not really. I have a dull headache from the ECT, but it goes away with some ibuprofen. I'm left with a sad, tired feeling.

Like I've found my way to the deep sadness within me that started all of this. I recognize it and must learn how to exist with it."

"That's very insightful, Susan, being able to recognize that sometimes we have to learn to live with some of these feelings, even if only for a time, in order to move through them and move on from them. How about you, Paul?" Bill turns his attention over to Paul. "How have you been doing since we last met?"

Paul looks at Susan before replying. "I'm hopeful," he remarks, "hopeful for our marriage, this life together, and Suzie's healing." Paul's eyes become red and watery. "I want to find a way for us to go forward, to move on from this and into a place where Suzie can find happiness."

Bill faces Susan. "How do you feel about that? Working toward a place of hopefulness? Of happiness?"

Susan is slow to respond, thoughtful. "Ultimately, I want that, too. I don't know if I'll ever be super happy again. I almost can't imagine it. But I want to move toward that. I want to find the strength to get through this and see what's on the other side. I don't know if I can do it by myself, though. I know this is an inside job, but I don't think I'm strong enough to fight alone. I guess that's some of the sadness I feel, too, that I'm not strong enough to do this alone. I used to believe I was strong enough to handle anything alone, and I don't know if that's true anymore. I don't want to be weak. And right now, I am weak," she finishes and looks at Bill.

"You have hit rock bottom and have fought hard to find your way up to the light again, Susan. No wonder you feel tired. This is no easy journey. Only you could have brought yourself back from the dark place that you went to. You are here now. Let us help you to continue your journey forward. You are not alone on your healing path, not by a long shot."

"I'm afraid to leave this unit," Susan responds to Bill. "I'm embarrassed to say that I'm afraid to go home. To be back out in the world. I honestly don't know who I am right now or how I'm supposed to feel. What will happen when I see mothers pushing baby carriages at the supermarket? What will happen when a child comes into where I work for their pre-school physical exam? What will happen each year on Mother's Day?" Susan starts twisting her fingers together where they had been resting in her lap.

Paul reaches over quickly and takes one of Susan's hands in his. He looks into her eyes and smiles at her. "You have me, Suzie. And I've got you. And I will help you through this. The staff here will help you through this. You have so many people who love you and care about you. We will carry you until you can carry yourself. I promise you."

"What about going back to my work? I don't know if I'm ready to be in that environment. Do they even know I'm in here? In the psych unit?"

"They know you're out with an illness," Paul says. "They are holding your position for you until you are ready to return."

Bill clears his throat. "Nothing says that you have to return to that job, Susan. Perhaps you will want to find a position, at least for the short term, with fewer triggers. When you're discharged from here, we will be putting in a referral to a partial hospitalization program. So it will be several weeks before you consider returning to your old position anyway."

"A partial what?"

"Partial hospitalization," answers Bill. "It's a day or half-day program for people leaving an inpatient psychiatric facility. It offers daily structure to help integrate what you've just been through and helps you return to your life outside these four walls. They have one-on-one as well as group sessions throughout the day. It typically runs Mondays through Fridays, and people attend for two to four weeks after they've been discharged from inpatient. Then they'll set you up with a therapist in the program who will follow you on an outpatient basis for individual therapy, couples therapy with Paul, and to manage your medications."

Susan nods. "And what about the head zapping treatments? Do those continue, too?"

"I believe Dr. Phillips wants you to have one more ECT treatment here, before you're discharged home. And then you will continue treatments on an outpatient basis."

"For how long will she have to get treatments?" Paul interrupts.

"It's different from person to person," Bill replies, "depending on how well Susan responds as the treatments continue. Some people have ten to twelve treatments, which is all they need. Others continue for a lifetime."

"I will *not* do this for the rest of my life!" Susan interjects. "No way am I scrambling my brain for a lifetime," she finishes bitterly, crossing her arms over her chest.

"And nobody is saying that you have to. Dr. Phillips will make his recommendation to your outpatient psychiatrist, and the two of you will decide what's right for you going forward. This is your healing process, Susan. You get to say what feels right, or not right, for your journey," Bill concludes.

It is Sunday, and the inpatient unit is relatively quiet. There are fewer staff and less structured meetings on the weekends. Patients visit with family in the common areas. Christmas is five days away. Susan is quietly reading in her room, the curtain drawn between her and her roommate; the roommate, who still keeps to herself, hardly speaks and, sadly, has no visitors. Susan has given up trying to get to know her and instead focuses on her last few days as an inpatient before being discharged home. Home in time for the holidays.

It is nearing lunchtime, and Susan wanders to the kitchen area, her little table of four chairs, wondering who will join her today. And who will not. She has not seen Russ for several days now and is growing concerned. She knows asking the staff about Russ will get her nowhere, as they must comply with privacy standards for all the patients. She picks up her tray and decides she will sit somewhere else today. She scans the small eating area and notices an empty seat at a table across the room.

Susan recognizes an older gentleman at the table; he has been on the unit for at least a week now. She walks over to the table, nods at the empty chair, and asks, "Anybody sitting here? Mind if I join you?"

"Nope. Go right ahead," he replies and goes back to his meal. Susan sits down, places her paper napkin on her lap, and readies herself to open the metal lid on top of her food. This is absolutely one thing I will not miss, she thinks, as she identifies a gray piece of meat alongside a pile of instant potatoes and mushy canned peas, all swimming in a puddle of light brown gravy. Susan replaces the metal cover over the food. She decides consuming the side salad and roll and butter will be safer.

The older man across the table looks up. "You not going to eat that?" He gestures to her plate.

"No. You want it?" Susan hands the plate to the gentleman, who eagerly lifts the metal lid and slides Susan's meal onto his almost empty plate. She watches him eat, seeming to delight in the bland meal, shoving in bite after bite, tiny bits of food getting stuck to his untrimmed white beard.

"Did you ever meet a guy named Russ?" Susan ventures to ask. "Tall, thin, dark hair. I haven't seen him around in a while. I was wondering where he went."

The man stops for a second. He runs his dinner roll around the edges of his plate, soaking up the remaining potatoes and gravy. His keen blue eyes focus directly on Susan. "You didn't hear?"

"No. Hear what?"

"That's the fellow who tried to kill himself last week. Yeah, they went into his room to do night check and found him hanging from one of the water pipes up near the ceiling. He made a noose out of his bed sheets. Nobody can figure out how he was able to climb up that high to get the sheet over the pipe, but he did it somehow."

Susan's hand flies to her mouth. "Oh, my God." Her heart is beating fast. "Did he kill himself?"

"When they cut him down, he was still breathing. But just barely." The older man enjoys seeing Susan grasping on to his every word.

"What happened to him? Where is he now?" Susan is starting to feel panicky.

"The last I heard," the older man has returned to wiping his plate with the remains of his dinner roll, "is that he's in the intensive care unit, brain dead, hooked up to a breathing machine. They're waiting for his cheating wife and his kids to come say goodbye before pulling the plug."

Susan can't believe what she's hearing. No. Not Russ. Not that sweet, gentle man. She quickly gets up from the table, her salad and roll untouched, and exits the kitchen, making her way back to her room. On her way down the hall, Susan bumps into Sandy, the day nurse. Sandy takes one look at Susan's ashen, tear-stained face. "What is it, Susan? What happened?"

"Russ," Susan manages to get out, gasping. "I just heard about Russ."

Sandy puts an arm around Susan's shaking shoulders and steers her past her room and down the long hallway. "C'mon with me. Let's find a quiet place where you can catch your breath. I'll stay with you. All right?"

Sandy finds an empty room and sits next to Susan on a bench by a window. Susan cries silently, thinking of her friend Russ, what brought him here, what brought him to the point of attempting to take his own life. It's too close to her own story. That could be her lying in the intensive care unit, hooked up to a ventilator, brain dead. What was the difference in their stories? Russ had no one to go home to, Susan acknowledges, and I do. She lets out a deep breath as if she has been holding her head underwater for the last several minutes. Sandy is gently rubbing Susan's back. "I have to get out of here," she suddenly tells Sandy, straightening up on the bench. "I want to go home."

Sandy sits back and looks at Susan. "I know," she says, "and we're working on getting your discharge plan in place. I'm glad to see this fighting spirit in you, Susan. I always knew you had it."

"You did? How?"

Sandy takes a breath and smiles. "I've been working on this unit for many years. I can almost always tell when a new patient arrives whether they've got what it takes to rise above their current situation and move on, or if they're stuck and may not be able to move forward. I saw a spark in you when you first arrived. And I knew. I knew you would fight until you came unstuck."

"Well, I'm glad you could see it in me, Sandy. Lots of times, I still don't see it in myself."

"You may not see it in yourself or feel it, Susan, but it's there.

And you are loved. That makes such a difference. You are so very, very loved."

Susan swallows. "I know I am," she says gratefully.

Chapter 14

Hillary

"Joanie?" Hillary reaches her hand out to her friend who has been sitting by the bedside.

Joan glances at her wristwatch and notices it is now two o'clock in the afternoon. Hillary has been laboring for almost twelve hours and looks exhausted.

"Yeah, Sweetie, what can I get you?" Joan is worried about Hillary. She has never given birth herself; she and her husband had long ago decided against children. But something in her gut is telling her that Hillary's labor isn't quite right; she's never heard of someone becoming so red and hot and sweaty during labor. Several times since she arrived, Joan has gently asked if it wouldn't be best to call the midwife. She's received the same response each time: not until the contractions are five to six minutes apart.

Hillary's lips are dry. Her mouth tastes papery. "How far apart are my contractions now?"

Joan glances from her friend to her wristwatch again. She has been timing the contractions and knows they are about eight minutes apart. She suddenly makes a decision within herself.

"They're about six minutes apart, Hon. Can I call Frankie for you?"

"They are?" Hillary brightens momentarily, raising herself on her elbow from her side-lying position. "Yes, six minutes apart is good. That's when they said to call my midwife." She has used up any little bit of energy that piece of news has given her and lays her head heavily back down on her pillow, the pillowcase wet and warm, smelling of sweat and her own body's odor.

Quickly, Joan stands up, realizing this is her moment to alert the midwife of her concerns. "Listen, why don't I get you another glass of cold water while I let Frankie know? Okay?"

Hillary doesn't argue and begins to grimace once again as her back, her sides, and her belly become rock-hard with another contraction.

Joan walks quickly out of the bedroom and down the hall. She starts dialing the midwife and makes her way rapidly down the stairs.

The phone rings once, twice. On the third ring, "Hello, Francesca Tobin, Midwife, how can I help you?"

"Hi, my name is Joan. I'm Hillary's friend. Her alternate birth partner." She pauses, waiting to be recognized.

"Oh, yes! Hi, Joan, you can call me Frankie. What's happening with Hillary? Is everything all right? Is she in labor? Is Peter there?"

Joan doesn't know where to begin, and her fears are unleashed. "I think something's wrong, Frankie. I've never had a baby, so I don't know. But Hill is in a tremendous amount of pain. And she is so hot she is red and drenched with sweat. Something isn't right. I just have this bad feeling."

"Okay, deep breath. Women often become hot and sweaty during labor. How far apart are her contractions, do you know?"

"They're like seven to eight minutes apart. But I told Hill they were six minutes apart. It was the only way she would let me call you. I've been trying to get her to reach out to you since this morning." Joan stops her rush of words and takes a deep breath. "Her water broke in the middle of the night. I'm really worried. How soon can you get here?"

"I'm on my way, Joan. Depending on traffic, I should be there in about half an hour. Is she doing her breathing to help get through the contractions? Is Peter coaching her?"

Without missing a beat, Joan responds, "Peter stepped out for a while." She decides there's no use hiding her feelings for Peter from Frankie. "I guess he decided that since I had arrived, he could go out and smoke cigars with the guys at the bar while the mother of his child is back at home suffering through each contraction. Sorry. I'm not a huge fan of Peter."

On the other end of the phone is Frankie's knowing voice. "No worries. Did you study any of the material I left with Hillary about the birth process and home births? She had told me you were the alternate birth partner."

"I watched a couple of the videos, yeah. We've been doing pursed lip breathing and box breathing. I've been trying to help her get into comfortable positions, propping her up with pillows."

"That's perfect, Joan. That's exactly what a birth coach should be doing. You're doing great. I'm on my way."

"There's one other thing," Joan interjects, her voice urgent. "When I helped her to the bathroom the last time, she was dripping water from between her legs. Not much, but it was brownish. And it smelled awful. I don't even know if Hillary noticed. If she did, she didn't say anything. She's been in excruciating pain. I wiped up the floor while she was in the bathroom."

"How long ago would you say that was, Joan? That you noticed the brown foul-smelling liquid coming from Hillary?"

Joan takes a breath, tries to calm her mind, and thinks back. "Let's see. I'd guess a couple of hours ago. She hasn't wanted to get out of her bed since then. I keep massaging her back and shoulders. That's not a good sign, is it, the brown fluid?"

Joan waits while Frankie pauses. "It could be a number of things. Stool from the mother or stool from the baby. Sometimes, it indicates the baby is under some stress in the birth canal. I'll check her and the baby out as soon as I get there. About twenty-five more minutes. You focus on remaining calm and helping Hillary get through those contractions."

At half past three in the afternoon, with a cool drizzle falling out of the gray September sky, Hillary tries to get herself out of bed once more to sit on the birthing ball Joan had run out to fetch from Frankie's car a few minutes ago. Hillary is not progressing. While her contractions keep coming at five to six minutes apart, the pain only seems to intensify with each passing wave. Frankie has told her that her cervix is not dilating as it should and that, with all of this effort, Hillary should be more dilated than she is. Hillary is trying not to feel the fear she sees behind Frankie's concerned eyes or to notice the anxiously knitted forehead lines her dear friend Joan has been wearing for the past few hours.

"Can you guys give me a hand getting on the birthing ball?" she says, sounding weaker than she meant to.

"Yes, of course. We are right here." Frankie's reassuring voice. "Let's see if some movement and repositioning will get this baby unstuck and advancing through the birth canal. Here, Joan, can you get on the other side of Hillary? Let's see if we can walk her around first."

As soon as Hillary is standing, she feels a trickle of fluid from between her legs. Chuckling, she says, "Sorry, ladies. Hope you don't mind a little pee to make this a more glamorous event."

Behind Hillary's back, Joan gives Frankie a worried look. The fluid is brown, no mistaking it. And the odor is enough to make both women turn their heads to get a breath of fresher air. Joan is beside herself, worried about her friend. She has watched as Frankie checked Hillary's cervix on and off throughout the afternoon and held her breath while Frankie placed her stethoscope on top of Hillary's belly, listening for the baby's heartbeat.

Frankie has been unable to detect a fetal heartbeat since she's been with Hillary this afternoon. Initially, she hadn't been overly worried, as often it is difficult to discern a fetal heartbeat with a stethoscope when the baby is in the birth canal. She is concerned about how hot and red Hillary is. When Frankie arrived, she checked her patient's vital signs, and Hillary's temperature was slightly elevated. She has had Joan apply cool cloths to Hillary's forehead for the better part of the afternoon. She knows the best place for Hillary and her baby right now is at the hospital.

Hillary had been adamant, more than adamant, if there is such a thing, about not going to the hospital to have her baby. Worried about contracting COVID, she had told Frankie no. She didn't want to risk anything happening to her or the baby. People were, after all, still dying in the hospitals from this virus, although advances in vaccines had been made quickly by competing pharmaceutical companies to immunize the masses. Frankie had received her initial COVID-19 vaccine. She knew she couldn't afford to be out of work sick or transmit the disease to her mothers and babies.

Frankie's focus quickly returns to her patient as Hillary lets out a long, low groan. "Another contraction? Breathe through it. You've got this, Hillary. This baby wants to come out into the world and meet his momma," she croons into Hillary's ear. "Let's get you sitting on the birthing ball."

"I don't think I can," wails Hillary. "I'm so tired, Frankie. Would it be all right if I got into my bed again? Maybe you could check my cervix and see if I've progressed any more. God, what's that smell?"

"Just a little accident," Joan quickly says, trying to keep her voice light. "I'm gonna clean up the floor, and we'll help you get back into bed, Sweetie." With her head bent as she wipes up the foul mess. "Hey, Hill, what do you say I give Peter a call? Let him know where things are at. He may want to come home and be with you now that..." Joan is at a loss for words. Now that what? Now that you're obviously in trouble? Now that you should have been in an ambulance on your way to the hospital hours ago? But she simply says, "I'm sure he'd want to be here. Why don't I call him while Frankie checks you out?"

Hillary, lying on her bed with her head and knees propped up on pillows, waves her hand wearily at her friend. "Yeah, sure. All right."

When Joan exits the bedroom, Frankie puts on another pair of gloves and turns on her headlamp. "Okay," she says from between Hillary's legs. "Let's see what's going on here." Immediately, she realizes that Hillary's cervix has not budged. She applies some lubricating gel to her fingers and inserts them into Hillary's vagina. She still cannot feel the top of the baby's head. The baby hasn't advanced down the birth canal as she had hoped when she had Hillary change positions and get up to walk around the room.

She takes a deep breath and glances at her wristwatch: four o'clock. "Hillary," she begins in a calm voice, "listen. I'm having some concerns about how slowly your baby is advancing down the birth canal. There hasn't been any movement since I last checked you." Frankie looks into Hillary's eyes and sees the exhaustion, the determination, and the flicker of fear behind all of that. "You and your baby need more advanced monitoring at this point—more than I can offer you here at home. Now, I know how much you wanted a home birth, and I understand your reasons for it. But in my professional opinion, we need to get you to a hospital. Sooner rather than later."

Hillary starts to protest, and Frankie continues. "Look. I know this isn't what you wanted. But I am concerned that if we wait much longer, it might have a negative outcome for your baby. I will be with you the whole time in the ambulance. But, really, we need to get you there, like now. Do I have your permission to call an ambulance?"

At that moment, Joan comes back into the bedroom. In a soft voice, with her lips turned up in a make-believe smile, she says to Hillary, "I talked to Peter. He's on his way home."

Hillary's mind is whirling. She can't believe this is happening. Every maternal fiber in her being is telling her not to deliver this baby in a hospital. This is not the birth plan she envisioned. And yet, Frankie is looking worried. And Joan has looked nervous for the past couple of hours. Maybe I should go, she thinks to herself. Maybe I'm being selfish, and my baby needs to be born in a hospital at this point. I want everything to be all right. I want this baby to be all right. I need him to be. But she tells Frankie and Joan, "I want to wait until Peter gets home and see what he wants to do." She doesn't miss the anxious gaze as it passes between the midwife and her best friend.

"He told me he would be home in fifteen minutes," Joan

chirps as she walks over to stand by Hillary's bedside and tries to fluff up the pillows behind her friend's head. She can tell Frankie is acutely worried, and her own heart beats faster. She gazes out the dormer window. *Where the hell are you, Peter?*

Joan stops pacing by the bedroom window when she hears a car door slam in Hillary's driveway. At last! Before Hillary can get a word out, Joan runs down the stairs. She flings open the door to the side porch and practically pushes Peter back outside as he bounds up the porch steps.

He steps back, startled. "What, the...?" He glowers angrily at Joan.

"Listen to me, Peter. I know we have our differences, and we don't see eye to eye on so many things, but if you love Hillary as much as I do, you need to stop for a second and hear what I have to say."

Peter drops his angry gaze and tries to walk around the side of Joan to enter the house.

She puts up a hand to stop him. "Out here." Joan indicates the porch with a nod of her head.

He squares himself against Joan, suspicion written all over his face. "Why? What's going on? Did something happen to the baby? I thought you said it wasn't born yet. Is it Hill? Is something wrong with Hill?"

"Calm down. I need to talk to you. What's going on is that there's a problem with the baby." She takes in a breath and continues. "He's not moving down the birth canal like he should. Frankie has been checking on the baby all afternoon, and there's been no progress. Hillary needs to get to the hospital before—"

"She won't go," Peter interrupts. "She's scared of her or the baby catching COVID and dying or something. Trust me, she won't go."

"I know. That's why we need your help, Peter."

A pause from Peter, then, "What do you mean?"

"Frankie has already told Hill she needs to get to the hospital. And Hill said she wanted to wait for you before deciding." Joan pauses and looks Peter straight in the eye. "You must do this for her, Peter, and for your baby. I've got a really bad feeling about things. I don't think Hill can wait much longer before something bad happens to the baby, or her. It's up to you, Peter. You've got to tell her the right thing is to have the baby at the hospital. You're the only one she'll listen to on this point. Please, Peter. This is really important." Joan reaches out to put her hand on Peter's arm, thinks better of it, and lets her arm fall to her side.

"Yeah. Okay. I'll see what I can do. You know how stubborn she is. She never listens to me about this baby anyways." He shrugs past Joan and, this time, makes it to the side door and enters the house with Joan on his heels.

"Don't let her know what I told you, Peter. For her sake."

"Yeah. Yeah. Whatever. Now let me get into my own damn house, will you?" He stops and turns back to face Joan. "Could she really lose the baby?"

Peter's lack of urgency exasperates Joan, but she answers calmly, "I don't know. But the midwife thinks she needs to be in the hospital." She follows Peter as he bounds up the stairs to the second floor.

Hillary lifts her head when she sees Peter's face in the doorway. "Hey, Daddy-O," she says tiredly. "Our little man is taking his own sweet time coming into this world."

Peter takes a breath of the acrid air in the bedroom and gazes over at Hillary, exhausted in her bed. "Listen, Babe," he starts as he looks over at the midwife, who nods in encouragement, "I think we need to get you to the hospital. They can take better care of you and the baby there." He sits on the edge of the bed, running his hand over his head. The smell in the room makes him want to gag. "Why don't I get your birthing bag together, and we can let the midwife call the ambulance."

Hillary looks up into Peter's eyes. She cannot read the expression behind his words but decides that he's being entirely sincere. "You think that's best, then, to have our baby at the hospital?"

Without missing a beat, in perhaps his most selfless act toward Hillary, thinks Joan as she watches from the bedroom door, Peter says, "I do, Babe."

Joan busies herself, tidying up the bedroom as best she can while they wait for the ambulance to arrive. She finds a plastic hamper in the bathroom, where she tosses wet and soiled towels, moist face cloths, and two nightgowns saturated with body fluid. She knows that the hospital rules governing births right now only allow for one family member to be with the mother during and after delivery, thus decreasing the risk of spreading the COVID-19 virus both in and out of the hospital. She knows she will have to say goodbye to her friend when the ambulance arrives, and she feels a great sadness within herself as she realizes how much this has meant to her: to be present with her friend, laboring, a rite of passage she has never experienced.

Frankie, who had gone downstairs to call the ambulance and notify the Obstetrics team at the hospital that Hillary will be coming in, now returns to the crowded little bedroom followed by two paramedics, one of whom is pushing a stretcher covered with a variety of portable emergency equipment.

Hillary perks up as they enter. "Hi, guys," she observes, trying to sound far more animated than she feels. "Is all this necessary? I can walk downstairs, you know."

"It's protocol," answers one of the paramedics, smiling at Hillary. "Mothers-to-be get the royal treatment. Let's get a set of vitals on you, and we'll help you onto the stretcher and have you and your baby on your way." He reaches into one of the duffel bags on the stretcher and pulls out a blood pressure cuff and stethoscope. Meanwhile, the second paramedic is over in the far corner of the room with a notepad in hand, taking report from an animated, concerned-looking Frankie.

Hillary is comforted by the kindness of the paramedics, a little embarrassed for all the attention being paid to her. I guess this is my circus, and these are my monkeys, she thinks to herself and smiles weakly, grateful, finally to be nearing the end of what has turned out to be a very long production.

Hillary is shaken as the paramedics pull the stretcher from the back of the ambulance onto the loading ramp of the hospital emergency department. She watches overhead as the lights in the ceiling of the hospital corridor flash by, one after the other, quickening as the paramedics pick up their pace to get her to the operating room for an emergency C-section. She tries to raise her head to find Peter. He is running beside the stretcher. She reaches out her hand to him and he grazes her fingertips.

Suddenly, the stretcher stops. Hillary hears a voice directing the paramedics through a set of double doors. She sees Peter's head through the small windows as the doors close behind her. "Wait!" she calls out.

There is a nurse in scrubs walking briskly alongside the

stretcher. "The baby's father will meet you in the OR after he's changed and scrubbed."

Hillary arrives in a green-tiled room, beeping equipment all around her, everyone moving in hushed tones. She feels the paramedics help to move her onto the operating room table. She looks up to thank them, but they exit the door as quickly as they have brought her through it. She turns her attention back to a nurse who is arranging the heart monitor leads and oxygen tubing that had been attached to her in the ambulance. She feels a band being fastened around her belly.

The room grows still as another nurse adjusts some dials on the fetal heart monitor. The silent pause lasts several long moments before the room erupts again in an organized frenzy. Someone is barking out orders in a commanding voice, and medication is injected into Hillary's intravenous line.

In seconds, Hillary starts to feel her legs go numb and her entire body relaxing. She notices herself becoming sleepy, her senses dulled. She tries to speak up, asking them to wait for Peter to come in, but finds her tongue is dry and thick in her mouth. She produces only a faint whimper, closes her eyes, and listens to the commotion around her.

"You're going to feel some pressure on your belly now, Hillary," a deep, male voice alerts her. She snaps her eyes open again, noting with some relief that Peter is sitting on a rolling stool beside her head, the color drained from his face, his eyes.

"What are they doing, Peter? Why isn't my baby crying!" Hillary tries to pull her body closer to the side of the operating table she is on to see what is happening beyond the sterile drape blocking the view past her chest. She can hear a quiet yet urgent stir from the hospital staff.

Peter grasps her opposite wrist and holds it hard, "Don't look, Hill. You don't want to see this."

Hillary yanks her arm away from Peter's firm grasp. It is almost impossible to move as her lower body is completely numb from the nerve block she had been given right before they performed the emergency cesarean section to deliver her baby.

Hillary is agitated. She had known her baby was in trouble. She had known it twenty-four hours ago when her water broke. There was nothing specific to foreshadow the strong fist of desperate panic that now grips her chest and holds it in a constricting vise; nothing, really, except a faint pink tinge to the splash of water that had spread across her bedsheets at home, heralding the beginning of birth; no physical sign except the strong force of her contractions; no signal whatsoever that her baby had already perished inside of her. But she had known.

She had known when Frankie had manually checked her cervix again and again. She had known when her contractions kept coming harder and longer and there was no progression of her baby's head down the birth canal. She had known when Frankie helped her change positions and contort her body in ways she never thought a pregnant woman could, in an effort to free up her baby. She had known after twelve hours of laboring when Joan and the midwife had spoken together in low whispers in the far corner of the bedroom. She had known when, finally, at almost twenty-four hours, she had looked into the anxious faces of Peter and her best friend and agreed to go to the hospital. She had known that her baby would not be born alive. She had known.

The fear inside of her reaches a crescendo, and Hillary vomits over the side of the operating table onto the floor. A nurse dressed in blue scrubs, hidden behind a surgical mask and cap, rushes over with a towel to wipe Hillary's mouth and mop up the floor. Peter pulls Hillary back onto the center of the table.

"Would you like something for the nausea?" the nurse asks.

"What's going on with my baby?" Hillary practically chokes on a second wave of nausea. "What are they doing to my baby? I want to see my baby!" She realizes she is yelling at the nurse.

The nurse has pity in her eyes when she looks down at Hillary. "They're doing compressions on your baby's heart. He doesn't have a heartbeat, so they are giving him medicine to help jump-start it, and they're breathing oxygen into his lungs for him."

"Is he going to be okay, though?" asks Peter meekly. "Are they going to get his heart started?"

"They're still working on him," the nurse replies. "They're doing everything they can."

Hillary realizes instantly, from the look in the nurse's eyes and those definitive words, "They're doing everything they can," that her baby's heart will not be revived. She feels the sides of the operating room closing in around her. Her vision gets smaller until all she can see is a long, narrow tunnel, a pinprick of light flickering at its very end. She can hear the voices of the doctors and nurses working on her baby, but they are muffled, almost like cartoon voices. They aren't making any sense. She thinks she hears the distant voice of a nurse say, "Quick, she's losing consciousness!" She imagines she hears Peter call her name. And, suddenly, the light at the end of the tunnel is snuffed out. A cold, dry wind surrounds her, gathers her, and ushers her swiftly away like a brittle autumn leaf. She succumbs without will.

Chapter 15

Susan

It is early Monday morning, and Susan is dressed in a johnny when the familiar wheelchair arrives to transport her to the pre-op area, where she will wait for her last ECT treatment as an inpatient. She greets the unit aide jokingly, "Ahh, my coach-and-four has arrived. Let's go for a jaunt through the countryside, shall we, Jeeves?" The aide chuckles, and they make their way off the unit and down the elevator.

As the aide pushes the wheelchair to the left, Susan glances down the first-floor hall to the right toward the light streaming through the doors at the main hospital entrance. Visitors and staff keep up a continuous circuit as they travel in and out through the automatic revolving doors, bundled up in their heavy jackets, faces buried in scarves to stave off the cold December air. Some carry wrapped packages for family members who will be hospitalized over the Christmas holiday. Susan smiles to herself.

Her attention quickly returns to the morning's mission as she and the aide turn another corner and finally enter the pre-op area. By now, the procedure is familiar to Susan; she climbs onto the stretcher and extends her right arm so the nurse can insert the IV catheter. She hardly flinches, her mind is so preoccupied with going home. She will be discharged tomorrow morning, and Paul will arrive to pick her up. She cannot wait to see Ginger. There is so much to do, she thinks to herself. I have about two and a half days to get ready for Christmas. The thought of pulling off a holiday meal and presents, even just for her and Paul, is almost overwhelming. Susan takes a deep breath and starts to relax. The anesthetic the nurse pushed into Susan's IV is taking effect.

By mid-afternoon, Susan wakes from her treatment. She slowly gets up, aware of the dizzy spells she gets if she stands up too quickly after receiving ECT. The clock on the wall reads two o'clock in the afternoon. She has missed lunch but knows the staff keeps crackers and peanut butter in the kitchen. Susan changes from her johnny into jeans and a sweatshirt and heads to the unit kitchen. She makes a few graham-cracker-and-peanut-butter sandwiches and manages to find a carton of milk after rummaging through the refrigerator. Susan dreamily gazes out the window while eating her snack.

"Oh, hi, Susan. I've been looking for you."

She turns and smiles. It's Bill. "Hi, Bill. Looks like you found me. What's up? Did I sleep through one of our sessions?"

"No. There is no session today. I'm leaving early this afternoon to start my Christmas holiday, and I wanted to catch you before I left."

Susan immediately feels a sadness creep into her chest. "This is going to be hard, Bill. I've never been good at goodbyes."

Bill sits down at the table across from Susan. There is no one else in the kitchen area. "You have done some incredible work here, Susan. You should be proud of how far you've come. I've set you up with a therapist in the Day Program, as we discussed in our last session. When they discharge you tomorrow, one of the nurses will review all of that, including your medications and outpatient ECT appointments. It has been my pleasure to work with you. I wish only the best for you." He smiles at Susan, the corners of his eyes crinkling with his genuine happiness for her.

"I don't even know what to say, Bill. I feel like you saved my life. And me and Paul, you saved our marriage. I know I wouldn't have gotten to this point without you. 'Thank you' doesn't seem like enough."

"You saved yourself, Susan. Don't forget how strong you are. Never forget that." Bill stands up and squeezes Susan's shoulder. "I've got to get going. I've got a flight to catch. Take care of yourself."

"I will. Merry Christmas, Bill."

"Merry Christmas, Susan. Be well."

Susan turns back to her crackers and milk as Bill leaves the room. She almost expects herself to tear up after saying goodbye to Bill. But instead, a slow smile spreads across her face. I made it, she thinks. I went through hell and back. But I made it.

It is Christmas Eve day. Susan has been home for two days, and it seems like forever since she was a patient in the psychiatric unit. She is sitting on the living room floor, Ginger snuggled up against her and snoring contentedly, surrounded by boxes, tissue paper, wrapping paper, and ribbon.

Thankfully, she had already purchased several gifts for Paul and hid them in the upstairs closet before she was hospitalized. Christmas music is playing on the CD player, and the smell of gingerbread wafts through the house as Susan has been on a baking frenzy since yesterday.

"Wow, what's all this?" Paul glances into the living room as he comes down the stairs, a grin on his face when he sees Susan happily wrapping gifts.

"Oh, don't look!" Susan says, startled. "These are for you."

"Okay, I'll keep my eyes closed and try to make my way to the kitchen. It smells delicious in here."

"Gingerbread," Susan replies absentmindedly, tugging at some ribbon on a large wrapped box. "I'm going to make homemade whipped cream to go on it. I know you love that."

"I do love that. And I love you. Come into the kitchen so I can give you a good morning kiss before going over to the shop."

"You have to go in to work today? I was hoping we could spend the day together."

"Just a half day, Suzie, then I'll be home. You'd be surprised at how many tools I sell on Christmas Eve; wives who've waited until the last minute before realizing their husbands aren't going to tell them what they want for Christmas." Paul chuckles, then asks, "Will you be all right at home by yourself until I get back? I have my cell phone, so I'm just a phone call away if you need me." He looks over at her, a concerned expression spreading across his face.

"Yup, I'll be fine," she replies, standing up and walking into the kitchen as bits of wrapping paper fall off her lap. "And I've got Ginger here with me. She won't let me get into too much trouble."

Paul pulls her into his arms. "Seriously, though, have you taken your meds this morning? Are you feeling depressed or sad? I'll stay if you need me."

Susan wiggles out of his arms and takes his face in her hands. "I'm good, Honey, I am. Stop worrying about me and go to the shop. I promise I will call you if I start to feel unsafe." She looks into Paul's serious brown eyes, smiles, and kisses him softly.

She returns to her wrapping after Paul leaves for work. Susan loves that Paul put up the Christmas tree and decorated it. The little white lights cast a warm and joyful glow from the corner of the room where the tree stands. She is excited about the holiday, excited for her and Paul's Christmas Eve tradition of homemade gingerbread and whipped cream while they each open up one gift from the other. And then tomorrow is Christmas Day!

Her sister Lizzie called last evening to ask if it would be all right for her and her husband to bring dinner mid-afternoon on Christmas Day. So it will be just the four of them, and Ginger. Lizzie had not been to see Susan when she was an inpatient because of Lizzie's work schedule. "I've been so worried about you," Lizzie said repeatedly during their phone call yesterday. "I just need to see you and see that you're doing good, as long as it's not too much for Justin and me to come over on Christmas. I don't want to add more stress or anything."

"No, not at all," Susan had replied. "We would love to spend the holiday with you guys. If you're bringing dinner, I'll be in charge of desserts. I promise it's not too much. You know how I love this holiday." She ended with a smile, hoping the happiness in her voice concealed the slight anxiety beginning to settle in the pit of her stomach. Lizzie and her husband, Justin, would be the first "real" people she would see since her suicide attempt, hospitalization, and ECT treatments. How much have I changed through all of this? she thought to herself as she ended the call. Who is the person the world sees now? And who is the person I *want* the world to see now?

Winter has passed, and it is the first warm spring day in

April. Susan is delighted to be heading out the door to her morning horseback riding lesson, a gift from Paul this past Christmas. She stoops to give Ginger a pat on the head before walking down the pathway to her car. Crocuses look up at her from the flower garden, deep yellows and purples. Susan smiles to herself.

These past few months have not been easy. She's not going to lie to herself. After much discussion with her therapist, Susan had decided not to continue the ECT treatments on an outpatient basis. "They do a number on my memory," she told the therapist. "I'm doing so much better, staying on my meds, coming to my weekly appointments. I'd like to see where this goes before continuing any head zapping. I promise I'll reconsider if I start feeling suicidal again." Her therapist had reluctantly agreed.

She steers her car down the dirt lane that leads to the stables. There is not another soul out on the roads. The COVID-19 virus has been relentlessly marching across country after country around the world, leaving grief, confusion, and hostility in its wake. Susan still cannot believe that the U.S. presidential candidates are using this disease as a poker chip on their way to the presidency. These are people's lives, she thinks to herself; people are terrified. It's no game.

Susan has recently been helping part-time at the COVID testing drive-through center under an enclosed tent outside the local hospital. She has seen and heard firsthand the grief left behind when family members and friends have been taken too soon by the COVID-19 virus. She has seen and heard firsthand the fear in people's minds as they roll down their car windows to allow a healthcare worker dressed in full protective gear to approach them and collect their swab sample. The general public doesn't know who to believe or what to think. There are so many theories floating around. She tries to reassure people the best she can as she works through long shifts with other nurses from the hospital.

Susan steps out of her car and waves to Bridget, the stable's owner and her riding instructor, as she pulls the loops of her facemask over her ears. Riding lessons are in the outdoor arena, and as long as students wear masks, Bridget allows lessons to continue.

"I've got your girl, Lady, all tacked up and waiting for you," Bridget calls to Susan as she and a beautiful chestnut mare walk over to the gate of the outdoor arena. "Here she is," Bridget pronounces as she hands the reins to Susan.

Susan smiles through her mask as she takes the reins and gently strokes Lady's soft neck. "Hello, sweet girl," she whispers into Lady's ear. "Ready for our ride this morning?" Lady lowers her head and softly gazes into Susan's eyes.

"You know she only does that to you, right?" asks Bridget laughingly as she watches the interaction. "A mare doesn't give her heart to just anyone, but when she does, it's forever."

"Oh, she just knows that I have a carrot waiting for her when the lesson is over," Susan teases back, mounting into the saddle as she and Lady begin their lesson.

When the formal riding instruction is over, and as Bridget re-enters the barn to muck out the horses' stalls, Susan asks if she and Lady can go out for a hack through the fields to cool off after their hard work together.

"Of course you can," replies Bridget with a smile as she disappears into the barn.

Susan and Lady head out through an open gate in the back pasture. The sun is shining, the birds are chirping, and the tree buds are just about to burst into full leaves. Susan leans slightly forward in the saddle, and Lady immediately cocks an ear back toward her rider.

"It's okay, go ahead, girl," Susan whispers as Lady picks up an easy canter. The path through the field winds gently up a hill, and when they reach the top, Lady slows to a walk and then to a halt; she and Susan take in the view of the valley below them. Susan allows the reins to lengthen through her fingers as Lady bends her long, graceful neck to nibble the bright green clover. Susan smiles. This, she thinks to herself, is heaven on earth.

Later that afternoon, Susan has returned home and is turning over some soil in the small flower bed in the front yard. Ginger is busy rolling in the grass, all four paws up in the air and a silly doggy smile on her face. Susan's cell phone rings. She quickly pulls off her gardening gloves and reaches for the phone in her back pocket. It's her sister.

"Hey, Lizzie, how are you?"

"We're good," her sister replies.

"We're good? What does that mean?" Susan is curious as to Lizzie's word choice.

"Well, there's something I, we, Justin and I, want to tell you. We want you to be the first to know."

"Oh, and what's that?" Susan asks inattentively as she scratches Ginger's soft belly.

"We're pregnant!" Lizzie blurts out. "I confirmed it last week at my doctor's office. I'm about eight weeks along. I just can't believe it! We're so excited! I haven't told Mom and Dad yet. Just you. You're the first one." Lizzie's voice rises with enthusiasm as she carries on her monologue.

Susan has trouble making out what her sister says after the word "pregnant." Her hearing becomes fuzzy, and she is suddenly nauseous. Her breathing comes fast and shallow. Oh, my God, this isn't happening, she thinks to herself as she tries to calm her breathing. "Keep it together," she says over and over to herself. "Just keep it together."

"Susan?" Her sister pauses. "Are you still there?"

"Yes. Still here," she speaks into the phone. Susan is aware of the world shrinking away in front of her.

"Isn't this exciting?" her sister asks again, clearly expecting more from Susan.

"Yes. It is. Exciting." Susan is beginning to hyperventilate. She has got to get off this call.

"Is everything all right?" Lizzie asks. "You don't sound like yourself."

"It's allergies," Susan lies to her sister. "Awful allergies. Let me call you back." She hangs up the call with her sister and quickly dials Paul at work.

Paul answers on the second ring. "Hey, Suzie. Everything okay?"

"No." She manages to pull in a deep breath of air. "No. I need you," another deep breath, "to come home."

"What? What happened?"

Susan can hear Paul's voice coming through the receiver of her cell phone, which has slipped out of her hand and lies on the ground beside where she has collapsed.

Paul's pickup truck tires squeal on the pavement as he flies into the driveway and jumps out of the vehicle. He sees Suzie seated on the front steps, her head in her hands, Ginger sitting beside her, staring up into Susan's face, worried.

"Oh, my God, Suzie! Are you all right? What happened?" Paul rushes to her side, kneeling on the bottom step, and peers into Susan's face.

"Lizzie," she answers meekly.

"Lizzie? Did something happen to Lizzie? Suzie, what happened to Lizzie?"

Susan lifts her face out of her hands, eyes swollen from crying, a small scratch on her forehead from where she landed in the grass when she fell. "She's pregnant."

"Oh, that's gr—" Paul starts, then stops and catches himself. "Oh, Suzie. I'm so sorry. And she told you just now? Over the phone?"

Susan nods, clutching her stomach, and almost doubles over in her anguish.

"Wow. I can't believe she would do that. Just tell you over the phone like that." Paul's indignation is growing now. "After all you've been through."

"Paul, it's not her fault. She doesn't know what I've been through. What I'm still going through. She's excited. She didn't do it on purpose. It just caught me off guard. It's hard enough when a friend tells me she's pregnant, but this is my own sister. It's just really hard."

"Oh, Suzie." Paul reaches his hand up to stroke the side of her face. "C'mere," and he pulls her to him, kissing the top of her head.

In a moment, Paul pushes away from Susan. "Wait right here. Let me get you some water."

"And a tissue."

"And a tissue," he smiles.

Paul has been gone for more than a few minutes when he finally reappears with a glass of ice water in one hand and a box of tissues in the other. "Here," he offers.

Susan takes a long, slow drink of water. "What were you doing in there?"

"You feel up for a little ride? I have something that I think will make you smile. A surprise."

"A surprise? What kind of surprise?"

"One that will make you smile. Now let's get Gingy girl in the house, and then I'm going to take you somewhere."

They climb into the cab of Paul's truck, and he slowly backs out of the driveway. They drive through town and turn down a long, winding dirt road.

"Hey, wait! You're taking me to the barn? That's the surprise?" Susan asks, a little bewildered.

"Well, sort of. You'll just have to wait and see," Paul replies with a mysterious grin as they turn off the road and onto the bumpy driveway to the barn.

Bridget greets Paul and Susan at the door of the barn. She, too, is wearing a big grin.

Susan stops and looks at both Paul and Bridget. "What's going on here, you two? I feel like you're in cahoots together."

There is a soft nicker from one of the stalls farther down the aisleway. Susan looks up at the familiar noise. "Lady! What's she doing inside on such a nice afternoon?"

"Why don't you go down and find out," says Bridget, as she and Paul turn to follow Susan.

"What's this on her door?" Susan asks, opening an envelope, addressed to her and taped to Lady's stall door. She reads aloud, "Dear Susan—You always bring me carrots, and you know all the spots I love to be brushed. You are my favorite person to go out for rides in the field with. We make a great pair. I'm yours. Love, Lady and Paul."

Susan's hand flies to her mouth. She drops the note on the barn floor and rushes into the stall to hug Lady. She turns to look at Paul, tears in her eyes and a huge smile on her face. "She's really mine?"

"She really is, Suzie."

"When did you plan all of this?" Susan looks from Paul to

Bridget.

"Oh, it's been in the works for a couple of months now," Bridget interjects.

"I was going to wait until next month, Mother's Day, and do it then," Paul says sheepishly, "but I think today was the perfect day."

"Is that what took you so long when you went in to get me a glass of water at the house earlier?"

"Yup. I called Bridget and asked her if we could make this happen today."

"And of course I said yes. I must confess, I wrote the note, not Paul or Lady."

"You guys..." Susan is at a loss for words, her heart replete with joy, and buries her face in the mare's chestnut mane.

Part II

Chapter 16

Hillary

Spring sunlight streams through the open windows to Hillary's bedroom, splashing across her face. Her eyes still closed, she turns to face its soft warmth. She can hear the twittering of birds from the treetops outdoors and for a moment, she's confused; no sounds of children's footsteps pounding down the hallway, loud voices as they clamber down the stairs, no sounds of traffic buzzing by on the road outside her window. And wait, is that the faint tolling of church bells in the distance?

Hillary opens her eyes and smiles slightly. Ahhh, it all comes back to her. She's in her antique brass bed, surrounded by puffy pillows and a warm white comforter. She reaches out one arm from beneath the covers, and her hand connects to the silky fur of her sweet kitty, Athena, curled in a ball on the pillow next to Hillary's head. She reaches her other arm from under the covers, stretches, and yawns. The smell of percolating coffee wafts into her nose. Time to get up and greet the day. She throws back the comforter and sits on the edge of her bed.

The wood floor is cold beneath her bare feet. It's still early in the season, and the nights are cool while the days are warm. Hillary loves this kind of weather, perfect for sleeping. She gazes around the room at all of her things, pieces of furniture she's recently collected while treasure hunting at tucked-away antique shops in the area. A new hobby. A new home.

As she makes her way down the creaky wooden staircase to her kitchen, Hillary finds herself filled with a new sense of purpose. She has left her old life behind, moved to a small rural town in New Hampshire, and is starting over. Beginning her life anew as the mother of a stillborn son, as a single woman who was able to leave what turned out to be an abusive relationship, as a leader in her computer firm with multiple foreign accounts, as a homeowner of a little cottage built over two hundred years ago and nestled in the countryside.

Hillary pours herself a mug of strong black coffee and gazes out the kitchen window to the back of her property. It's a small plot, easy to manage, surrounded by a forest on two sides and an old stone wall on another. The road past the front of her house is long, winding, out of the way, occasionally traveled. Some days, she feels like she's hiding out here. Other days, she relishes the peace this house affords her: the gentle sunlight, the quiet breezes, the deepness of the woods behind her. Not where she imagined herself if someone had asked her a year ago.

Her cell phone rings, and Hillary startles, then reaches over to the counter where it's vibrating. "Good morning, Joanie. How is life in the fast lane?"

"Good morning yourself," responds her friend. "Just checking in on you, out there in the wilderness. How are things?"

"Things are things. I'm doing good, Joanie. Trying my best to move on, you know. I have not forgotten about losing Schuyler, but I'm moving on with him always in my heart. Trying to identify as a woman, a mother, who lost a child and a partner. Because when I left Peter, I lost that, too. Someone recovering from all that and trying to emerge from the other side." Hillary pauses, then adds, "That probably sounds corny, doesn't it?"

"Corny? No. Strong, wise, determined? Yes," replies her friend. "You amaze me every day, Hill. Not too many women I know could pull themselves out of the tragedy you experienced, look to the horizon, and move on. You've got a strength I will never have. That much I can tell you. You, Sweetie, are a rare breed."

"God, you make me sound like a horse, Joanie. For heaven's sake! But thank you. You know I couldn't have gotten through the loss of Schuyler without you. And I wouldn't be where I am, literally where I am here in my little house in New Hampshire, without you. I couldn't ask for a better friend." A breath, and then, "When will you have some time to come and visit me? The house is so cute now that I've got it all set up. I'd love for you to come out some weekend and stay with me."

"Oh, my gosh, let's try and get something on the calendar. I'd love to spend a long weekend at your place! See you and your pony. Speaking of which, how is Calypso doing at her new barn? It's been, what, almost four months or so since you moved her? I miss riding with you, Girl."

Hillary pauses to reflect before answering her friend. Once she had finally realized that her and Peter's lives were never, ever going to go back to what they had been before the birth and death of Schuyler, she was gripped by the strongest impulse to get out, get away, and move on. An old friend from college had inherited her grandfather's horse farm up in the hills of New Hampshire. Without much forethought, Hillary had reached out to Bridget to inquire about the possibility of boarding Calypso there. Her college friend had been more than receptive and was even able to provide a lead on a couple of houses for sale in the area. Hillary couldn't believe how determined, how assured, and how utterly calm she had been, putting all of this in place. Putting all this distance between herself and her old life in place.

"Oh, you know Calypso, as long as she has a large paddock to run around in and a pile of fresh hay, she's a happy girl."

"How is the new barn? Are you liking it?"

"It's different, I'll say that. No indoor riding ring. Fewer boarders. It's quiet, but the care of the horses is great, and I've met some nice people at the new barn. There's this one woman, she's a little older than me. She's also a boarder. Has a beautiful Morgan mare named Lady. She makes tea out of loose-leaf herbs for her horse!"

"She what? Does her horse drink the tea?"

Hillary laughs. "Well, yes. After it cools. It's for the horse's stomach. Apparently, Lady is prone to ulcers. She's earthy-crunchy, this woman. Loves to trail ride, be out in nature, collect crystals. You know I love all that stuff."

"I know you love herbal tea. I'll give you that." Her friend laughs with her. "But I've never known you to ride Calypso outside a riding ring. You think you'll go trail riding with this woman and her horse?"

"I just might," replies Hillary matter-of-factly. "It's the new me, you know. One never can guess what I'll get into next."

"What's that supposed to mean?" Joan is suspicious.

Hillary pauses again, gathering her thoughts. Choosing her words, she replies, "I've been thinking, Joanie..."

"Oh, I don't like the sound of that," her friend interrupts.

"No. Just listen. I don't think Schuyler is supposed to be my only child in this lifetime."

"Oh, Lord, don't tell me you've been reading more about past lives and future lives and all that stuff because you know I don't understand all that gobbledy-gook."

"I know you're not into that line of thinking, Joanie, and that's all right. But I believe there is a reason Schuyler came into my life, even briefly. I think he isn't the only one, though."

"The only one what?"

Hillary gently places her empty coffee mug in the sink, cradling the phone in the crook of her neck as she slices off a piece of banana bread she made last evening. "The only child I'm supposed to have." There, she said it. It was out there.

"Listen, Sweetie, you are just getting yourself back on track after a horrible, make that a couple of horrible, major life events. Give it some time. You will meet someone again who undoubtedly will want to have a child, or children, with you."

Hillary swallows her bite of banana bread. Too sweet, she thinks to herself and makes a mental note to add less sugar to her recipe next time. "That's just it. I can totally see myself having another child. I absolutely cannot see myself in another relationship any time soon. If ever."

"Hey." Joan's voice is soft, a little patronizing, still loving. "You don't have to decide anything today. It is a gorgeous Sunday morning. I'm off to have a riding lesson on my little spitfire in a few minutes. Give your pony some kisses from me. And be careful if you go out trail riding. Jeez, I worry about you!"

Hillary smiles into the phone. The big sister she never knew she needed. "I love you, too, Joanie. Talk soon." She ends the call and places her cell phone on the kitchen table.

Looking down, Hillary momentarily watches Athena making slow loops around her feed dish, loudly purring.

"Okay, Princess, breakfast is coming. You're not very subtle, you know," she murmurs with a smile.

It is later than Hillary had planned by the time she drives down the rutted dirt roadway to the barn, and the four parking spaces in front of the riding ring are already taken. She pulls her little red Subaru up behind her friend's pickup truck in the driveway by the farmhouse. Bridget won't mind, Hillary assures herself as she opens the car door and is practically run over by Bridget's hound-mix puppy.

"Roscoe, down!" she hears a voice shouting from inside the barn. Hillary turns and looks up as Bridget jogs out to take Roscoe by the collar. "Sorry about that. I know you're a cat person." Bridget says, a little breathless, as she hugs her former college roommate. "You're in luck today, though. I think I have a fix for that." Bridget's eyes twinkle as she steps back from Hillary, still holding onto the bouncing, panting puppy.

"A fix for what?" Hillary is momentarily confused.

"Oh. I should be more clear. For the cat lovers among us," she says with a big smile. "An old tabby cat has been hanging around the barn since the snow melted. He's a little on the skinny side. And one of his ears is torn. Looks like he might have been a gangster in another lifetime!" She laughs again. "The ladies have decided we need to keep him. And what can I say? I'm in desperate need of a good mouser."

"Is he feral?" Hillary wonders out loud.

"He seems to like a warm lap and a few pats. But don't let him fool you. He will start purring madly while you scratch his head, and then out of nowhere, he will go on the attack and get you with his claws."

Hillary falls in step with her friend as they make their way through the muddy lot and toward the barn, Roscoe leaping ahead of them chasing a butterfly. "Oooh, sounds like my kind of guy," she says cheerily, "the independent sort."

"Never easy to find in these trying times," jokes Bridget. They both giggle.

Hillary's eyes have just adjusted to the dimmer light in the stable when she sees her new friend, Susan, dash by her and bang through the tack room door.

"Morning, Hillary!" Susan calls breathlessly as she makes her way by. "Sorry, in a rush. Gotta get some antiseptic wash and a Band-Aid. Gangster-kitty strikes again!"

"Oh, God," moans Bridget. "Who did he get this time?"

Susan replies from behind the door, where she is rustling through her trunk of horse things to find her first-aid kit, "He got Meghan, poor kid. She was innocently petting him, and he turned on her. I hope he's up to date on his shots. Little bastard!"

Hillary looks back toward the aisleway in the barn to see a teenage girl, red hair pulled back in a braid, following Susan into the room filled with saddles and bridles. Hillary smiles at the young girl. "Good thing we've got a resident nurse here at the barn." The girl gives Hillary a quick smile in return.

"Yes, I'll be hanging out my shingle later today. Bumps, bruises, cuts, I can fix them right here in our little tack room. No charge," calls Susan as she examines Meghan's scratched hand. "I'm happy to offer talk therapy as well," she laughs, "but there is a charge for that!"

Everyone chuckles. Therapy, thinks Hillary, now that's the best part of a barn full of ladies and their horses. That and the friendships we form. Strong, warm, life-time friendships. Suddenly, she misses having her friend Joan to ride with.

Bridget notices Hillary's somber eyes and reaches out a hand to rub her shoulder. "Hey," she says gently. "Your girl is out in her paddock waiting for you. All the ponies are spicy today in the spring air. You may want to work her in the long-lines before you get in the saddle. Just a word to the wise!"

"Duly noted." Hillary returns from her wistfulness. She strides down toward the back set of barn doors, inhaling deeply the familiar scent of sweet feed, pine shavings, and saddle oil as she walks past the horse stalls. Just as she exits the barn, she catches a quick flash of the tabby cat running back into the barn, a dead mouse dangling from his mouth.

"Ahh, so you must be the little rascal they're all talking about." She pauses to watch the tabby. "Nice job with the mousing, Sir." And she heads to the paddocks out behind the barn, calling to Calypso.

The mare looks up from her hay pile as soon as she hears the sing-song cadence of Hillary calling her name. She starts toward the paddock gate at a trot, then breaks into a canter, throwing a few bucks along the way and sliding to a stop as she reaches her nose to nuzzle Hillary's outstretched hand.

"Mmmm, you are full of it today, silly girl." Hillary reaches up to caress the horse's strong, elegant neck. "Let's get you brushed, tacked up, and put you to work today. Get some of that energy out of your system." The mare lowers her head, allowing Hillary to place the halter over her nose and ears.

Susan has her horse, Lady, on the cross ties at the other end of the barn, busily currying the horse's chestnut coat. A cloud of dust hovers around Susan's head from her vigorous grooming.

Hillary laughs as she sets up Calypso on another set of cross ties, opens her brush box, and begins her grooming routine. "Looks like your girl must have rolled in the mud," she calls to Susan. "I can barely see your face through all that dried-up dirt and dust!"

Susan turns toward Hillary and gives a slight cough to clear her throat. "She's like a dirt magnet, my girl. I groom her regularly, and as soon as I turn her back out again, she will happily find any patch of mud she can and roll in it until she's filthy." Susan smiles at her new friend. "Hey, Lady and I are going for a ride up through the fields, if you'd like to join us. We can keep our pace at a walk if your girl is feeling her oats in this springtime weather."

Hillary notes the expectant look in Susan's eyes. Reluctantly, she replies, "Maybe another day. Calypso was bucking and prancing on her way across the paddock just now. I'm not sure how she'll do out on the trail today. I think it's probably best if I school her in the ring. You know, somewhere surrounded by fencing!" She hopes she has not offended her new friend, who has already asked her several times if she and Calypso would like to go out on a trail ride. She suddenly offers, "I've honestly never been much of a trail rider. I've only ridden my girl outside the ring a couple of times. To tell you the truth, I'm a bit of a chicken when it comes to trail riding. Lions and tigers and bears, you know?"

"I totally get you, and no worries," calls Susan who has returned to Lady and is placing the saddle on her back and tightening the girth. "It's not for everyone. I really think you would love it, though. The trails are beautiful here. The fields. The woods."

"No, I want to. Sometime. It's good to get out of your comfort zone every once in a while."

"Don't I know it." Susan leads Lady out of the barn by her bridle. "It's the only way to reach for the stars."

Hillary watches out the barn door as Susan and Lady trot past the paddocks, gathering speed as they canter up the hill and disappear into the woods beyond.

"Someday," she whispers to Calypso as she adjusts the mare's leather bridle. "Someday, we will be off and chasing after the stars, too."

Chapter 17

Susan

A light but constant drizzle is pelting the kitchen windows as Paul pushes through the door, a panting, muddy-footed Ginger close on his heels. "I always thought it was 'April showers bring May flowers,'" he says to Susan as he scoops up the wiggling dog to wipe off her feet. "What do May showers bring?"

"Pilgrims. Oh, wait, June flowers, I guess," answers Susan, preoccupied with soaping and rinsing the breakfast dishes in the sink.

"Are you still going to the barn to ride with your friend this morning? The Weather Channel says the rain isn't going to let up until this evening. You guys will get soaked." He gently sets Ginger down, kicks off his boots, walks up behind Susan, and kisses the back of her neck. "We could stay home today. Just the two of us...what with all this rain?" He grins.

Susan dries her hands on a dish towel and turns into Paul's embrace, "I would love to, Honey, but I already texted Hillary. We're going to give the ponies a spa day today and then clean our saddles and bridles. We decided to bring crackers, cheese, and a little sparkling water to the barn, and snack while we clean the mud off our tack."

"I guess I'm okay being stood up for pony spa day," Paul replies, pretending to be dramatically offended. "I've got to get going on some stuff in the basement anyway."

"How can you even find anything in the basement?" Susan laughs. "It's so cluttered with all your tools and half-started projects. Do you even know what you're working on?"

Paul pulls away from Susan and smiles at her. "Why, yes, I do. I plan to do some organizing this morning and then build you those window boxes you've been asking for. We should be able to get them up and planted in time for Memorial Day."

"Oh, that does sound like a worthy project. Carry on, my wonderful husband. Will you be sure to take Gingy out while I'm at the barn? I don't know how long I'll be there this afternoon."

Paul nods. "Yup, of course. Hopefully, the window boxes will be put together by the time you come home. If not done and painted."

"Thanks, Honey." Susan is organizing a pile of cheeses and an assortment of cracker boxes on the kitchen counter. She chooses several and throws them into a large lunch cooler, along with a bag of freshly washed grapes and a couple of bottles of seltzer. She looks up at Paul, who is still watching her. "What?"

"Oh, nothing. Just you. I love watching how happy you are when you get ready to go to the barn."

Susan returns his smile. "I do love it there. I'm never not happy being around the horses." She tosses a few wrapped chocolates on top of the other items, closes the lunch cooler, gives Paul a peck on the cheek, and bends to give Ginger a pat on the head.

"Be a good girl," she says to Ginger, "and keep Daddy out of trouble while I'm gone."

"Bye, Sweetheart," Paul says to Susan's back as she shuts the mudroom door behind her.

The driveway to the barn is full of muddy puddles as Susan navigates to the parking area. It has been such a wet spring, raining most of April and now into May. She hasn't gotten to ride Lady as much as she'd like to but has instead gotten to know her new friend Hillary better, as they seem to have similar work schedules and tend to be at the barn at the same time. Susan notices Hillary's red car is not parked in front of the barn. She's late as usual, Susan thinks to herself and admonishes herself, recognizing that she is the exact opposite, always ten minutes early to any planned event. She gets out of her car, and her barn boots sink to her ankles in oozing brown muck. "Delightful," Susan says under her breath as she pulls her hood over her head and marches into the barn.

She hears a few quiet nickers from the horses when she opens the front barn doors. The barn is dark and damp as Susan breathes in her first scents of hay, old wood, and horsehair. She lets out a long breath, feeling any tension release from between her shoulder blades. "Good morning, ponies," she calls down the aisle, making her way to Lady's stall.

Lady's head reaches out when Susan pulls back the stall door, the mare's soft muzzle aiming for her coat pocket. She laughs softly and kisses Lady's forehead. "Yes, I do have a carrot in there for you, spoiled pony." She holds one end of the carrot out as Lady crunches the other end, her deep brown eyes looking directly into Susan's. "You do know your way right into my heart, don't you," she murmurs to the mare, holding Lady's gentle gaze.

From down the partially lit aisleway, Susan hears a hearty, "Hello, Friend! Where are you?" as Hillary enters and makes her way to the tack room with a couple of bulky boxes and bags.

Susan pats Lady's nose, closes her stall door, and turns to her friend. "Good morning to you! Can you even believe this weather? At the rate we're going, we'll be lucky to get out and ride by June. Good grief." She reaches out to her friend and gives her a light hug. "It'll be fun to spoil the ponies today, though," Susan concedes. "What's all this stuff you brought?"

Hillary dumps her armload of items onto the wooden table in the tack room, straightens up, and smiles. "I started looking through my cupboards for snacks to bring to our little two-person party here and realized I need to clean out my cabinets more often!" She lifts a small glass jar. "Fig jam, for example. Perfect to go with our crackers and cheese." Setting down the jam, Hillary opens a metal tin for Susan to see inside. "A half-eaten tin of butter cookies."

"So perfect," agrees Susan. "I brought some cheddar and a little bit of leftover Brie. Oh, and some fancy chocolates for after. We have a veritable feast on our hands."

"Yum. I can't wait. Let's leave our food here and get out our stuff to groom Calypso and Lady." Hillary reaches for an unopened brown paper lunch bag amidst the other goodies on the table. "And this," she smiles as she holds up the paper bag, "is for Rascal."

"The barn cat? You brought the barn cat snacks, too? You're so funny, my friend."

Hillary steps out the door and into the aisleway, Susan following behind her. "Of course I did. You know I can't help myself when it comes to cats."

"Hill, if you keep feeding him fancy canned food, he's never going to take his job as a mouser seriously!"

"That may be," replies Hillary, making soft kissing noises as she scrapes the canned food into a little bowl on the floor at the far end of the barn, "but poor Rascal looks like he's had a rough life. He deserves to be spoiled a little, don't you think?"

"I suppose we all do, for that matter." Susan watches quietly as the timid tabby shoots out from behind a pile of stacked hay bales and commences eating the cat food with gusto.

Hillary looks over at her friend, a big grin on her face. "See that? Progress. He'll be purring in my lap in no time."

"Or you'll be in the ER needing stitches and a tetanus shot after he attacks the hand that feeds him." Susan chuckles and shakes her head. "C'mon, let's start grooming."

The two friends gather their brush boxes and other grooming supplies, take their mares out of their stalls, and begin currying and brushing the two impatient horses.

"My, but these two are feisty today!" Hillary exclaims as Calypso paws the barn floor with her front hoof.

"What do you expect? They've been cooped up for the better part of three days now with this monsoon we've been having. These girls need to get outside and run around, kick up their heels." Susan stands up from cleaning Lady's hooves and straightens her back. "I wonder if Bridget would mind if we just let them loose for a few minutes in the outdoor ring? The footing is sandier, so it's less muddy there than in their paddocks."

"Good idea. Let's ask her." Hillary has taken her cell phone from her back pocket and is already texting the barn owner.

Susan walks over to Hillary, both staring at the cell phone while waiting for Bridget's reply.

A loud ding! Hillary squints to read the text aloud to Susan. "Okay to let the girls out so long as they don't get too crazy out there and tear up the footing in the ring."

"Let's do this!" Susan is already unclipping Lady from the cross ties, ready to lead her outdoors.

"They're going to get filthy out there, you know," sighs Hillary. "All of our hard work..."

"They will be so much happier, though, once they can get out and stretch their legs a bit. We can brush the mud off them when we bring them back in. Let's go before the rain picks up again." Susan continues to the barn's back door, leading a prancing Lady beside her.

The two horses are full of antics, bucking and running as soon as they're let loose in the outdoor ring, chasing one another, snorting and pawing at the wet sand. "Oh, my God, the two of them!" Susan laughs out loud.

"The shenanigans!" cries Hillary, laughing just as heartily as the two mares blast by her and Susan, galloping hard, ears pricked, and tails streaking out behind them.

By the time Hillary and Susan have corralled the steaming horses, have led them back to their stalls and brushed off what mud they could, the two friends are as muddy as their equine companions, if not more so.

"C'mon," calls Hillary, "let's get into the tack room where it's warmer and see if we can dry off while we have our crackers and cheese."

"I'm right behind you. I might even take off my boots and let my wet socks dry out by the heater. If you don't mind the smell of muddy barn socks, that is!"

"Not at all, my friend," Hillary replies, sitting in one of the wooden chairs at the small table, shrugging off her wet raincoat as she does. "I'm starving. Let's eat!"

Once her boots are removed and set out to dry, Susan opens her lunch cooler and begins arranging the crackers, cheese, and grapes. Hillary does the same with her food packages, and the two sit down to snack and chat. Hillary is curious about Susan's life outside of the barn; she doesn't know much about her new friend besides her being a nurse at a local health clinic.

"You're a nurse, right? What kind of nursing do you do?"

Susan looks up. She has started working one of the buckles on Lady's leather bridle, trying to loosen it in an effort to scrub it clean first and then oil the soft leather. "Yeah, a family medical practice. Nothing too exciting. How about you? You work from home, is that right?"

"I do. Yes. I'm a consultant for a computer company based out of Albany, New York. I started working in their corporate office, and then when COVID hit, we all ended up working from home. When I moved out here, they wanted me to stay on with them, so they allowed me to continue working from home."

"Hey, that's a nice deal. How long have you been doing that kind of work?" Susan gives a final tug to the buckle and is able to pull the leather out of the fastener. She begins diligently rubbing saddle soap into it with a soft rag.

"Oh. Gosh. Well, there's a long story..." Hillary sighs and looks up from the leather girth she's polishing.

Susan senses Hillary's pause, stops scrubbing, and glances at her friend. She cannot read Hillary's expression; a look of melancholy, perhaps, resignation even? Susan slightly smiles at Hillary, "I've got all day, if you want to share." She looks back to the bridle in her lap and continues cleaning.

In the space Susan has created, Hillary begins. "I grew up out that way, near Albany. I lived with my stepmother and half-sister on the outskirts of the city." Hillary notices Susan is watching her again, her eyes kind and questioning. She doesn't normally open up to people about her life, the one she left behind. But she feels a comfort in this new friendship, a caring. A kindred spirit, perhaps. Hillary continues.

"My dad died when I was in middle school. He had already married my stepmother."

"Oh, I'm sorry about your dad," Susan interrupts softly. "Where was your mom? Your birth mom? Or is that too personal a question?"

"No, not at all. She died when I was very little. Cancer, I think. My dad never talked about her much. I don't really remember her."

Susan leans in toward her friend, sadness in her heart. "Gosh, that's awful, Hill. What was your stepmother like?"

"Well, when you think of the wicked stepmother in any fairy tale, Anita's like the poster child for that role!" Hillary laughs and then goes on, "I won't bore you with that whole story. Needless to say, we're not super close."

Their attention is suddenly captured by a light scratching at the tack room door. The friends look at each other questioningly. Hillary stands up, lays the leather girth she's been cleaning across her chair, and cautiously tiptoes to the door. They hear the scratching sound again. "Somebody definitely wants to come in here," she whispers and slowly turns the doorknob. As Hillary pulls the door open a crack, in pops the curious head of the barn cat.

Immediately, Hillary lowers herself to the floor and begins the soft kissing noises she makes when feeding Rascal. "Hey there, handsome kitty," she croons. "Come to join the girls in here where it's warm?" Rascal enters cautiously, his tail up, the tip flicking back and forth. He quickly strides over to Hillary's empty wooden chair, hops up, and sits across from Susan, gazing at the food on the table.

"Oh, hey there, Buddy," Susan says in a low voice. "Cheddar? Brie? What's your fancy?" And she reaches across the table to gingerly offer the tabby a chunk of cheese. Quickly, he takes it in his mouth, jumps off the chair, and dashes back out of the open tack room door to find a dark, safe place to enjoy his treasure.

"All right," Susan admits with a chuckle, "I think there's hope for him yet! How funny was that?"

"Let's leave the door open a little and see if he comes back for seconds." Hillary gets up from her crouched position on the floor and resumes her seat at the table, layering a cracker with a bit of Brie and a dab of fig jam. She tosses the entire thing into her mouth. "Mmmm. Delish!" she exclaims, licking the sugary jam off her fingers.

"So where was I," she pauses and looks at Susan, who is also creating a cracker and cheese tower to pop into her mouth.

Susan swallows her tasty creation. "Your stepmother. Albany."

"Oh, right. Yeah. Well, we didn't have a lot of money for extras, as she was a single mother and all after my dad died. I used to ride my bike to a local stable in the summers. It started as a way to get out from under her roof, igniting my passion for horses and riding. That's where I got my start. At that little backyard stable around the corner from my house. How about you? How long have you been riding?"

Susan takes a quick sip of her seltzer, thoroughly enjoying this conversation. Most of her friends are fellow nurses and don't share her horse passion. "Lady is my first horse, actually." She watches Hillary's eyebrows lift in surprise. "I used to take riding lessons as a kid but never had my own horse. My husband got her for me last year, after I started spending time riding here with Bridget."

"Oh, my God, you're so lucky to have a husband that gets your horse passion like that. Trust me, most guys don't." Hillary frowns. She's given away a little more of herself than she intended to with that statement.

"I know. I'm fortunate," Susan replies tentatively, not sure she wants to share how it came to be that Paul bought her a horse and the circumstances that led up to that.

Susan regains her composure and begins arranging another cracker and cheese combination. "So, you left Albany. Can I ask why?" She senses Hillary's hesitation, doesn't look up at her friend, and waits to see where the discussion will take them.

Hillary sits back in her wooden chair and gazes out the tack room window at the relentless raindrops sliding down the glass panes. She looks at the empty paddocks, brown with mud, the green taking over the hay fields and distant treetops. The dark woods at the edge of the hay fields. The dark woods where she hasn't ventured, but where her new friend seems to find a sense of comfort and safety that Hillary can't imagine. With some trepidation, she goes on.

Still looking out the window, Hillary continues in a far-away voice, "I had a baby. Last year. While I was living out there. His name was Schuyler. And he died. In childbirth." A hard lump forms in her throat. She can't look at her friend. There, it's out. The truth. Saying it again makes it real. Again. Hillary feels her heart rise, expand, and cave in on itself.

Susan is stunned. She had absolutely no idea. Quickly, she regains her composure and realizes she has to say something to acknowledge this confession, honor this moment, and respect what happened here. She reaches across the table and lays her hand gently on her friend's arm. "My God, Hill," she murmurs.

Hillary startles slightly at Susan's touch. It breaks her preoccupation, and she finally turns and looks away from the window into her friend's face. There is no judgment there, no pity, no question. She allows her gaze to find Susan's eyes. They look right into Hillary with an expression Hillary recognizes. It shocks her. She reads understanding in Susan's deep gaze. Hillary's heart rights itself in her chest and continues beating in its regular rhythm. Courage flows through her.

"I had hooked up with this guy at work, Peter. And we had a relationship. I got pregnant."

Susan is still, her heart aching silently for her friend. "And this Peter. He must have stayed back in New York, I'm guessing?"

"Yeah." Hillary takes in a deep breath. "We moved in together. He asked me to live with him and his two kids." She pauses and looks away again. "We were going to have a family."

There is a long silence. Susan watches her friend gather her thoughts and sees the pain flash across her face. Gently, she prompts, "But that didn't happen?"

"He is an alcoholic. He gets mean when he gets drunk—verbally. He didn't want the baby in the first place. Not really. It was all about him, you know, how this baby would be just another mouth to feed, how he had his whole life ahead of him. He blamed me. For getting pregnant. For ruining his life."

"Asshole."

Hillary laughs, allows her shoulders to relax, picks up her discarded girth, and starts vigorously oiling the dark leather. "Pretty much," she concedes.

"What about his other kids? Did they live with their mother?"

"Oh, gosh, no, they lived with us, too. Their mother was in and out of rehab. It was kind of a shit show. Once I moved in with Peter, I became like their mother. You know, cooking all of their meals, making sure they got off to school on time."

"And what did Peter do?" Susan is appalled. "He just left everything to you? And you weren't even their mother."

"Yeah, basically."

Susan sees a look of nostalgia pass across Hillary's eyes, one green, one hazel. She feels a small cavern open within her, and things shift inside. Family. Children. She has done her best to avoid these types of conversations. She gently shakes her head and offers her friend a small smile, an opening to continue. She needs to tell me this more than I don't need to hear it, Susan thinks to herself, and wills herself to remain composed, at least on the outside.

Hillary hasn't missed the change that comes over Susan, her red-rimmed eyes, her tight composure. "You okay with me telling you this?" she asks. "I don't have to. It's a lot, and I don't mean to dump it on you."

"Oh, not at all. Really. I'm here. I'm listening. I want you to tell me." She gathers herself up. "So, what happened with the baby?"

Hillary leans back in her chair. "I had a midwife. It was during COVID, and I didn't want to have my baby in the hospital. I didn't want to risk any sickness for myself or my baby."

"So, you had a home birth?"

"I did."

The nurse in Susan is curious. "And did something happen? Were you full term when you delivered?"

"I was. It was an uncomplicated pregnancy. I went into labor at home, and the midwife came. It was a hard labor. A long labor."

"How long?" Susan is all nurse now, knowing that after a certain point, medical intervention in a hospital was probably needed to save the life of this mother and her baby. She cringes inside, anticipating the rest of Hillary's story.

"Twenty-three hours." Hillary again turns her head away, reliving that long day. Wondering if the outcome would have been different had she gone to the hospital earlier in her labor.

Wondering for the thousandth time if it was her fault that Schuyler had been born dead.

Twenty-three hours! Susan thinks to herself in alarm. That's too long. Why didn't the midwife get her to a hospital sooner? She can't help but blame the midwife. She says none of this to Hillary.

Reading Susan's thoughts, Hillary goes on. "It wasn't the midwife's fault. I was set on not going to the hospital. She had wanted me to go earlier on in my labor, but I wouldn't go. I just couldn't. I wanted Peter there. And he wasn't. And I had heard of women losing their babies because of blood clots from COVID-19. Losing their own lives even." She takes a shuddering breath.

Susan gets up from her chair at the table. Quietly, she walks around to Hillary and encircles her with both arms. This woman blames herself. "Hillary. Look at me," she says softly.

Hillary looks at Susan and sees the tears running down her cheeks.

"You didn't do this to your baby. Things happen—things we will never understand. Even the most perfect circumstances can turn out the most painful results. Tell me what happened to your baby."

"Peter finally came home. He had been out drinking at a bar." She pauses for a split second and then goes on. "We decided to go to the hospital. And when we got there, there was something wrong with the baby's heartbeat." Hillary has a lost look in her eyes, reliving her horror, her fright. "They rushed me in and did an emergency C-section. And my baby was dead."

Susan is rubbing Hillary's back. Small, gentle circles. Her heart is breaking. She holds the ripe and aching silence for her friend, feeling as if she, herself, will break at any moment. Tears stream down her face.

"They did CPR on Schuyler at my bedside to try and bring him back. For over an hour, they worked on him. And he never took a breath."

Susan gathers Hillary tightly in her arms. "Oh, Sweetie. I'm so sorry."

Hillary is weeping into Susan's body. "I never heard my baby cry," she whispers, barely audible.

The two women hold each other in this profound embrace for several long minutes, each lost in her own thoughts, her own loss, and their connection. They rock gently back and forth, two branches of the same tree, bending, dipping in the wind, righting themselves again. Deep roots. Deeper still, that they are now entwined.

A faint mewling pulls the friends apart. They look about to focus in on the sound. Hillary is the first to smile. She wipes her still-moist eyes on the sleeve of her barn jacket. "Oh, for heaven's sake, Rascal!" she admonishes the barn cat who has reappeared and is watching the two of them, "Way to steal the moment." Hillary gently gets down on the floor near the tabby, stretching out her hand. He continues to watch her. Curious. Not afraid.

Susan has also regained her composure, looks at her friend and the cat, and smiles. "Well, look at you. The cat whisperer!"

They both laugh lightly, releasing any further tremulousness in their hearts from the previous sharing. The moment remains close. Susan is the first to pick up their conversation, unsure if the timing is appropriate, but feeling it is safe all the same. She notices a sleeping voice start to rise within her, compelling her.

"You're going to think this is weird," are the words that

surprise Susan when they spill out.

"What's weird?" replies Hillary, who has managed to coax the cat onto her lap and sits, legs folded under her, on the tack room floor.

"I understand you."

Hillary looks into the face of her friend. Her visage determined, without question.

"It's not the same. But in a way, I have lost a child, too. I cannot imagine how you have picked yourself up after the loss of your baby, carried on in the world, then started over here, someplace new. But I do know what it is to carry the weight of that loss inside of you, the weight of your womb, the heart of a woman, dense and filled with sorrow."

Hillary stops scratching Rascal's ears. Her complete attention is on Susan now.

"I always wanted a child. I always knew I would have a child. Be a mother, you know?"

"I do," Hillary mutters softly, still holding Susan's gaze.

"I married my husband because he told me he would give me a baby. And then, after we got married, he took that back. He changed his mind."

"Oh, my God, Susan, that's awful! What happened?"

"I lost my mind is what happened." She peers down at her friend, sees the puzzled look on her face, and continues, "I tried to kill myself. I had to be in an inpatient psych unit for almost a month until I could figure myself out again."

"I'm so sorry." Hillary reaches up and places her hand on Susan's knee. "Did you stay with your husband?"

"I did. Most people wouldn't understand it. But I did. We went through a lot of therapy together. And I decided to stay with him, that there was enough of our relationship with each other, without having a child, to stay together. I love him with all my heart." Susan pauses and looks away as more tears well up in the corners of her eyes. "Not having a child, though, is the biggest regret I will take to my grave." Her familiar refrain.

"So I know what it's like," she continues after the briefest pause, "to have to paste on a fake smile when your girlfriends gush as they announce to you that they're pregnant. And I know what it's like to be invited to a baby shower and sit in the back of the room weeping while the expectant mother opens her shower gifts." Susan's words are a torrent, a flood of raw anguish from her broken heart. She has never felt so close to someone who absolutely understands this desperate sadness she has been living with.

Hillary gently removes Rascal from her lap, brushes herself off as she stands, and returns to her chair across from Susan. She reaches for her friend's hand. "It's so hard to carry on and live, I know."

"And I know," Susan can't stop the wave of words coming out of her, "what it's like to be left out of raising a child that you long to know and love."

Hillary is momentarily confused. "What do you mean?"

"My sister. She got pregnant. And, honestly, it nearly killed me all over again. But I rallied. Her pregnancy opened my heart to the possibility of loving a little niece or nephew. Of mothering in that way." Susan takes a deep breath and holds it in a long pause.

"And?"

Susan lets out a forceful stream of air. "I never see that baby, my nephew. Since he was born, my sister and her husband have kept to themselves and their new little family. I've often offered to see the baby and spend time with them. They never take me up on it."

"She never comes to visit you? With the baby?"

"No. They will get together for the major holidays, but that's kind of it. I don't even know that baby."

Her friend's confession takes Hillary aback. She never would have guessed, from the outside, what Susan had endured. Indeed, their stories, their sorrows, are so similar. "Did you ever talk to your sister about it? Tell her how you feel?"

"It's not like that between me and her," Susan replies, sniffling. "We've never shared stuff like that. We're both so different." Susan looks at her friend, their hands still clenched, reaching across the table. She gathers herself together and smiles weakly. "So you are not alone, Hill. I want you to know that. It's not the same thing, but I do understand you."

"And I you, my friend." Hillary returns a fragile smile.

Susan straightens up and begins gathering the cracker packages, re-wrapping the cheese parcels. She is completely unprepared for what Hillary says next.

"Without a doubt, I know that Schuyler wasn't supposed to be my only child. I plan to get pregnant again."

Chapter 18

Hillary

The Fourth of July is hot and pasty. Hillary stands in front of her open refrigerator door, relishing the feel of the cool blast of air on her face. She selects a pitcher of cold lemonade from the shelf, her favorite summer drink, and pours it over a glass of ice, then adds a slice of lemon on the side. Like I'm at a restaurant, she thinks, and walks out her back door onto the screened-in porch. A ceiling fan lazily churns the thick, humid air. She plunks down into an old wicker chair and idly picks up a novel she has been reading, but can't focus on the story, the words flitting into incomprehensible sentences in front of her on the page. "Oh, to hell with this!" she mutters, planting the open book face down on a side table. Athena, disturbed from her nap on an accompanying wicker chair, picks up her head and looks at Hillary, obviously perturbed. "Go back to sleep, Your Majesty. Your mother is just in a tizzy, is all. I guess I'm going to have to tell someone before I explode with this secret." Hillary stomps back into the house, perches on the edge of her loveseat directly in front of the air conditioner in her living room, picks up her phone and dials.

Before her friend can even offer a greeting, Hillary blurts, "Joanie, I have something to tell you."

In the brief pause before Joan can gather her thoughts and respond, Hillary hears the sounds of laughing, splashing, and the shouts of children in the background. Damn! she chides herself in that quick second. It's a holiday. Joanie is probably with family poolside today. I'm such a dork, she thinks.

"Hill! Hi. Is everything all right?" Joan is slightly out of breath.

"I am so sorry, Joanie. I totally lost track of the days. Are you at your family's pool celebrating the Fourth? I didn't mean to bother you. I can call you another time. It's nothing important."

Joan laughs into the phone. "Yes, it is the Fourth of July. Yes, I am poolside, with a drink in hand. Thank you very much! And, yes, you know you can always call me anytime, anywhere. What's going on, Girlfriend? Are you doing anything to celebrate the holiday today? Any barn picnics or anything?"

"Oh, gosh, no, nothing like that. It's pretty quiet up here in these New Hampshire hills. I think there are fireworks over the lake in town tonight, but I'm not sure I'll go. I don't really know anyone. It would look weird to show up as a single person to watch fireworks. Like I'm a stalker of some kind. A fireworks stalker!" They both chuckle.

"It's so good to hear from you, Sweetie. I feel like we've both been so busy with work and life that we haven't had a good girlfriend talk since I came out to visit you and beautiful Calypso last month. So, what's new with you? How's work? Has Peter tried to reach out to you again? The jerk!"

Hillary pushes herself deeper into her loveseat, turns down the air conditioner behind her, pulls a cushion onto her lap, and tucks her legs underneath her. Where to begin? "So, for starters, work is going really well. They gave me another damned promotion, if you can believe that."

Joan squeals on the other end of the phone. "You go, Girl! Way to show those boys how it's done!"

"As for the other...," her voice trails off.

"Peter," confirms Joan.

"Yeah, well, there's Peter. He has reached out to me a couple of times. Texting at first and then a couple of calls."

"What the hell does he want?" Joan is annoyed all over again by Peter. "Why can't he just leave you alone?"

"For one thing, we still work on the consulting team together, so it's inevitable that we have to talk to each other about work stuff." A pause.

"I'm sensing a 'but' here," Joan correctly reads the pause.

"But the last time we talked on the phone, he got all mushy and apologetic..."

"Oh, please!"

"He said he wants to get back together." The words come out in a cascade. She waits to be chastised by her friend.

"And you said no, I hope?" Joan's voice is becoming impatient.

"Of course I said no. What do you think? That I could ever go back to him? Too much has happened for that. Too much water under the bridge. Never again! Not for me. But you know what, Joanie?"

Joan's voice softens, "What, Hill?"

"It felt nice to be asked. To be thought of that way again."

"To be desired?"

"Yeah. To be desired." Hillary can hear the volume pick up behind Joan, the family holiday melee going on by the pool. "Listen. Let me let you go. We can finish catching up another time. Okay?"

Joan, who has known her friend for many years and through

many renditions, recognizes that there is something more to this phone call.

"No, I've got a few more minutes before the hot dogs and hamburgers come off the grill. What is it? Tell me."

Now that an opening has presented itself, Hillary feels at a loss as to how to begin. Her oldest friend. It shouldn't be this hard. "It happened. Again."

"Honey, you're being a little vague here. What happened? Again?"

"Me. It. I'm pregnant. Again," Hillary adds with determination.

There is the longest silence from Joan, who has one eye out for stray water balloons, which have started flying across the pool deck at her family picnic, and the rest of her attention glued to the information Hillary just spat out. Joan gathers what she hopes sounds like enthusiasm and shouts into the phone,

"Wow, Hill! So, it worked? The intrauterine insemination? It actually worked?"

Hillary has a huge smile on her face, so relieved she has finally been able to share her wonderful secret. "I know, right? There is only a ten percent chance of becoming pregnant this way, and it happened! The fertility clinic confirmed it yesterday." Her voice trembles, overflowing with the long-held tension of the past, the fragile web of hope for the future. "I've got a second chance to be a momma, Joanie."

Joan is about to open her mouth to congratulate her friend when a water balloon hits her broadside. "Ooph!" she shouts, laughing. "I just got soaked! Let me call you back later after the festivities are over. I want to hear all about it. Love you, Girl."

"Love you, too," whispers Hillary into the phone, though the call has already ended from Joan's side.

In spite of the very wet spring earlier in the year, summer in New Hampshire is hot and muggy, with little relief outdoors unless you are out first thing at dawn or last thing at twilight. Hillary finds herself standing on the patio one evening, watering the wilted tomato plants she placed in buckets, trying her hand at gardening now that she is a country girl. "You guys look like shit," she says, talking to her tomato plants. She then regrets it, remembering from some psychology class in the distant past that plants can hear you when you speak to them and respond to what you say. Quickly, she adds, "In a good way. Drink up!"

The temperature is finally comfortable in the late day air that is gently pushed across Hillary's bare arms by a soft breeze. She looks up and watches a few shadowy bats swoop and dart through the sky on their never-ending quest to feed on insects. "Go get 'em, boys," she calls. "Best mosquito control anyone could ask for!" She has put up a bat house on the south side of the garden shed in her backyard, carefully following the instructions. So far, she has never seen a bat entering or exiting the bat house. She watches the first star blink in brightness as it appears in the dimming western sky.

"I wish I may, I wish I might," Hillary speaks to the little star. "I wish for my baby to be strong and bright." Gently, her hand finds its way to her belly. Once, her hand had felt secure there, comforting the little one inside her. Now, Hillary notices a slight trembling in her fingertips. A warning, perhaps: Don't get too close to this baby. Not yet. Look what happened last time. She pulls her hand off her belly and reaches up to tuck a strand of her long black hair behind her ear. A faint sliver of the moon has appeared, looking as if it's ready for a game of chase with the little star across the darkening night sky. Twilight is so fleeting, thinks Hillary, as she gathers up her garden gloves and watering can, a brief moment between time, between worlds. She swears she can hear Schuyler's sweet baby laughter ringing in her ears.

"Good night, Schuyler," Hillary calls softly over her shoulder toward the velvety sky. She blows a soft kiss toward the little star as the screen door to her kitchen closes with a gentle creak behind her.

One cool morning in late September, Hillary is awoken by the jarring Beep! Beep! of her alarm clock. Annoyed, she reaches a hand out to her bedside table, knocking over a box of tissues as her fingers blindly search for the source of the pestering sound. She finds her mark, pushes down hard on the button on top of the clock, then sinks back into the dreaminess of her still-warm quilt. Suddenly, she pulls back the covers and jumps out of bed. "Oh shit! I have to get going! No sleeping in today." She trips over her slippers, left neatly by her bedside when she tucked herself in early last night, knowing she'd have to be up with the sun to make it to the barn this morning.

Glancing over at the alarm clock, Hillary hops on her left foot while massaging her right big toe that she stubbed. Ouch! Laughing at herself, she notes the time. Not too late, she assures herself, not as late as I usually am. She doesn't want to disappoint her timely friend Susan this morning, not with what they have planned for today: a horseback ride on the beach, something Hillary has always longed to do and never imagined she'd have the courage to attempt, along with being able to bring spicy Calypso with her.

It was Bridget, the barn owner, who had suggested a couple of months ago that the three of them—Hillary, Susan, and Bridget—load their horses into Bridget's three-horse trailer and drive across the state to one of the beaches that allow horseback riding after Labor Day, once all the regular beach-goers have returned to their respective school and work lives. At first, Hillary had politely declined; she still hadn't ridden her mare outside of the ring and had visions of Calypso galloping off into the sunset at the first sighting of a seagull, with Hillary clutching her mane for dear life.

Susan had convinced her otherwise, and slowly but surely, over the past few weeks, Hillary and Calypso had joined Susan and Lady on their hacks out and about the property surrounding the farm—first, just a gentle walk beyond the paddocks. Calypso had been "looky" but had behaved herself. And just last week, a canter up the hillside beyond the hayfields. Calypso had stretched out under the saddle, her neck long, ears pricked; Hillary felt the mare suddenly gather herself and leap into the air. She bucked several paces before Hillary could pull her back down to a walk again.

"I'm so impressed you were able to ride that!" cried Susan, she and Lady coming up at a canter several paces behind. Susan slowed her mare to a stop beside a heaving Calypso.

"I probably shouldn't risk too much more of that the further I get along in my pregnancy," panted Hillary. "That was really fun, though; I felt like I was ten again!"

The two had walked their horses slowly back to the barn, allowing the mares to nibble clover as they went. The horses had cooled considerably by the time they made it back to their stalls.

That had sealed the deal for Hillary. If she could bring Calypso back to a walk from a dead run and sit some pretty good-sized bucks, she felt she could manage to ride her on the beach. She scrubs her face and pulls her hair back into a long ponytail. Deciding it will take too much time to make her bed, she leaves Athena asleep on a pile of pillows, grabs her decaf tea, a granola bar, and an apple, and makes her way to her car and on to the barn.

Before Hillary even turns down the drive toward Bridget's, she sees the long gooseneck horse trailer attached to the farm pickup truck waiting in the parking area. Damn! Susan is already there. She had wanted to surprise her friend and get to the stable before Susan did. The best laid plans, she thinks to herself, slowing her car to a crawl in case Roscoe the puppy pulled one of his mighty-dog maneuvers, flying over the hedge by the house to chase the cars down to the barn.

Susan looks up from stowing her saddle in the horse trailer and hurries to Hillary's driver's side before Hillary can get out of her car.

Hillary puts down her window. "What? What happened?"

Susan has a serious look on her face. "Bridget's barn help called out sick this morning," she states matter-of-factly, as if that statement alone draws all possible conclusions regarding her facial expression.

Hillary is baffled. "What?"

"Her barn help. The kid's not showing up to do stalls and care for the horses today, so Bridget can't go to the beach."

Hillary's heart sinks. "Oh, I'm so bummed!" Her forlorn look prompts her friend to continue:

"But she said we can take the trailer and go, just the two of us! I've driven it before. I'm not great at it, especially backing up this beast, but I can get us there and home in one piece." Susan gazes expectantly into Hillary's face.

Hillary shrieks, jumps out of her car and hugs her friend. "My God, yes! We must still go. Let's get the horses loaded up and be on our way. Road trip!" she shouts, grabbing Susan by the arm and happily pulling her toward the barn.

As the truck and trailer carefully lumber onto the highway, Susan being an overly careful driver when hauling their two most prized possessions, she reaches over to turn down the radio knob and asks, "Are you sure it's safe for you to be riding? Does your obstetrician know what you're up to?"

Hillary cautions, "You keep your eyes on the road, my friend!" Then explains, "No, my obstetrician doesn't know what I'm up to. I, for one, am not going to tell her." A pause, and then she laughs, "And neither are you. Honestly, Susan, I wouldn't miss this for the world. It'll be all right. I rode right through my first trimester with Schuyler. Thanks for checking in, though. You're such a good nurse."

Susan smiles at that, focusing on the road ahead, not wanting to miss their exit for the beach. It's a perfect day, cool but not cold, with a bright blue sky and puffy white clouds. Truth be told, Susan wouldn't want to miss this, either, but felt she had to do her due diligence as a healthcare professional and check in with her pregnant friend. The traffic is light at this early hour, and the two chat about this and that. Susan circles back to Hillary's pregnancy. "So, are you getting excited?" Instantly, she hears her voice fall flat. God, what a dumb thing to ask, she thinks to herself.

"Hmmm. I don't know if 'excited' is the right word. I'm hopeful. I don't want to let myself get too excited, you know, just in case. I won't believe it's real until I hear my baby cry."

Susan is thoughtful for a moment, then responds, "I don't know how you're doing this, Hill, moving on like this after losing

Schuyler. You are one of the bravest women I know."

Hillary settles into her passenger seat, shifts her legs in their leather riding boots, and sips her decaf tea. "It took me a long time to process what happened with Schuyler," she starts, staring straight ahead out the windshield. Suddenly, she turns her head and asks Susan, "Do you believe in past lives?"

Susan is startled by the unexpected turn of conversation. Curious to see where it's headed, she replies matter-of-factly, "I guess. In a way. Honestly, I've never delved into too much about past lives." She gathers her thoughts, realizing she's pedaling down several tracks at the same time in her mind. "I don't not believe in past lives. How's that?"

Hillary smiles, her eyes lit up. "I do love you, my friend. Open to explore anything, even the otherworldly. I have been interested in past lives for a long time. I read this book called *Journey of Souls* when I was pregnant with Schuyler. Have you heard of it? By this guy Michael Newton."

"Nope. I can't say that I've ever read it. What's it about?" Susan's interest is piqued, and she has to force herself to focus on driving and getting them all to the beach safely. She takes a breath and slows her thoughts.

"So, he did all this research with patients. I guess he was a therapist, and he would hypnotize them and record them going back through their past lives."

"Wow. That is interesting. What did the patients tell him?"

"It was fascinating. To a one, they all had very similar experiences of their souls existing beyond what we understand as the human body and its ties to the earth." She pauses, realizing this may be a bit out-there for Susan, although imagining it is not. She can't stop, though, as her truth comes to light. Hillary continues, "Anyway, these patients described how their souls chose their particular destiny in this lifetime. Often, they had something from a past life that they had to learn, overcome, or solve, and so when they chose their host for this lifetime, it was on purpose to resolve whatever had happened in the past."

"So, you're saying we have chosen our current lives for a reason? Chosen our destiny, in a way?" Susan's brows are knit together as she puzzles this concept out.

"Yes, exactly!"

"How does that relate to Schuyler? And to you?"

"I believe," Hillary begins, "that there was a reason Schuyler came into my life. And I believe there was a reason he left it so quickly. A reason why he died."

Susan feels the tone of their discussion tipping, becoming slightly lost and frantic. "And what would that be?"

Deadpan, Hillary responds, "I must have done something in another lifetime to a child, or a baby. I must have neglected a child I had been responsible for or hurt one, or..." Her voice trails off.

Susan holds her breath and waits, sensing what is coming next.

"Or killed one."

"No. Hillary! I don't think that's how this works. Are you saying you feel like Schuyler came into your life as a—" What? She can't imagine. "As a punishment for something you did in a past life?" she spits out, incredulous that her friend would rationalize the death of her firstborn this way, and realizing, too, that Hillary continues to, and always will, in part blame herself for the death of her baby boy. Susan feels her heart tearing once more for her friend, for this tragedy. Perhaps there is no getting past that when you have carried and birthed a child, even when you have not. Any woman, any womb, carries this great universal responsibility. And with that responsibility comes the guilt of failure. Susan reaches over to find Hillary's fingers on the truck seat, squeezing them.

"I know it sounds weird, but it's the only thing that makes sense to me. It's also why I must bring another child into this world. My lesson with Schuyler was to suffer the greatest loss imaginable. My lesson with this baby," Hillary pauses to move her hand and place it on the slight rise of her stomach, "is to get it right. To do everything right this time around." She becomes silent, her eyes soft, and she has a knowing smile as she looks down toward the hand resting on her belly.

Hillary's confession flattens Susan and what she recognizes of herself in it: the guilt, the punishment, and the longing. She gathers her thoughts: "Like an amends, sort of?"

"Well, more than that." Hillary is absentmindedly rubbing small circles over the spot where her growing child is. "Like bringing new light into the world, new goodness. Being able to be the bearer of that."

"Bearing love into the places of darkness?" Susan concludes for her friend.

Hillary looks over at Susan, her eyes wet with tears, and whispers, "Yes. That."

Chapter 19

Susan

The horses are wide-eyed, their nostrils flaring as they step off the trailer, their necks high and their ears at attention. Calypso is pacing small, quick circles at the end of Hillary's lead rope. The breeze is heavier here by the ocean than at the farm, whipping up the scents of salt water, sand, and dried grass, and frothing the distant waves into crashing spires of foam. The mares have seen nothing like this in their lives, and their instinct as prey animals is toward flight.

Susan has Lady somewhat calmed down and is saddling her up by the side of the horse trailer. She offers her horse a handful of chopped carrots in an attempt to regain her wild focus. "There's my girl," she softly murmurs into Lady's ear. "You will love the ocean. I promise." She scratches behind Lady's ears as the mare drops her head, a calming gesture in horses.

For her part, Calypso is still trying to gather herself together under Hillary's gentle words. Susan cannot hear what Hillary is saying to her mare, for the thunderous waves in the distance are strong and rhythmic, overpowering any voice other than the squawking seagulls circling overhead. She looks over at her friend and raises her voice above the wind, "You going to be all right with her?"

Hillary is slowly able to approach her mare and lay a gentle hand on her neck. Susan watches as Calypso's head lowers, and her eyes soften, widen, and take in the human she trusts most. Susan smiles knowingly to herself. Such is the connection between women and horses.

"Yup, she's good now," Hillary calls over her shoulder to Susan, her gaze never breaking that of Calypso's.

Eventually, they are both in their saddles and walking the cautious horses closer toward the surf. The tide is out, and there is a wide swath of moist, packed sand along the water's edge. Perfect for a good gallop, thinks Susan. She laughs at Lady's reaction to the waves, reaching toward her hooves and just as quickly receding. The mare, puzzled, drops her muzzle to the wet sand and is met with a splash of salty foam. Quickly, she jumps back as if bitten by a snake.

"Which way do you want to go?" cries Hillary, who has kept a dancing Calypso on a short rein.

Scattered hoof prints lead off in either direction from where Susan and Hillary are standing. The wind is coming from the west. Susan turns Lady toward the east, the sun in their faces, the ocean breeze at their backs. "This way," she calls happily.

After several minutes of walking along the water's edge, the horses relax, as do their riders. "I have wanted to do this my whole life," shouts Hillary gleefully, glassy-eyed and staring at the distant horizon. Susan smiles, watching her friend.

Without warning, Calypso and Hillary suddenly blast off into a canter, gathering speed. Susan barely has time to collect her reins before Lady madly dashes after her equine companion. Dear God, thinks Susan, Calypso has taken off with Hillary! We will never catch them. The mares are thundering down the beach now, hooves flying, their tails in long ribbons behind them. Susan has bent close to Lady's neck, and tendrils of chestnut mane are whipping the skin of her face. She lifts her stinging eyes and feels Lady's muscles gather and lengthen underneath her. The mare is running for all she's worth. They are in a dead gallop. There is nothing for it but to hold on for dear life. She buries her hands deeper into Lady's mane, tears streaking down her cheeks from the wind and the sand in her eyes, her breath coming in great deep gasps as the salty air is forced into her lungs. Susan cannot tell whether she is laughing or crying in this rapturous moment.

Susan lifts her head again, trying to keep an eye on Hillary and Calypso ahead of them. They are coming into focus now as Lady begins to slow her pace, and Susan notices that Hillary has brought Calypso down into a collected trot. She rides up beside her friend, winded and gasping. Susan turns and looks over at Hillary, fearing her friend will have been terrified after Calypso's wild abandon just now. She catches the biggest grin on her friend's face. Hillary had never been out of control for one minute of that breathtaking dash.

"You did that on purpose!" she shrieks, urging Lady back into another gallop. The chase is on once more. Laughing and calling down another length of beach, the riders continue their run, feeling the rush, the freedom one can only experience from the back of a spirited horse, the sound of the wind and the waves in their ears, the warmth of the sun on their joyful faces.

Hillary and Calypso quickly pass them, and they are a few paces ahead of Lady and Susan when they abruptly come to a halt. Hillary jumps off her mount. "What is it?" calls Susan, trotting up beside her friend. "What happened?"

Her gaze follows Hillary's, and Susan sees a collection of starfish washed up on the beach from the tide going out. They are lifeless on the sand, motionless despite their five arms, without being buoyed by the ocean water. She imagines the starfish, there must be thirty of them, pale orange and various sizes, silently accepting their fate, even as the spray from the saltwater in the distance continues to shower them with tiny intermittent droplets—not enough moisture to keep the starfish alive, but enough to reveal the capriciousness of the ocean waves, which gently shelter the creatures who exist in their depths, while also bearing the strength to mercilessly deposit the starfish there on the sand.

Hillary turns to Susan, who has also dismounted from her horse by now, and shoves Calypso's reins into Susan's empty hand. "You hold her," she says with gravity, glancing toward the large mare. "I have to save them." Hillary then rushes toward the helpless starfish and, one by one, begins to pick them up and gently run them to the water's edge, where the waves gather them as a mother would her errant children and pull the little starfish back into her watery embrace. Susan recognizes the desperation scattered on the beach before them and loves her friend all the more for her determined efforts to alter fate.

Susan continues to watch Hillary move farther along the beach in her attempt to save all of the starfish lying there. It has been a good thirty minutes, as Hillary carries each starfish individually across the sandy swath, delicately depositing it back into the waves. The mares are becoming impatient, having grown somewhat accustomed to the wind, water, and ever-crying gulls. They are pawing, ready to move on. But Susan keeps them still, whispering softly that they must wait a little longer. If the starfish are tossed hastily back into their watery home, they might lose an arm and return to their former starfish lives, at least for a while, not whole.

In the distance, Hillary rises after rinsing her hands for a final time in the cold New England salt water. She walks toward Susan and the two restless horses with a small smile and tears in her eyes. "Sorry I took so long," she starts as she reaches Susan.

"You don't have to explain a thing," her friend replies softly, handing Calypso's reins back to Hillary.

The ride home is quiet and reflective. Traffic on the highway, while certainly more congested than earlier that morning, is still not at the worst it will be when evening rush hour arrives. Susan is tired, in a comforting way, the way one feels after being out in the wind and the wild; it makes you physically fatigued yet emotionally sharpened. She swallows a bite of apple, then says, "Well, we did it. How do you feel, my friend?"

Hillary turns her gaze from the passenger side window, her face glowing with happiness. "This," she replies, "has got to be one of the very best days of my life." She grows contemplative for a moment. "Thank you for sharing this day with me, Susan. Wouldn't have wanted to spend it with anyone else."

Susan smiles. "So, tell me, what is your plan going forward, with your pregnancy and all? Will you keep riding?" She crunches into her apple again.

"No, I don't think so," Hillary murmurs. "Nothing can top this ride, and I don't want to risk anything with my baby."

Susan sighs, relieved to hear her friend say this.

"Although I don't know what I'll do with Calypso," Hillary goes on. "I really don't want her sitting for that many months until I can ride again. She's a horse that does best with consistent work."

Susan thinks about this and then has an idea. "Have you

thought of leasing Calypso to someone to ride while you're pregnant and when the baby is first born?"

"I've actually given it a little bit of thought," Hillary responds. "There aren't too many people I would trust with Calypso. She's such a sensitive girl and is highly trained. I wouldn't want anyone to mess up what she already knows."

"What about one of Bridget's more advanced students? A high schooler or something? Someone who has some years of riding experience under their belt. I bet it wouldn't be hard to find a kid who would jump at the chance to lease a horse like Calypso. You could always put in the lease agreement that they have to take one riding lesson a week on her. That way, you know somebody's got eyes on both the kid and the horse."

"You're right, you know. I'm going to have to do something. And I like the idea of having them take a lesson on Calypso every week. I'll reach out to Bridget this weekend and see if she has anyone she would recommend. She knows Calypso, what she's capable of, and her training and talent."

Susan continues thinking about the logistics of Hillary and what she will do once the baby arrives. As far as Susan is aware, her friend has no family in the area to help with childcare. She is sure Hillary has been working this out in her own mind as well. Instead of delving into that topic, she asks, "So, do you know yet if the baby is a boy or a girl?"

A wide grin spreads over Hillary's face. She has been waiting to share this news. Practically bursting with it. "A girl." Her hands again rest protectively over her belly. "A little girl."

"Oh, that is so happy! And have you thought of any names?"

Hillary pauses for a quick second. "I have," she says. "Her name will be Twyla."

"What an unusual name. I love it! Is it after somebody in your family?"

Hillary looks to her friend, knowing she will completely understand what she is about to explain. "You know in the evening? When the sun is about to set on the horizon, and the moon and stars are just beginning to rise? There is that moment when all the colors of the sky mix—the magentas, the oranges, and the purples—right before darkness comes?"

"Ahhh, twilight. I love that time of day."

"It's like in that moment, there is an opening between one world and the next. Just for a fleeting second, like you can reach across it and touch those on the other side, glimpse what might have been."

Susan understands. "The holiest hour."

"Yes, it is. So, Twyla. For the twilight time."

"That's so beautiful, Hill." Susan's heart feels complete, and happiness is overflowing for her dear friend. The nurse in her asks, "Everything is going well so far? With your pregnancy?"

Hillary takes a swallow from her water bottle, repositions herself, and responds enthusiastically, "Yes. I've been going to the specialty obstetrics group at the university medical hospital. They're watching me closely because of what happened with Schuyler."

"And you'll deliver in the hospital this time around?" Susan asks hopefully.

"That's the plan. They're going to do a scheduled C-section at thirty-seven weeks. Twyla's arrival date will be toward the end of April."

"Oh, my gosh, this is so wonderful." Susan is about to become gushy and reins in her emotions, aware that her friend has rightfully put up some protective walls around this pregnancy. Susan does her best to respect them, although she feels a closeness to this baby that she hasn't allowed herself in a long time, perhaps ever. Out of the corner of her eye, she notices

Hillary has turned in her seat and is staring at her. "What?"

"I have a question for you."

"Okay." Susan is cautiously curious.

"Will you be my back-up birth partner?" The words spill out as Hillary continues. "My friend Joanie, from back in Albany, plans to come out and be with me during the birth and for a few weeks after. But if the baby comes early, and Joanie can't get to New Hampshire in time for the birth, would you mind being on standby?"

Susan is elated. "Mind it! It would be my privilege. Of course, I would love to be your back-up birth partner."

"It could be in the middle of the night."

"I'll be there."

"It could be halfway through your workday."

"I'll be there."

"It could be in the midst of a tornado."

Susan laughs playfully at her friend, "Would you stop? If you need me, I'll be there."

Hillary sighs, "Oh, yay! I was hoping you'd say that." She returns to viewing the scenery outside the truck window. They are nearing the farm now, the highway is behind them, and they are on back-country roads following the woods, fields, and stone walls that make up the heart of New England. Hillary realizes she has about fifteen minutes before they pull into the driveway to the barn. She gathers her courage and looks once more directly at Susan. "I have one more question for you."

Susan's attention is back on the road ahead, and she absentmindedly says, "Yeah, sure, what is it?"

In a low voice, yet suffused with emotion, Hillary begins, "You know I'm not very close with my stepmother?" There is no question of this. "And I don't know the baby's father, of course." A heavy pause. "So, I'd like to ask you to be my baby's grandmother." She takes another breath, holds it, and waits.

The truck and trailer slow as Susan's heartbeat slows. The question has plunged her deep within her psyche. She feels a familiar pain begin to grow hot within her. The old ember glows and brightens, but this time, it does not scorch her and instead begins to spread and rise within her, illuminating the darkest and most forgotten corners of her soul. The warmth continues rising through her heart and leaking out of her eyes. As tears begin to fall, Susan looks to her friend. "I would be honored," she answers with gratitude, her voice cracking, barely above a whisper.

Chapter 20

Hillary

Hillary steps out of her cozy little house and into the frigid morning air, small puffs of her breath visible as she makes her way out her front door and to her car. She is taking tiny steps since the stones of her walkway are slippery and covered with frost from last night's temperature drop. She gazes down at the dry brown grass of her lawn, the withered flowers with straw-like stems bent at odd angles. She never did get around to putting her gardens to bed earlier in the fall as she had hoped, what with her busy work schedule and her ever-growing belly getting in the way, literally, of her yard work. Ah, well, Hillary imagines, *once Twyla is born in the spring, I can have her out beside me in her stroller while I dig around and straighten up these flowers.* She opens her car door, lands in her seat with a thud, and drives north to the medical center for her monthly obstetrics appointment with the specialist.

After the now perfunctory abdominal ultrasound, Hillary is waiting in the exam room when the door opens and Dr. Machado, her obstetrician, walks in, a clipboard held tightly to her chest. Hillary looks up as the doctor enters and smiles reassuringly at Hillary in greeting. However, Hillary realizes that only the bottom half of Dr. Machado's face bears a smile and her eyes remain intensely focused. Immediately, Hillary's heart skips a beat. Without thinking, she blurts out, "My baby's all right, isn't she?" She is gripped with panic.

The obstetrician sits on a rolling stool across from Hillary and gathers Hillary's hands in hers. "Yes. Absolutely. Your baby is fine." Finally, the corners of Dr. Machado's eyes crinkle as she tries to soothe her patient. "What I'm seeing on your ultrasound is that the placenta is partially covering your cervix." She looks expectantly at Hillary, almost as if she is willing her patient to understand this perfectly logical summary.

Hillary waits for the doctor to go on. Dr. Machado continues to smile, her eyebrows slightly raised in anticipation. Hillary is trying to pick up on what the doctor is saying, her tone, her facial expression. But she cannot, so great is her fear of losing this baby, too. Finally, annoyed at Dr. Machado's apparent inability to read the emotional tension in the room, Hillary demands, "So, what does that mean, exactly?"

Dr. Machado eventually drops her eyebrows, releases Hillary's hands, and, still sitting, rolls her stool across the room to her laptop computer. She clicks some keys, turns the screen to face Hillary and begins pointing out various landmarks on the ultrasound of the developing fetus before them. "Here you can see," she explains as if to a classroom of medical students, "the fundus of the uterus. Healthy. And just below that," she moves her finger a fraction of an inch lower on the screen, "we see the top of your cervix."

Hillary gazes at the grainy black-and-white representation of the insides of her pregnant belly, trying to follow along with what Dr. Machado is describing. She sees her baby's large head, curved spine, and little fingers and toes. Her baby. Her Twyla.

She imagines holding this little life in her arms one day soon, dressing her in the prettiest of baby clothes, and teaching her to ride a horse. Hillary has briefly stopped listening to the obstetrician.

"And so," concludes Dr. Machado, wrapping up her short dissertation regarding the ultrasound image before her, "while at this precise moment, the placenta is partially covering the outlet for your baby, and there is a risk that the placenta will attach to the scar tissue from your previous C-section, making a second C-section somewhat more perilous due to the possibility of hemorrhage..." She takes a large breath in as she culminates in triumph, "we remain optimistic, knowing that the placenta, much like the lovely sea anemone, often uproots itself and moves to a newer, more satisfactory location."

Hillary stares at the doctor, stupefied. Sea anemone? What the hell is she talking about? She tries to wrap her head around what she has gathered from the conversation. "So, what you're saying is that if I had to have a C-section right now, right at this very moment, it might be dangerous because of where my placenta is? But there's a good chance my placenta will move?" Hillary thinks back to high school biology class and does not recall ever hearing about any sort of journey of the placenta. The hilarity of this image is playing at the corners of Hillary's mouth as she thinks to herself, I must've been out sick that day.

"Exactly!" Dr. Machado proclaims, standing with a flourish of her long white doctor's coat, wrapping up the visit now that her patient has finally understood her mini-medical lesson. "I see it happen all the time. Let's get you scheduled for another checkup in two weeks."

Driving home, Hillary speed dials Joan and puts her on speaker phone to update her friend on her visit to the obstetrician.

Joan is laughing hysterically, "'The lovely sea anemone'? What in God's name kind of doctor is she? Oh, Hill, I don't mean to find humor in this, but really, it is hilarious!"

Hillary is relieved that, one, her baby is developing perfectly, right on schedule, and two, that she survived Dr. Machado's medical lecture. She lets herself go and begins to laugh along with her friend. "I know, it really is!" She is giggling helplessly as the two of them carry on about all things related to Hillary and the baby's health, the lovely sea anemone notwithstanding.

Hillary watches out her living room window while heavy snowflakes fall gently as feathers, covering her yard in a fluffy coat of white. It is Christmas Day night, and Hillary has turned on her outside spotlight so she can watch the snow fall. It has been a lovely day spent over at Bridget's house with Bridget and her new significant other, Tim, and a couple of local friends of theirs.

Although Joan had begged Hillary to come out and spend Christmas with her at her family's house in upstate New York, Hillary had declined, not wanting to travel that distance, in snowy conditions, with the throng of other holiday drivers who would be sure to be on the road, many of them inebriated. "I don't want to take any chances," she had replied to her friend, who said she understood, if somewhat reluctantly.

Susan had also invited Hillary to spend Christmas with her and her husband. She told Hillary she was hosting her parents, her sister and husband, and their young son. As much as Hillary would have loved to spend the holiday with her dear friend, she understood the importance of this healing time together for a family that seemed, like all families, really, to have some tears and holes in the fabric of their togetherness. She had wished Susan a very Merry Christmas and had secretly hoped that Susan would be able to find some time to connect with her sister and her little nephew.

With thoughts of family turning in her mind, Hillary places her cup of pregnancy tea in its saucer on her coffee table and dials her stepmother's number. She waits...one...two...three...four...

On the fifth ring, Anita growls into the phone, "Well, it's about time you called, Hillary! I've been waiting all day to hear from you. It's Christmas, after all. Does your family mean nothing to you?"

Oh, here we go, Hillary sighs to herself. "Merry Christmas to you, too, Mom. Of course I was going to call you today. I figured you'd be busy attending church in the morning and hosting the holiday meal this afternoon."

Her stepmother puts herself on center stage. "I certainly could have used your help with the meal, Hillary. We had a houseful: Your cousin Christina from Connecticut came with her husband and three little ones, and your father's mother from the nursing home was here. God help me. I don't ever want to end up like that! And your sister, of course, with her latest boyfriend. He wore all black leather, with an earring in his nose. He was covered with tattoos! Can you believe someone would show up to Christmas dinner like that?" She gives a slightly forgiving laugh and adds, "But you know your sister, always saving some poor rescue from the gutters of the city."

No, that's probably not the case, thinks Hillary. More likely, this boyfriend grows his own marijuana in his basement, and the two of them have a direct source of the very best leaves. But sensing her stepmother is about to go on a long-winded diatribe concerning the "youth of our country," as she refers to anyone under the age of thirty, Hillary asks, "So what did you serve your guests today, Mom? You're such an amazing cook. I bet it was delicious."

Back in the spotlight, Anita goes on to list the plated hors-d'oeuvres she had been preparing since earlier in the week, the main dish of roast tenderloin encrusted with garlic and herbs, the many vegetable sides, the rolls, the accompanying wines, and the desserts, which included a flaming plum pudding doused in brandy. "Everyone said it was the best Christmas meal they could ever remember," she finishes with pride. "And what about you, my dear," she finally concludes. "How was your little holiday get-together at your friend's house?"

Hillary squirms, hearing the condescending tone to Anita's question. But, she thinks, it's Christmas after all. I have to take the high road. She answers, "It was so nice, Mom. There were just six of us, and everybody brought a dish. We ate and drank wine. Well, I didn't drink any wine, of course. And then we played board games." Knowing where her stepmother's train of thought will go next, Hillary adds, "I made it home safely before the snow slicked up the roads."

"Well, it would have been nice to see you here, Hillary," referring to the family's house in Albany. "But in your present condition, circumstances as they are, I guess I can make an exception."

Hillary feels her stepmother baiting her. Try as she might to keep her tone light and conversational—this was supposed to be a quick holiday hello call, after all—Hillary replies incredulously, "My present condition? What's that supposed to mean, Mom?"

"You know, pregnant out of wedlock." Anita pauses for dramatic effect. "Again."

Any sense of decorum has fled from Hillary. She is fuming.

In a voice louder than she intended, she responds, "Seriously? Seriously, we're going down this road again, Mom? This is my life. I am not here to live it for you, or your expectations, or your friends' expectations." Her voice is shrill now. "If you don't want me or my baby to be a part of your life, if we are too much of an embarrassment to you, then just say the word, and we don't have to be a part of it at all!" Hillary tries to temper her emotions and involuntarily mutters, "For the love of God, Mom."

"How dare you, Hillary, speak to your mother that way! And on a high holy day, no less! I am a good Catholic, Hillary. I go to church. I try to help people. God knows I took care of you and raised you as my own after your father up and died." Hillary is sure she hears a fake sniffle from Anita's end. "Leaving me with two little girls and a whole lot of debt." The sniffling continues. Her stepmother is a brilliant actress, as Hillary well knows. "The least you can do, the very least, is show me some respect, Hillary." Anita makes a show of loudly blowing her nose as a conclusion to this masterpiece of verbal manipulation.

Regrouping after a sip of tea, Hillary slows her breathing. It's just not worth it with her stepmother. It just isn't. She sighs, giving in to what she knows her stepmother wants to hear, what she knows will placate her. "I do respect you, Mom," she offers, tasting the acid in the back of her throat. "I could never, ever repay you for what you've given me." Her stomach turns, and she wants to vomit. But mostly, she wants to end this call, which is going nowhere. Anita has won this game once again. She is a clever player, and Hillary has never quite been up to her stepmother's strategic emotional volleys.

Anita emits a satisfied sigh. "I hope you do, Hillary. Family is all we have in the end, you know. We have to stand by each other no matter our own personal trials and tribulations. It is what Christ teaches us."

Hillary rolls her eyes, covers the mouthpiece of her phone, and groans.

"What's that, dear? Did you have something you wanted to say?"

"Just that I've got to get going, Mom. And Merry Christmas."

"Merry Christmas to you, too. Let's talk again soon. As much as you don't believe me, I do worry about you all alone in that house up in the hills."

Now her stepmother is just playing the martyr. It's a familiar track that the conversation is on. Hillary decides to set boundaries by terminating the call and trying to enjoy the rest of this holiday evening. "Okay, Mom. I'll talk to you soon." She concludes the call, puts the phone down, and stretches her pregnant body along the couch, bumping her feet into Athena, who is once again curled up asleep in a pile of throw pillows.

"C'mere, kitty," Hillary mutters as she pulls Athena onto her lap and scratches behind her velvety ears. The soft light from the twinkling Christmas tree in the corner of her living room casts a warm and gentle glow against the wind and darkness outside.

"Merry Christmas, Twyla," Hillary whispers, wrapping a warm quilt around them.

One sunny afternoon in mid-April, as Susan returns from the paddocks where she has just turned Lady out after a glorious ride through the woods, she feels her cell phone vibrating in her back pocket. Quickly she responds to it after glancing at the caller. "Hey, Hill," she answers tentatively, knowing that her friend had a scheduled appointment with the obstetrics specialist that morning for her thirty-five-week checkup. "Everything all right?"

"Well, yes. And..."

Susan hears the animated emotion in Hillary's voice. "Aaaand...what...?" She is worried. Has something gone wrong at this appointment? Hillary had confided last month to Susan that her placenta, that wandering, lovely sea anemone—everyone was in on the joke now—had rooted down in a new location, far from the danger zone of Hillary's scar tissue left by her previous C-section. Susan knows that, at thirty-five weeks, the baby's lungs should be developed enough to survive outside the womb. What could it be? The suspense is killing her.

"And she's coming! Twyla is coming. Today. They are doing the C-section today!" The words rush out in an excited explosion.

"Oh, gosh, today? I thought you weren't scheduled for your C-section for another couple of weeks. Is something wrong?" Her voice betrays her concern.

"Well, I was at my appointment with Dr. Machado this morning, and she noticed that the baby had some mild distress. So she told me they didn't want to take any chances. They're going to perform the C-section today." Hillary is breathless on the other end of the phone. She continues, "I asked if I could go home to get my birthing bag and come back for the procedure, but Dr. Machado said no, they want to keep me monitored until Twyla is delivered."

Susan, ever organized in handling unexpected health crises and prepared to be a part of this baby's birth, has already started checking things off in her mind. "Do you need me to go to your house and get your birthing bag? Bring it to you at the hospital?" She assumes that, based on this news that the baby is in some distress, the C-section will be imminent and Hillary's friend Joan will not make it out in time to be the birth partner.

"No, you don't have to. I already called Joan; she's in her car and on her way. The C-section won't happen until late this afternoon, so she should be able to pick up the birthing bag at my house and make it to the hospital in time." Hillary pauses, unaware of her friend's mild disappointment on the other end of the phone. "Oh, Susan, I am just so happy that this is finally happening. I wanted to tell you right away! Listen, I've got to go. One of the nurses just walked in. I'll keep you posted, okay?"

"Okay," Susan murmurs into the phone, her heart somewhat deflated, though the call has already ended. She pockets her cell phone and walks through the barn to the tack room, picking up her saddle and bridle. Meghan, one of Bridget's more accomplished students, is sitting at the little wooden table in the tack room when Susan arrives. She is desperately tugging at her riding boots, trying to pull out of them after her ride on Calypso just now.

Susan places her saddle and bridle on racks along the wall and turns to Meghan. "Here, let me help you with those," she offers, grasping the heel of one of the boots in her palm and tugging on the toe of the boot with her other hand. After much struggling and a few grunts, Meghan's foot eventually slides out from the tight boot.

She wiggles her toes. "Ahhh, that feels so much better," she sighs.

"How was Miss Calypso for you today? I saw her giving you a few fresh bucks in the ring earlier when Lady and I were coming back through the field. Still happy with your decision to lease her while Hillary is getting through her pregnancy?" As soon as she says the word, Susan perks up her head and says to the young girl, "By the way, I just got a call from her, and the baby is coming. Today!" Susan is grinning from ear to ear, despite her wish that she, and not Joan, would be present for the actual birth of the baby.

Bridget walks in at that precise moment. "Oh, my God, you guys. I just heard. This is so exciting! I can't believe it's happening already. It seems like just yesterday Hillary was telling us all about the attributes of the sperm donor she'd chosen."

"Yes." Susan picks up this thread of conversation in a lighthearted way, recalling Hillary reading to them the description of this mystery man: "'Born in Europe, pastimes are hiking and beekeeping, he has honey-brown hair, sculpted lips and rakish eyebrows.' What in the world are rakish eyebrows, anyway?!" The three dissolve into peals of laughter.

That evening, Susan has been texting Bridget and checking in from time to time to see if she has heard anything from Hillary. So far, neither has heard a word. Susan is snuggled on the couch, her head resting on Paul's shoulder, inattentively rubbing Ginger's belly while they watch a TV show together and wind down from the day.

"She's going to be all right," Paul says gently, reading Susan's thoughts. "She's at the hospital, and they are closely monitoring her and the baby. And if something does happen to go wrong, she's at a top-level medical facility. She's in the very best hands. Your friend and her baby are going to be just fine. I can feel it."

Susan knows that Paul is aware of her immense concern and worry, but how could he ever know, not only what the birth of this baby means to Hillary, who silently blames herself for the loss of Schuyler, and now has a chance to find some redemption for her tortured soul; but also, for Susan and the chance she never thought she'd have to be in a mothering role to any child. Susan feels she, too, has finally been chosen; her own heart is no longer forsaken. She realizes Paul will never fully understand this. How could he possibly? She sinks deeper into Paul, loving him for who he is, and with her whole heart she silently forgives him.

Finally, at half-past eleven—Paul having long ago retired to their bedroom after falling asleep watching TV together, and Ginger, too, lightly snoring by Susan's side—her phone lights up with a text message.

It's from Joan: "Twyla has been born. She is healthy! She took her first breath. She cried loudly when she entered the world. She is well developed. She is perfect. And right now, Hillary is resting comfortably with little Twyla tucked in beside her."

Susan stares at the screen of her cell phone through a wash of grateful tears, praying that at this moment, Hillary senses something has been reversed, that her friend has done what she felt she must do in this lifetime to make up for whatever past transgressions Hillary believed had led to Schuyler's death. That in this holiest of hours, she is forgiven and can now accept with complete joy, her living baby.

Hillary and Twyla have been home for two days now. She is exhausted, elated, and madly in love with this little girl who sleeps peacefully beside her. There is a light knock on her bedroom door as she gazes down at Twyla's long blonde eyelashes, perfect upturned nose, and seashell pink fingernails.

"Hey there, sleeping beauties," Joan calls softly, peering into the dimly lit bedroom and locating Hillary and the baby amidst a pile of pillows and quilts. "I'm going out for a bit to get some groceries and a few things we need to stock your refrigerator while I'm here. I wanted to check and see if you need anything specific from the store."

"I would love an iced coffee from Dunkin's if you don't mind going through the drive-thru. Decaf."

"Yeah, sure, Sweetie. You got it. Anything else? Any special foods you are craving?" Then, with a wry smile, "Cream for your sore nipples?"

Hillary giggles quietly at this. "Very funny, Joanie! Yes, as you well know, my nipples are sore, but little Twyla and I are getting the hang of this nursing thing." She glances back at the perfect little bundle nestled in the crook of her arm. "You go ahead and get out of here, take a break from being my nursemaid. My friends Susan and Bridget will stop by in a bit. I want to introduce Twyla to them. Can you leave the front door unlocked for when they get here?"

Joan is grateful to be able to step out for some fresh air and feels safer knowing someone will be stopping by to check on her two charges while she runs errands. "Right. I'm off, then. I have my cell phone if you need me." She closes the bedroom door gently behind her as she leaves the room.

Hillary slowly untangles herself from the bedcovers and places Twyla on her back in the center of a ring of pillows. The baby makes a soft whimper as Hillary climbs out of the bed. "Momma will be right back, Sweetheart," Hillary whispers as she gently rubs the soft down of Twyla's head. "I've got to splash some water on my face and change out of this nightgown before the girls get here." The baby settles beneath her mother's touch, and Hillary cautiously walks to the bathroom, holding her sore belly with both hands as she makes her way down the hall.

Almost as soon as Hillary returns to the nest of a bed that she and Twyla have been living in since their return home from the hospital, she hears the doorknob of her front door twist and the excited yet hushed voices of Bridget and Susan as they make their way up the stairs and to the doorway of Hillary's bedroom. They are all smiles as they gaze at their friend, who softly cradles her baby to her breast.

Susan is the first to enter. "Oh, Hill," she sighs, "look at her. She is so beautiful." Susan reaches out to touch Twyla's little fist. The tiny hand opens and immediately grasps onto Susan's finger.

"Meet your granddaughter." Hillary looks up at her friend with an expression that Susan has never seen on her: one of pure love, wisdom, and otherworldliness. Her friend has been transformed, and she has come into her own as a mother. "Would you like to hold her?" Hillary carefully wraps Twyla in a swaddling blanket and offers her up to Susan.

Susan takes her granddaughter in her arms and walks over to the rocking chair in the corner of the bedroom. Gentle afternoon light falls on her and the baby from a skylight above. Susan gazes at the sleeping baby's face as she settles into the rocker. She whispers to Twyla, "Hello, Beautiful. Your grandma loves you forever and always." In this blessed moment, Susan is overwhelmed with tenderness for this baby. I will give you the moon, she acknowledges. I will give you anything you wish for, my little granddaughter. Susan's heart is lost to this tiny being. She lifts her tear-stained face to look at Hillary, watching from her bed. "Thank you," she murmurs.

Chapter 21

Susan

Susan slams on the brakes to her car as a flash of hound dog appears in her peripheral vision, leaping over the boxwood hedge in front of Bridget's house and landing squarely in front of Susan's vehicle.

"Damnit, Roscoe!" she shouts at the windshield, smiling and shaking her head back and forth. "Your Super Dog routine is going to be the death of you!" Roscoe, who is fully grown now, has come over to the side of the car and is staring at her through the driver's side window, his doggie lips pulled back in a wide grin, pink tongue lolling, tail thwacking the side of her car. She creeps along to avoid bumping the excited dog and pulls in behind Bridget's pickup truck.

"He's such a nut, your pup," she says by way of greeting as Bridget hops into the passenger side of Susan's car. Once assured that Bridget's boyfriend has a firm grip on Roscoe's collar, Susan slowly backs out, and the two return up the driveway.

Bridget, who is turned halfway around in her seat in an effort to untangle her seat belt, notices the pile of wrapped packages in the backseat of Susan's car. "Oh, my God!" she cries. "Are those all for Twyla?"

Susan smiles. "Yup. I can't help myself. I love to spoil that little grandbaby of mine. And today we're celebrating her six-month birthday, so there's all the more reason to come bearing gifts." Susan looks at Bridget, "You brought the cupcakes, right?"

"You bet. All the ones that Tim didn't get his hands on." She laughs. "I swear, between the dog and the boyfriend, I'm lucky I got out of the house with a dozen of these frosted beauties." She indicates the box covered in aluminum foil resting on her lap. "We'll order pizza and salad once we get to Hillary's house?"

"White pizza. Just like we always do when we visit with Hillary and Twyla. It's sort of become our thing." The car rumbles down the back roads of the small New Hampshire town. It is fall, and once again, the leaves on the oaks, maples, and birches take center stage in their riot of reds, yellows, and oranges, made brighter against the drab grayish-brown backdrop of the fallow hay fields they are passing. "God, this view never gets old," Susan mutters as she turns down the road to Hillary's house.

"So, how is the nanny that Hillary found working out for her? I think Hill's only come to the barn to see Calypso once or twice since Twyla was born, so I never get to catch up with her. I feel like I'm out of the loop." Bridget chuckles.

"Oh, Flora? She is a godsend to Hillary and Twyla. Honestly, I can't believe Hill agreed to let someone else care for her sweetheart. But eventually she had to go back to work. Thankfully, her computer company still lets her do everything from her office at home."

Susan thinks back to the conversation she'd had with Hillary after she had interviewed Flora, one of a long string of nannies who answered Hillary's ad, none of whom had met Hillary's standards: the eighteen-year-old who had no résumé and showed up in a T-shirt and pajama bottoms, the older woman who shared her strict methods of child-rearing, the young woman with no nannying experience to speak of and who was asking to be paid double what the going rate was. The list went on. Eventually, Hillary interviewed a woman who had been a nanny previously, was in her middle years, and was open to working the hours Hillary needed to cover. Hillary would work in her office upstairs during the day, and Flora and Twyla would set up the living room with Twyla's portable crib and all of her toys and books. They were right near the kitchen for bottles. Hillary had happily confided to Susan that Twyla seldom slept in her portable crib, however. Hillary would come down from her office to check in on Twyla and Flora, and Twyla would be fast asleep on Flora's shoulder; Flora, eyes closed, humming softly, just loving her work. "And," her friend had continued with a laugh, "it's just as well because Athena has claimed the portable crib as her royal throne."

"Flora. Right. Isn't she from South America or something?"

"Mexico, actually. Her family immigrated to the U.S. when she was younger, I guess. I haven't met her yet. Hillary is hoping Flora will teach little Twyla how to speak Spanish."

"Of course she is," Bridget quips. "Why wouldn't Twyla grow up speaking more than one language?" They both laugh, knowing how loved this baby is and the wishes and dreams Hillary has for her daughter.

Hillary's living room is festooned with streamers and balloons, all dazzling to Twyla, who reaches up toward them, enraptured, from her high chair. Bridget bustles through the front door and leaves the box of cupcakes on the kitchen counter. She scoops the giggling baby into her arms and walks around the room to examine the pretty, shiny birthday decorations. "That's right," murmurs Bridget to the delighted little girl, "Auntie and Grandma have arrived. Let's get this birthday party started!" In response, Twyla grabs a fistful of Bridget's long braid and stuffs it into her mouth.

Susan carries in her many wrapped packages, managing only to knock over a few stuffed toys as she arranges them on the coffee table. "You are the very bestest Grandma," Hillary says, eyeing the gifts and giving a small laugh. "Your timing is perfect. I just called the pizza place and ordered our takeout."

"Yum. I can't wait," replies Susan, taking a seat on the couch next to Hillary. She notices that her friend looks rather pale. Before Susan can question Hillary, her friend goes on.

"Twyla has started teething. She is miserable! We've both been up all night. Sorry about the mess in here." She waves a hand wearily toward what Susan notices to be a rather tidy living room.

Bridget joins them on the opposite couch, bouncing a still laughing Twyla on her knees. "So, how've you been, Hill? I feel like I haven't seen you in forever. Meghan is doing great with Calypso, by the way."

"Oh, I know," replies Hillary. "Meghan is just the cutest. She keeps sending me pictures of her and Calypso diligently practicing their figures in the ring; both of them covered in suds while she tries to bathe Calypso; the beautiful braid she made in Calypso's tail, tied off with a large burgundy ribbon. I couldn't have asked for someone better to lease my pony." She leans back into the couch cushions and smiles.

Twyla starts to whimper in Bridget's lap, reaching her arms toward Hillary, who quietly rises from her seat on the couch and gathers her baby girl into her arms.

"I'm right here, Sweetheart. Momma's right here," she whispers softly, kissing Twyla's blonde head. "I've got you." The baby quiets instantly as she nuzzles into her mother's neck.

Watching the two of them, Susan notices that one of Twyla's blue eyes is starting to turn hazel. She's going to have her mother's eyes, Susan thinks to herself, wondering if Hillary is happy about their twinness or disappointed. Early on in her pregnancy with Twyla, Hillary had mentioned that she hoped her baby had both eyes the same color and went on to describe the merciless teasing she endured as a young girl because of her heterochromia iridium.

The doorbell rings, startling all of them and causing Twyla to let out a loud wail. Susan quickly rises and makes for the door before the pizza delivery driver rings the bell a second time. She hands him some money and turns to her friends. "Follow me, ladies. The birthday feast has arrived."

They gather around the kitchen table, passing plates of pizza and salad. Hillary is trying to juggle a squirming baby on her lap with one hand while eating a slice of pizza with the other.

"Here, let me take her," Susan offers, reaching for Twyla. "I'll hold her while you eat, and then we'll switch." As soon as Twyla settles on Susan's lap, the baby reaches toward a piece of abandoned pizza crust on a paper plate in front of them. "Oh, no, Sweetie," Susan laughs and pushes the plate farther across the table and away from Twyla's grasping hands. "No pizza for you. Not yet, anyway."

"I don't think a small piece of crust will hurt her," Hillary announces. "As long as we watch her and just let her gnaw on it. Go ahead, Susan. It is her six-month birthday pizza party, after all."

Susan offers the baby a section of crunchy crust, which Twyla immediately thrusts into her mouth and begins to chew on. Her little face brightens, and the friends laugh at Twyla's reaction to her first taste of pizza. Susan kisses her granddaughter on one of her chubby cheeks. "You're a pizza lover too, huh? You take after your grandma!" More laughter around the table.

Bridget swallows her last bite of salad and pushes her chair back from the table. "I know I say this every time, but that has got to be the best white pizza ever." She sighs contentedly. Then, switching subjects, "So, I'm thinking about making some changes at the farm, and I wanted to see what you guys think."

Both Susan and Hillary look up from their plates expectantly. "What kind of changes?" Hillary asks, around a mouthful of lettuce.

Bridget pauses dramatically, then announces, "I'm thinking about putting up an indoor arena at the farm." She grins, waiting for a response from the other two.

Susan picks up the thread of excitement from Bridget. "Oooh, that sounds like an awesome idea, Bridget. Have you looked into getting one built? Where would you put it?"

"Well," she continues, "I was talking with Tim about it. He's in construction, you know, and we were thinking we could put it up right by—"

"What made you come up with this idea?" Hillary interrupts, looking directly at Bridget, a scowl on her face.

Susan is puzzled by Hillary's out-of-character reaction but remains silent, waiting to see how Bridget will respond.

"The farm is losing money," Bridget admits, looking down at her hands on her lap. "Not huge amounts by any means, but enough to make me realize that I've got to do something to increase my revenue stream to keep the place going. It was actually Tim's idea," she says with some pride at her boyfriend's solution.

"Well, of course he would suggest you build something huge like an indoor on your property," Hillary scoffs. "It's your money, and all of it would be going right into his pocket. I'm assuming he recommended himself as your contractor?"

"Umm, yes. He did." Bridget is at a loss as to how to respond to Hillary's critical tone. Everyone in the room is holding their breath.

"Instead of taking out a loan to build an indoor ring, you need to hire another instructor, an advanced-lesson instructor, and build your clientele that way," Hillary snaps.

What is going on with Hillary today? She just totally insulted Bridget, Susan thinks, as she watches two bright red splotches appear on Bridget's cheeks. Susan stands up and hands Twyla back to Hillary. "Hey, Bridget, want to help me clear off the table? Then we can gather in the living room for cupcakes and presents," she suggests in a hail-Mary attempt to change the temperature of the conversation.

Bridget passes a bewildered and somewhat hurt glance over to Susan. "Yeah, sure. Let's get this stuff cleaned up."

"So, what is everyone doing for the upcoming holidays?" Susan asks after they settle onto Hillary's couches again and watch as Twyla gazes at herself in wonderment in a plastic mirror, which is part of the new baby-activity set Susan bought for her, recommended as one of the top ten baby must-have toys of the year. Susan had done her research.

Clearly afraid of what Hillary might say next to her, Bridget stuffs a huge bite of cupcake into her mouth, forcing Hillary to answer the question first.

Hillary looks down at Twyla on her lap, still staring at her reflection in the baby mirror. She smiles. "This little beauty and I are planning a road trip to visit my cousin Christina and her family in Connecticut for Thanksgiving. They've got three little girls all under four years old, bless them," she chuckles, "and I want Twyla to have a chance to meet her cousins." She pauses, seeming to have dropped her earlier animosity toward Bridget. "My stepmother invited us for Christmas, but I'm not sure if we'll end up going. She's been so obnoxious on the phone lately, and I don't want to expose Twyla to that negativity."

"You and Twyla are welcome at our house for Christmas if you'd like," Susan mentions, offering her friend a warm smile. "As for Thanksgiving," Susan shakes her head in disbelief, "my sister Lizzie has invited the whole family to her house for dinner."

"Oh, that's so awesome," Hillary acknowledges, with obvious happiness for her friend. "So, things are starting to work out between you and your sister?"

"They are. We had that turning point about a year ago, and we've been able to really connect since then. In fact, she invited Paul and me to Thanksgiving before we even had a chance to make any other plans. I'm pleased about it."

"And how about you, Bridget?" Hillary turns her attention to their other friend.

Bridget pauses and collects herself, trying to discern if there is anything loaded behind Hillary's question. Deciding it's safe to answer, she replies, "Well, Tim and I are hosting our regular Christmas Open House for friends and neighbors." She lets out the breath she had been holding. "You and Twyla are invited to our house as well if you don't end up going to see your stepmother."

"My idea of a perfect Christmas Day," offers Hillary dreamily, "would be for Twyla and me to spend the entire holiday at home, just the two of us. We could get up in the morning, change into matching Christmas jammies, order Chinese takeout, and watch Christmas movies all day."

"That sounds like a perfect holiday to me!" Susan responds with a little extra exuberance, trying to keep the conversation lighthearted. "You should totally do that, Hill. You and Twyla are your own little family now. Time to make your own Christmas memories."

Picking up on what Susan is doing, Bridget chimes in, "I think that sounds like the very best kind of Christmas tradition." The high color has left her cheeks, and she smiles earnestly at Hillary.

"Yeah, well, we'll see," Hillary replies distractedly as she quickly pulls a small toy out of Twyla's fingers that the baby clearly intends to pop into her mouth. "That plastic doggie is not edible, my love," she says playfully to her daughter. The friends chuckle at Twyla's expression of pure indignation.

The holidays have come and gone in a festive blur of family, friends, and food, and now it is February, the thick of winter. The sky is steel gray, and snow is piled up in deep drifts against houses and trees. Susan has been unwell for several days, and a home-testing kit proves positive for COVID. She dials Hillary.

"How's the best grandma ever doing today?" Hillary answers in a sing-song voice. "Are you and Bridget still going to come by for a little party with our favorite Valentine this weekend? I found her the cutest dress, by the way: red, with pink hearts. It even has a matching headband," she concludes with obvious delight.

Susan gives a muffled cough and replies in a scratchy voice, "I am so sorry, my friend. I just tested positive for COVID. I feel like I've been hit by a truck, and I have no plans on leaving my couch any time soon. And anyway, I need to quarantine at home for a few days." She dissolves into a coughing fit.

"Oh, my gosh, Susan, you poor thing! I completely

understand. Can I do anything for you? And thanks for keeping me and Twyla safe from any COVID-19 germs. I feel so bad for you."

Susan groans. She aches all over. "It's not the end of the world. Thanks for offering. Paul has me set up with tissues, cough drops, a decongestant, and Gatorade. He is trying to be a good nurse, but I told him not to quit his regular day job." She attempts a light laugh and ends up coughing all over again. When she can finally regulate her breathing, she continues, "Let's plan something after this virus passes. Hopefully, it will be a little warmer by that point, too."

"Absolutely, we will. Well, your grandbaby and I send you love and kisses. Feel better soon, my friend."

"I will. Tell that little sweetheart her grandma loves her forever and always." Susan is mildly out of breath as she ends the call and burrows down into her blankets, with Ginger, ever devoted, right by her side.

By the time Susan feels that the effects of the virus are entirely behind her, another month has gone by. The days are longer, and the wind coming from the south and west is a bit warmer than it had been. Susan is grateful for the change in weather and arrives at the barn after work one evening to give Lady a handful of apples and a good brushing. Bridget is sweeping up the barn aisle as Susan enters.

"Oh, hey, as I live and breathe!" she calls out to Susan. "How are you feeling?"

Susan sets her bag of apples by the tack room door and walks over to hug Bridget. "Much, much better, thank you. I've missed my girl, though. Thanks for taking such good care of her while I was recuperating. God, that COVID-19 can be a nasty bug!"

"My pleasure. She is such a good pony. She missed you, though. I can tell."

"How's that?" Susan asks dubiously.

Bridget glances at the horses contentedly munching their evening hay in their stalls. "Take a look. Her head popped right up the second she heard your voice." Lady is staring attentively at Susan, her brown eyes deep and liquid, her muzzle quivering in a low nicker.

"Oh, Lady, my love," Susan utters to her mare in a tender voice and moves to unlatch the stall door. "Let's get you out on the cross ties so I can curry you and stuff you full of treats." The mare nickers again.

Bridget is busy tidying up the barn and organizing buckets of horse feed in the grain room for tomorrow's breakfast. "Hey, have you heard anything from Hillary recently?" she calls out.

Susan pauses in her grooming with a passing sense of concern. "She texted me about a week ago," she calls back toward Bridget, "said she hadn't been feeling well, and she and Twyla were taking it easy. She said she had been having headaches and dizzy spells and thought she might have the flu. I offered to stop by with some chicken soup, but Hillary said she didn't feel up to visitors just yet."

"Another thing," continues Bridget as she exits the grain room, brushing hay off her coat front and coming to stand next to Susan, "is I haven't seen any pictures of Twyla on Facebook in the past couple of weeks."

"Now that you mention it, I haven't, either. I just chalked it up to Hill feeling under the weather. But it is definitely out of character," Susan goes on, a small knot forming in the pit of her stomach. "I mean, usually, she posts a new picture of Twyla doing something adorable at least every couple of days."

Susan catches Bridget's eye and sees she is also concerned about their friend. "You know what we should do tonight? We should both text her separately. At the very least, she'll know we're thinking of her."

"Yes, let's do that. I hope everything is all right. It's got to be tough to be a single parent with a little one and be down and out with the flu."

"Hopefully, Flora is able to help with the day-to-day," answers Susan, finishing up her grooming and leading Lady back to her stall.

That night, Susan can't sleep. She has tried adding more blankets for warmth and then removing the added blankets because she's become too hot. Finally, she climbs out of bed and tiptoes downstairs at two o'clock in the morning to brew a cup of chamomile tea and attempt to read the new novel she recently started, hoping it will make her drowsy enough to fall back to sleep. She can't focus on the story, however; something is niggling at the back of her mind. Her earlier text to Hillary has gone unanswered.

Susan closes the novel on its bookmark, perches on the edge of the couch, and starts flicking through the most recent updates on Facebook. Suddenly, a post catches her eye. She gives the wording a cursory glance, and her heart freezes in her chest. It's a post from Hillary, the first she's seen in a couple of weeks.

"Sorry I have been so secretive," it reads. "I have a brain tumor. The prognosis is not good." Hillary's post asks for time and space from contact with friends.

Susan falls back heavily into the couch cushions, feeling as if she has just been punched in the stomach. She has no breath. Tears are streaming down her face. How can this possibly be? Hillary has a brain tumor, of all things. Good God! Immediately, Susan's mind goes into nurse mode, and she thinks: I wonder if

Hill has started treatment? Is she getting chemo or radiation? And then, with horror, who is taking care of little Twyla?

Even though it is the middle of the night, Susan immediately texts Bridget: "Have you seen Hillary's post on Facebook yet?"

Instantly, Bridget texts back: "I just read the news. I'm sobbing."

"I can't believe this," Susan responds. "How can Hillary, beautiful, vibrant mother to our Twyla, have gone from the flu to a brain tumor?"

Bridget writes back, "And she asked us not to reach out to her in her Facebook post. How will we get any answers?"

The two continue communicating late into the night, weeping, dumbfounded, holding on to what little they know. Despair creeping into the quiet places of their hearts.

Another Facebook post, an update, appears the following morning as Susan tries to pull herself together and prepare for work. She puts down her hairbrush and gazes at her phone vibrating on the vanity. Quickly, she scans the post.

It's from Hillary's sister, Eva. Susan reads: "Hillary is coming to terms with her diagnosis, and Twyla is safe and being cared for. We want to let everyone know that Hillary is scheduled for surgery on her brain tumor. Right now, Hillary is fighting for more time with Twyla."

Susan sets the phone back down and stares at her tear-streaked face in the mirror above the bathroom sink. It has to be very serious, she concludes knowingly. It has to be so bad that the brain surgery Hillary will undergo is in hopes of adding time—time, and not life. A loud sob escapes her.

She manages to make it through her workday at the medical clinic, oblivious to the cries of the pediatric patients she has to vaccinate, oblivious to the frantic look in a father's eyes as he discusses how he and his wife are painfully moving on after the death of their son due to a drug overdose, oblivious to the needs of her own body as she works straight through the day never realizing she hasn't stopped for lunch. So great is Susan's sorrow for Hillary—for Twyla.

Her fellow nurse, Norma, is worried about her and pulls her aside before they leave work for the day to ask what's wrong. But how can Susan explain? There are no words.

That evening, it is all Susan can do to drag herself into the house, change into her sweats and go through the motions of getting dinner ready for herself and Paul. She stares blankly into the refrigerator, trying to make sense of its contents, trying to put together a dinner menu for tonight, when Paul comes up behind her and gently wraps his arms around her. Susan turns to him and buries her face in his work shirt. "This is so not fair," she utters. Her voice comes out muffled.

"I know, Suzie, I know," Paul murmurs into her hair as he brushes it with his lips.

Susan pulls back from their embrace and closes the refrigerator door behind her with a bang. She is angry. "What the hell!" she rants. "Her life has already been filled with so much suffering after the loss of her first baby. And that stupid boyfriend who didn't support her. And now," her voice is rising, her eyes flashing, "now she will never see her little girl grow up, never see Twyla take her first steps, go to kindergarten, become the wonderful person Hillary wishes for her to be."

Paul takes her hands in his, steadying her. Susan hadn't even realized she had been pummeling his chest with her fists in her fury at the injustice of it all. "I'm sorry," she whispers, her eyes large and defeated. "What makes it worse is I can't even reach out to her, you know, and ask her how she's dealing with all of this. Tell her that I'm here for her, that I love her. And I don't know her family at all. I'm standing here on the sidelines while my friend is dying, and I can't do a thing!"

"I'm so sorry, Suzie. It must be difficult for a nurse to stand by and watch without any answers." Paul's voice is low and soothing. "Didn't you say there was a nanny? Could you reach out to her? She may know a little more about what's happening."

The tension in Susan's shoulders relaxes slightly. She hadn't thought of this. She feels herself regaining some composure. "You're right, Honey. I could find her on Facebook and message her." The shuddering inside her begins to subside. She can take this small action.

Paul pulls her to him again and kisses the top of her head. "Why don't you sit down and work on finding the nanny? I'll make us dinner."

Susan chuckles despite herself. "You? Make dinner? You never cook. The only thing I've ever known you to make is breakfast." She looks up at him and sees his love for her reflected in his eyes.

"Then we'll have breakfast for dinner," he replies, smiling down at her. "And while you're at it," Paul says to Susan's retreating back, "Why don't you just send a text to Hillary saying simply that you love her? She doesn't have to reply to you. You're just putting it out there for her to know."

God, how Susan loves this man, her beacon in any storm.

Within a couple of days, Susan hears back from the nanny. "I am so happy you reach out to me," she texts. "I hear so much about you and the other lady from Hillary over the past months. I feel like I already know you." Flora goes on to inform Susan that Hillary has been transferred to a large medical center out near Albany, New York, and that she underwent an eight-hour surgery yesterday where the surgeons were able to remove about fifty percent of the brain tumor. Sadly, the procedure left Hillary completely paralyzed on one side. Flora concludes her message by writing that she has been staying with Twyla at the house in New Hampshire and that soon the family would be moving Twyla to Hillary's sister's house, where Twyla would go to live.

"I'm horrified at the very thought of Twyla being exposed to that family," Susan texts Bridget that evening, during their now nightly ritual of catching each other up on what they've learned about Hillary and offering support to one another as the two of them navigate this time of uncertainty and grief, standing as they are, outside of the circle of Hillary's family and friends from Albany.

"Right? Hill never would have wanted this," Bridget concludes in her return text. "Can't Twyla stay in New Hampshire and Flora look after her? Maybe now with the surgery, Hill can make it home to be with Twyla."

Susan reads the desperate hope in Bridget's words. Reluctantly, she types back, "Flora confirmed that the kind of tumor Hillary has is a glioblastoma. There's currently no cure for that type of cancer. She won't be coming back from this." Her gut twists as she presses the send button on her phone.

There is a long pause before Bridget's text response appears. "I can probably cover the costs for Calypso for a couple of months. But if it goes beyond that, I will have to devise another plan for her."

"I will give you half the money for Calypso's monthly expenses. Please let me help you with this. You may want to try to contact Hillary's friend Joan out in Albany. I've never met her but Hillary told me they grew up riding together. I think Joan still has a horse. She may be able to help in the long term. I saw her name on the recent Facebook thread with updates from Hillary's sister."

"Okay, good idea. I will do that," comes the reply from Bridget.

A couple of days later. another Facebook post appears from Hillary's sister, Eva. This post includes a picture of Hillary. Susan studies the image of her friend. She still has all of her long black hair! Susan had imagined they would have had to shave her head for the surgery. In the picture, Hillary is propped up in a hospital bed, one limp arm resting on a pillow. Twyla is sitting on the bed beside Hillary, who is concentrating on feeding a bite of apple to her little girl with her non-paralyzed hand. The post reads, "Hillary is doing as well as can be expected. We anticipate moving her to a rehab facility in the next couple of weeks. In the meantime, Hillary would be so happy to have friends come by for short visits."

As soon as she reads these words, Susan reaches out to Bridget, and they plan to take a day off from work next week and drive out to Albany to visit Hillary. Susan can get the following Tuesday off from work, and Bridget can find someone to help with the farm chores that day as well. They are both relieved to finally see their friend, to tell her in person how much they love her and will do anything they can for her, anything at all that she needs.

Monday evening, Susan reaches out to Hillary's sister by text to confirm that she and Bridget, Hillary's friends from New Hampshire, plan on leaving early the following morning, hoping to arrive at the medical center to visit Hillary in the late morning or early afternoon.

Almost instantly, Susan's phone pings with a reply from Eva. "Hillary has taken a sudden turn for the worse. Only family at the bedside at this time."

Susan is stunned. A turn for the worse? What exactly does

that mean? Would she never get to see her dear friend again? Would she never get to say goodbye to her? Her head spins with all of these questions and the answers deep within her that she knows to be true.

On Tuesday morning, a text from Flora confirms what Susan had guessed: Hillary has slipped into a coma. She isn't expected to recover, and plans are being made for her to be discharged on hospice to her stepmother's house. Flora has been staying at Eva's house to help Twyla adjust to her new living arrangements.

"This can't be what Hillary would have wanted!" Susan cries as she throws her phone down on the kitchen counter, startling Ginger, asleep in front of the sunny sliding glass doors.

Just then, Paul comes downstairs. "What's that?" he asks, concern in his voice. He glances down at Ginger, who has scooched under one of the kitchen chairs. Paul squats down by the chair, puts out a hand, and gently strokes the top of Ginger's head.

Susan continues, as more tears splash down her face. She has cried a river, it seems, since she first found out about her friend's terminal diagnosis. "The Hillary I know would never have wanted Twyla exposed to her family. Something must have happened. I would have thought she'd have planned for Twyla to go live with her cousin in Connecticut. It's so out of our hands, Paul." Susan pauses to grab a tissue from the box on the counter and wipes her eyes. "Bridget and I know Hillary's true wishes for her daughter. And it's not this. It would never be this!" Her face crumples again as a new wave of desperation overtakes her.

"Shhh, Sweetheart," Paul softly responds. "It is absolutely, positively out of your and Bridget's hands now."

Unable to stop her indignation from rising, Susan says, "And what about the crazy stepmother? Showing up at the eleventh hour to bring Hillary home to die? I hope Anita doesn't think this act will absolve her of all the horrible things she did and said to Hillary over the years."

"Maybe she is thinking that. Maybe the best she can do in these final moments of Hillary's life is to rise to the occasion and finally be there for her stepdaughter. We'll never know. Please don't waste your energy, Suzie, being angry at her family, the universe, or the cancer. Instead, use it to send all the love you can to Hillary. She needs it now more than ever."

"You're right, you know. She does. How did you get to be so wise?" She gazes at Paul through her tears and gives him a faint smile.

His knees creak as he straightens up from petting Ginger, who has by this time come out from her hiding place and is staring up at Susan with worried eyes. "It's not my first rodeo," he replies, looking right at her.

Three more days pass with no updates on Hillary's condition. Susan glances at her phone upon first waking on the fourth morning, realizing with gravity that it is just one week until Twyla's first birthday. Oh, the plans we had! Scrolling through her messages, Susan finds a new text from Flora. Hillary is gone. She has died in the night, surrounded by her family. Peacefully. Beautifully.

"Goodbye, dear friend," Susan whispers into the still air around her.

Hillary has left us, Susan quietly acknowledges, an overwhelming sense of peace settling in her heart. She has left her family, and she has left her baby girl. She is now home with Schuyler.

Susan imagines their greeting: Hillary in a white cotton gown, her raven hair loose and flowing, an angel with arms outstretched as she kneels to embrace her sweet boy. He would be about two years old by this time, thinks Susan, and in her mind's eye, she watches him run on chubby little legs, a huge smile of recognition on his face. He has been so lonely waiting for his momma to come and find him. They are finally together.

Chapter 22

Susan

In the deep, hazy blue light, just as night is lifting and right before dawn, Susan opens her eyes, gently turns back her covers so as not to disturb Paul, who is still asleep in their bed, and quietly makes her way to the bathroom to wash and dress for the day. Last night, she had laid out her cream-colored silk blouse, black cashmere sweater, and black dress pants. She will wear her pearl stud earrings with the matching single-strand pearl necklace. Her low-heeled black leather slingbacks wait by the door. Funeral attire, she thinks, as she scrubs her face in the mirror, brushes her teeth, and styles her short brown hair. She wishes she hadn't agreed to go with Bridget today.

Tiptoeing back through their bedroom to find her gold watch, Susan hears Paul stir from beneath the blankets. "So, today's the day," he says sleepily, looking at her through half-closed eyes. "You ready for this, Suzie?"

Susan fastens her watchband and sits on the edge of the bed beside Paul's reclining form. "As ready as I'll ever be, I guess. I've always had difficulty attending funerals. I know it's the time to pay my respects to the deceased, but I've always felt that the wake or memorial service is for those left behind. Not really for the person who died, you know?"

Paul props himself up on one elbow, watching Susan, listening.

After a thoughtful pause, she continues, "Hillary is elsewhere now. Everywhere. If Lady and I go for a ride into the forest, I will find her there; if I stand on the top of a mountain overlooking the scenery below me, I will find her there; if I walk the sandy edge of the ocean and feel the waves on my feet, the smell of saltwater in the air, I will find her there. She will be in the rising and setting of the sun. She will be the wind through the leaves before a rainstorm. The shooting star streaking through the sky on a cold winter's night." Susan wraps her arms around herself, lost in her longing for the friend she grieves, their friendship, the blessing that it all was.

Paul reaches up and rubs her back. "You are amazing, you know."

Susan turns her head to look at him questioningly as Paul continues, "I don't think I've ever met someone who loves so deeply, loses their heart so completely to another. She was lucky to have you as a friend."

"And I, her," Susan sighs and reluctantly rises from the bed. Bridget will be here soon to pick her up. They will make the long drive to Albany together in the early morning. She bends and kisses Paul lightly on his cheek. He is already halfway to dreaming again. She reaches over him to pat Ginger, curled up in the middle of their bed, and solemnly makes her way downstairs to wait for Bridget.

The two are quiet and introspective as they travel west toward New York, chasing the dark curtain of night as the sun rises behind them. "I made us some lavender tea," Bridget finally announces. "I figured we could use something to relax our nerves on the way there."

"Oh, that was good thinking." Susan glances at the steaming travel mugs in the center of the truck console. After a moment, she says, "I don't know what I'm going to do if Eva brings Twyla to the services. I don't know if I'll be able to bear watching her searching the faces of all those strangers, looking for her momma. It's likely the last time we'll see Twyla."

"I was thinking the very same thing. In Hillary's family's world, we do not exist. I am not her Auntie Bridget, and you're not her grandma—Eva and Anita have those titles. This is going to be really hard." Bridget turns to look briefly at Susan. "I'm glad we're going together." And softly, almost under her breath, as she turns her attention back to the highway, she whispers, "We never got to say goodbye to her."

Several more minutes go by as they speed along, the sunlight reaching its arms from east to west and revealing signs of spring around them: the green grass, the tender flowers, the tiny leaves unfurling at the ends of tree branches. All of these new beginnings. And birds. So many birds flying and swooping. It is going to be a bright day, a warm day, a perfect day, Susan thinks, except for—

"I finally connected with Hillary's friend Joan." Bridget's voice calls Susan back from her mind's wandering.

"Oh? And what did she have to say?"

"We actually had a pretty long conversation. Joan told me Hillary had a will."

"She did?" Susan is surprised. "I didn't know that." She thinks on it momentarily, then adds, "Although it makes sense when you have a family, a child, to have a will. And Hillary was always so organized with her finances and things like that."

"I was surprised to hear that, too," Bridget goes on, recalling her conversation with Joan. "Calypso is left to Joan. So she and I are working together on the particulars of that. I guess Joan isn't sure she can afford both her horse and Calypso." Bridget sighs. "She's going to look into some things, talk with her husband, and let me know. Joan says she will have a plan for Calypso by the end of the month. It worries me, though. I love that mare."

Susan reaches out to place her hand on Bridget's arm. "Bridget, you and I have pooled our resources to keep Calypso at your place. We both know we can't afford to do this in the long term. And she is such a nice horse, with so much potential. We have to believe Joan will act in the best interest of Calypso. I mean, do you doubt that she'll honor Hillary's final wishes?"

"No. Absolutely not. When I talked with her, it was obvious how much Hillary meant to Joan. She said Hillary was like a younger sister to her. I am just concerned that if Joan can't take her, Calypso might end up getting sold down the line to—"

"We can't even think that way," Susan interrupts. "I'm sure she will do the best she can by Calypso. She knows how much that horse meant to Hill."

Bridget takes a sip of her lavender tea. "She also told me something else very interesting."

Susan's curiosity is aroused. She turns in her seat to face Bridget. "What's that?"

"Well, you know how you and I were wondering why Twyla ended up with Eva and not the cousin in Connecticut?"

"Yeah? Did Joan talk to you about that?"

"I kind of asked in a roundabout way." Bridget raises her eyebrows.

"Do tell."

"Joan told me that in Hillary's original will, Twyla *was* supposed to go and live with the cousin in Connecticut, just as we thought. But," she pauses for emphasis, "right before Hillary was due to go in for the brain surgery, her sister brought a notary to the hospital and had Hillary change the will so that Twyla would go and live with Eva."

Susan is incredulous. "How could they even do that! Hillary most likely wasn't of sound mind at that point. Wouldn't the notary have had to confirm that somehow?"

"I don't know the details. That's as much as Joan was willing to tell me. Between you and me, I think the sister did it for the money."

"The money?"

"Yeah, Hillary's entire estate is going to Twyla. I bet Eva thought that if she became Twyla's legal guardian, all that money would fall into her lap."

Susan chews the inside of her lip, thinking about the logistics of this theory.

"Joke's on her, though," Bridget sputters. "The estate can't be touched until Twyla turns twenty-one, Joan said."

"At least there's that," Susan replies, looking up as they turn down the long drive to the funeral home.

The parking lot is packed, and Bridget has to find a space in an overflow lot across the way. After the long ride from New Hampshire, they climb out stiffly, each taking a moment to smooth out their funeral outfits. Then Susan and Bridget make their way to the funeral home entrance. They shuffle along behind the large crowd. As they enter the vestibule, Susan inhales the overwhelming scent of incense. In the corner is a lone pedestal, flanked by potted ferns, upon which rests a guest book. Susan and Bridget stand in line to sign their names. An usher hands them each a prayer card with Hillary and Twyla's picture on the front of it and indicates with a nod that they are to move along into the viewing room.

Susan is immediately overwhelmed by the number of people gathered in groupings of three or four, some crying, some talking in hushed whispers, others having rather boisterous conversations. There are pictures everywhere of Hillary: Hillary as a child, Hillary and Calypso, Hillary and Twyla. Susan reaches into her purse for a tissue and dabs at the tears forming in the corners of her eyes.

Bridget reaches out to Susan and puts a hand on her back. "Come on, let's get ourselves into the viewing line, all right?"

Susan meekly follows Bridget up to an altar draped in folds of dark green cloth. In the center of the altar is a small cedar box surrounded by dozens of flower arrangements and more potted ferns. Susan is aware that Hillary was to be cremated. She is not prepared, however, for the inscription on the side of the wooden box: 'Hillary and Schuyler'. Susan completely breaks down at this point. She can't swallow this. Hillary must have kept Schuyler's ashes with her all this time. Susan had never known. She begins to weep openly, gasping in her immense grief, her heart—held together with fragile threads these past two weeks—torn wide open again. She cannot take a step forward. Time has no meaning, and time has stopped. So consumed is her soul with this vast sorrow that her mind is completely blank.

"Susan," she hears faintly in her ear. Then, more loudly, "Susan! Let's get you out of here." It is Bridget, with her arm firmly wrapped around Susan's waist, forcing her to turn away from the cedar box and back toward the vestibule. "I think you need some air, Hon," Bridget says, marching the two of them past the curious looks of the people standing behind them in line.

Slowly, Susan feels herself coming back. Back into this time, this place. She lifts her gaze from the floor where she has been carefully watching her footsteps so as not to trip and fall in her altered state. She glances across the room to the far wall. An older woman is standing there, her hair dyed a garish shade of red, effusively comforting an olive-skinned man, tearful, with a neatly trimmed goatee. The woman is quite obviously basking in his attention. That must be Anita, thinks Susan. And Peter.

Standing beside them in the receiving line, Susan guesses must be Eva, a large lady, both tall and wide, presenting a grim countenance. Perched on her arm, in a black velvet dress, is Twyla. Next to Eva, a young woman converses with passing mourners, her eyes obscured beneath a stylish veiled hat. "Could that be Joan?" Susan wonders aloud.

"I imagine so." Bridget turns to acknowledge the woman. "Joan would be considered family at a time like this. She's known Hillary since they were kids."

Susan casts her gaze back to Twyla. "Goodbye, Sweetheart. Grandma loves you forever and always," she whispers.

The air is less heavy as they emerge into the vestibule, and a bank of windows offers a glance into the light-filled world beyond the finality of death. Bridget keeps a steadying hand on Susan's back as they approach the exit. When they pass a small cluster of women dressed in black and speaking in hushed tones, Susan notices one of them peel away and head toward her and Bridget. She is a small woman with coffee-colored skin wrinkled by the sun. Her deep-set eyes are a rich brown. Her thick black hair is swept up into a neat bun at the back of her head. The woman smiles as she steps forward, her hand outstretched in greeting. "You are Hillary's friends from New Hampshire?" she asks with a smile. "Susan and Bridget?"

"Yes," Bridget answers tentatively. Taking the woman's outstretched hand. "And you are?"

"I am Flora. The nanny." She is still smiling brightly at Susan and Bridget. "I know it must be you the minute I see you," she says in her heavy accent. "Hillary, she tell me all about you. How very sad we meet here today." She gazes around the vestibule at the endless supply of potted ferns and the many mourners, "like this."

Susan feels an instant connection to this woman, and before she knows what she is doing, she has her arms around Flora in a long embrace. When they pull apart, both women have tears in their eyes.

"Thank you," Susan says, her hands still on Flora's shoulders, "thank you for caring for both of them."

"Of course." Flora brushes at her eyes with the back of her hand, a small smile still on her face. "I love them both very much. This is the best job I ever have."

"What will you do now, Flora?" Bridget steps in closer to form their tight little circle of three.

"I stay with the baby at Eva's house for the next two weeks. To help her with the change." She pauses, then adds wistfully. "Then I am out of a job."

"I am so sorry, Flora." Susan reaches out to touch Flora's arm, as if this announcement, too, requires condolences.

"I find something else. I always do." She brightens again and lays her other hand on top of Susan's. "She loved you dearly, you know. She did not want you girls to know how sick she feel."

"We thought she had the flu," Bridget adds, almost apologetically. "What happened?"

"Come. Sit with me over here, out of the way of these people. I tell you." Flora gestures to a row of plush chairs lined up facing the windows. "Your friend, she start to have weakness. And she become dizzy. She have some falls. I try my best to get her to see the doctor. She would not. She very stubborn, Hillary." Flora shakes her head and looks into the faces of Susan and Bridget. Susan has the strongest sense that Flora is looking to them for forgiveness of some kind.

"There was nothing more you could've done, Flora," she says

in what she hopes is a reassuring voice.

Flora continues, "One night, I am out to dinner with my sister. She work as a medical assistant at the hospital. We are eating our dinner, and my cell phone, it buzzes. It is from Hillary. It say, 'HELP ME.' My sister and me, we leave our dinner right there on the table and drive as fast as we can go to help Hillary." Flora flushes, blinking back more tears. "She had fall on the floor with the baby. She so weak she cannot stand up."

Bridget's hand covers her mouth as she pictures this.

"The baby is crying. So, I say to my sister, 'pick up the baby.' I check Hillary. She is not hurt. She lay on her back, so I cover her with a blanket. Then I call 911."

"That must've been so scary, Flora," Bridget offers.

Flora keeps talking as if she has not heard. "We, my sister and me and the baby, we all go to the hospital with her. We wait and wait in the Emergency Room. At last, the doctor come out. He say they do a scan of the head and Hillary have a very large tumor."

Susan offers Flora a clean tissue from her purse. Flora wipes her eyes and nose. "Thank you. You are very sweet. Just like Hillary tell me about you."

"And so, then they must have admitted her to the hospital, right?" Susan asks.

"They did. Hillary ask me to call a friend, Joan. Then I send my sister home with the baby. I wait with Hillary at the hospital until Joan is there. I hold her hand the whole time and tell her everything going to be okay." Flora's heartbreak is written all over her face. "But it is not to be."

"I'm so sorry you had to go through that, Flora," Bridget responds.

"You did everything you could for Hillary and Twyla. I can't imagine what would've happened if you weren't there for them,"

Susan adds.

"Her life in God's hands," Flora concludes. "For some reason we never know, He call her back to Him."

"Yes, He did," is the only reply Susan can think of, although it seems lacking in so many ways. She looks at Bridget.

"Thank you, Flora, for sharing that with us." Susan again takes the nanny's hand in hers as the women stand and gather their belongings.

"Can I ask you one last thing, Flora?" Bridget is buttoning her coat.

"Of course."

"This may not seem important in light of everything that happened, but I've been worried; what happened to her cat?"

A smile reappears on Flora's face. "I take her home to live with me and my husband. She is one very spoil kitty now."

They can finally laugh, a small happiness on this otherwise solemn day.

"Well," Bridget announces, "we have a long ride ahead. We'd better be on our way. It was so nice to meet you finally, Flora."

Bridget and Susan push their way out through the heavy wooden doors of the funeral home and are released into the brilliant afternoon sunlight.

Susan sees Paul through the windshield of the farm truck as Bridget pulls into the driveway. He is sitting on the front steps of their house, waiting for her in the fading light, holding a barking, wriggling Ginger on his lap. "Thanks for everything today, Bridget," she calls to her friend as she slides out of the passenger seat, "I'll see you at the barn sometime this weekend." Susan stands in the driveway and waves as Bridget backs the truck out and continues down the road.

As soon as the driveway is clear, Paul releases the half-crazed Pomeranian, who comes flying across the yard and stands on her hind legs, front paws stretched up toward Susan. Susan scoops up Ginger, whose fluffy tail is wagging madly. Laughing, she cries, "You have to stop licking my face, puppy! I can't see where I'm going," and makes her way to the front steps to sit beside Paul.

He puts his arm around Susan's shoulders and pulls her in tightly. "You made it through today, Suzie. How'd it go?"

Susan leans her head into Paul's chest, gazing at the colors of the evening sky, the pinks deepening to magentas, deepening to purples. "It was long, and it was hard. But I was able to get some closure. I don't want to talk about it right now, though. I want to sit here with you and watch the sunset."

They are quiet for a time, Susan's head still resting on Paul's chest, listening to the steady beat of his heart, feeling the safety of his arm around her. The light trill of peepers starts up in the wetlands behind their house. Susan loves this familiar sound, heralding the return of spring.

After a time, Paul speaks into the fading light around them, "I got a call from Parker today."

Susan sits up and looks at him. "Oh, yeah?"

"Yeah. He wants to stop by and visit this weekend. Maybe we could have him over for dinner, if that's all right with you?" Paul has a tentative smile on his face as he looks at Susan.

"Yes, of course. It'll be nice to share a meal, just the three of us," she replies, with genuine happiness in her heart.

"Well, four of us, actually."

Paul answers Susan's puzzled look, "He's bringing his boyfriend for us to meet."

"Oh, that's wonderful, Honey! This is a big deal. I'll have to make us something fancy so we can impress him and his boyfriend." In her mind, Susan starts going through her repertoire of dinner recipes.

"Whatever we have will be perfect, I'm sure," Paul replies, his smile even more prominent, as he stands and pulls Susan up off the front steps.

Paul takes her by the hand and leads her through the dimming twilight back into the house. Ginger darts in between them and through the front door as Susan gives a last look into the evening sky. One bright star has appeared on the Western horizon. And as she gazes into the coming darkness, another star appears faintly beside it. Susan smiles and whispers to the heavens, "Good night, Hillary. Good night, Schuyler." And she closes the door softly behind her.

Epilogue

And so, my love, life carried on for the rest of us after the death of your momma, in its regular cycles and rhythms. None of us were the same, though; we faced each day with a new sense of reverence, of grace, and of gratitude; giving a little more of ourselves than we might have done previously, savoring the simplicity found in the quiet peace of a deep forest, the hushed calm of a snowfall, the glory of colors in the rising and setting of the sun.

In the end, Joan could not afford to keep Calypso, as your Auntie Bridget had feared. But she did right by your momma's horse and honored your momma's wishes for Calypso always to be loved and cared for. I found out soon after we returned from Albany that Joan had reached out to the parents of young Meghan and offered them the opportunity to lease Calypso indefinitely. So that beautiful mare remained with us at the farm, loved beyond measure by her new person.

We started an annual tradition that fall, your Auntie Bridget, and Meghan, and me. Right after Labor Day, when the summer tourists have returned to their school and work lives, and the beach opens up to horses and riders, the three of us trailer our ponies to that very same place your momma and I went to so many years ago. We gallop along the packed sand, calling and laughing to each other above the crash of waves, blinded by the salty wind rushing at us, the horses' manes lashing at our faces as we bend low on their necks, urging them on faster, faster.

In all the years we have returned to that beach, I have never again come upon a cluster of starfish scattered along the shore; the ocean has kept her promise to the creatures who survive in her watery embrace. Something in the universe had shifted that day so long ago; the stars aligned, and a fate was altered.

Just as it was on the day of your birth.

I no longer question the ability of the universe to shorten itself, lengthen, change time or distance, or, yes, even fate. I have seen it happen. We call these occurrences miracles and assign them an air of magic. But, really, there is no magic involved; miracles are part of the fabric of life. They are to be expected, watched for, noticed. They will happen in the quietest of moments, without song or fanfare. Be vigilant for them, my love.

I do not doubt that on some ordinary day, doing some ordinary thing, perhaps standing in line at the café on the corner, I will look up to place my order for a breakfast croissant and cup of black tea, and I will recognize your momma's eyes in the face of the young woman taking my request. I will have found you. Another miracle. I expect it.

Until then, sweet child, never forget that Grandma loves you forever and always.

Happy fifth birthday, Twyla.

A Note to the Reader

This book was born out of a dream. Shortly after my friend Meg passed away, I dreamt one night I had been diagnosed with cancer. In the dream I was getting ready to undergo some sort of radiographic testing, and the technician asked if there was any possibility I could be pregnant. I answered earnestly, "No, there isn't." My dream-self thought for a moment and added, "Well, I suppose I could be..." Then I awoke. Puzzled as to the meaning of this, I shared the contents of my dream with a coworker, a nurse, who astutely asked, "Is there something in your life you're trying to give birth to?" Without hesitation, I replied to her, "Yes, I think there is." And in that moment, the idea for this novel was born. My hope in sharing this story with you, dear reader, is not only for my friend and her courageous life to be remembered, but also that someone reading this who has found themselves to be unexpectedly a childless mother, who has experienced suicide in some way, who has lost a baby to stillbirth, or whose life has somehow been touched by cancer, will find understanding in these pages, solace, and hope. You are not alone. I have listed here some of the many books I read during the writing of this novel in order to gain insight into the thoughts and feelings of my characters. I hope you will find them beneficial.

- Day, Jody. Rocking the Life Unexpected: 12 Weeks to Your Plan B for a Meaningful and Fulfilling Life Without Children. Amazon.com, 2013.
- Eckl, Cheryl. A Beautiful Death: Keeping the Promise of Love. Flying Crane Press, 2015.
- Hanson, Emma. Still: A Memoir of Love, Loss, and Motherhood. Greystone Books Ltd., 2020.
- Callahan Smith, Maureen. Grace Street: A Sister's Memoir of Grief and Gratitude. Gray Dove Press, 2021.
- Heinman, Elizabeth. Ghost Belly: A Memoir. The Feminist Press, 2014.
- Hendler, Sue. Dying in Public: Living with Metastatic Breast Cancer. Michael Grass House, 2012.
- Mele-Bazaz, Leah. Laila: Held for a Moment. Kat Biggie Press, 2022.
- Newton, Michael, PhD. Journey of Souls: Case Studies of Life Between Lives. Llewellyn Publications, 1st ed., 1994.
- Partridge, Stephanie R. Baby Bump, Cancer Lump: A Memoir of Fighting Cancer While Pregnant. Peartree Imaginations L.L.C., 2018.
- Richardson, T. B. Honeysuckle: From Discovery to Death. T. B. Richardson, 2009.
- Riggs, Nina. The Bright Hour: A Memoir of Living and Dying. Simon and Schuster Paperbacks, 2017.
- Smith, Jennifer. What You Might Not Know: My Life as a Stage IV Cancer Patient. Jennifer Smith, 2013.
- Taylor, Brooke D. Unimaginable: Life after Baby Loss. Brooke D. Taylor, 2020.

For additional information and links to helpful sites, please visit my webpage at: www.CarolynHochardAuthor.square.site

Acknowledgments

My sincerest thanks to the team at Compass Rose Publishing: to Daniel Williams, Director of Author Services, a most stalwart and patient guide, who led me through the independent-publishing process. To my copy editor, Diane Hinckley, whose keen eye and attention to detail allowed me to write the best version of this book. Much appreciation to my proof editor Chele Pedersen Smith for your clarity and warm encouragement. Many thanks to Danielle Kane, whose graphic editing talent produced the beautiful cover design layout. And my very deepest gratitude to Diane Kane: content editor, friend and mentor, who not only championed this novel from the get-go, but brought her incomparable optimism and insight to every meeting.

I would be remiss if I did not recognize the immensely talented Polish artist, Dorota Kudyba, whose cover art is everything I imagined.

Early readers helped me keep my focus and story line pointed in the right direction. To my friend Beth Picone-Topper: Thank you for poring over countless drafts and never failing to provide me with loving encouragement. To my friend Jane Moss: Thank you for reading through the hard stuff and never looking away. You each helped me keep the writing momentum going.

A heartfelt acknowledgment to Heather Zebrowski, who shared my grief at the passing of our dear friend Meg, and whose love and friendship are woven into the fabric of this story.

Thank you to Sara Beagan Guptill, psychic extraordinaire, whose gift allowed me to reach from this world into the next and touch both lost stars and found souls. Your support of this project has been unflagging, and for that I am eternally grateful.

To the many animal friends I've known since childhood;

guardian angels, each and every one of you. To the dogs: Ginger I, Maxwell, Duke, Mike, Frisbee, Zoom, Ginger II, Hershey, and Dino. And to the horses: Katy, Patrick, Commander, Ellie, and Slate. I am forever indebted to you for your protection and guidance through the darkest of nights.

To my sister, my very first horseback riding partner. Who would've thought that naughty Shetland pony, Heidi, would lead us to a life-long love affair with horses? Thank you for sharing the good rides, and the falls, too.

To my parents: Two city kids who moved to the country and indulged their daughters' love of animals and the outdoors, and who eventually grew our little hillside farm from a dog and a cat or two, to more than forty sheep and several horses. I am quite sure my career choice as a nurse had something to do with those middle-of-the-night sheep births in the freezing cold of February. Thank you for your love and support, always.

Lastly, to my husband, John: My deepest gratitude for being my partner through illness, the anguish of lost motherhood, and the eventual re-emergence into life. Thank you for being by my side and for letting me write about such a personal moment in our lives. Your unwavering love will forever be my North Star.

In her debut novel, Carolyn S. Hochard shares her personal journey of self-acceptance and healing as she navigates a society historically equating womanhood with childbearing. She compassionately examines themes of suicide, stillbirth, and terminal cancer with the experience of a seasoned Registered Nurse. Carolyn resides in Massachusetts with her husband, two Tibetan Spaniels and her Kentucky Mountain Saddle Horse. She is currently engaged in writing her next novel.

Many thanks to you, the readers,

for your love and support of

The Stars We Could Reach.

Please ask for it

at your local library

or bookstore.

Reviews on

Amazon or Goodreads

are greatly appreciated.

Follow me on

FACEBOOK

and

INSTAGRAM

Check out my website:

www.CarolynHochardAuthor.square.site

Contact me to schedule library or book club events.

Email: csh3741@Comcast.net

www.ingramcontent.com/pod-product-compliance
Lightning Source LLC
Chambersburg PA
CBHW030918140626
46545CB00016B/1392